The Complete Guide to Protecting Your Financial Security When Getting a Divorce

Alan Feigenbaum

Heather Smith Linton

D0907769

McGraw-Hill

New York   Chicago   San Francisco   Lisbon   London
Madrid   Mexico City   Milan   New Delhi   San Juan
Seoul   Singapore   Sydney   Toronto

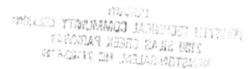
Copyright © 2004 by Alan Feigenbaum and Heather Linton. All rights reserved. Printed in the United States of America. Except as permitted under the United States Copyright Act of 1976, no part of this publication may be reproduced or distributed in any form or by any means, or stored in a database or retrieval system, without the prior written permission of the publisher.

1 2 3 4 5 6 7 8 9 0   AGM/AGM   0 9 8 7 6 5 4

ISBN 0-07-141032-5

This publication is designed to provide accurate and authoritative information in regard to the subject matter covered. It is sold with the understanding that the publisher is not engaged in rendering legal, accounting or other professional service. If legal advice or other expert assistance is required, the services of a competent professional person should be sought.
> —*From a Declaration of Principles Jointly Adopted by a Committee of the American Bar Association and a Committee of Publishers and Associations.*

McGraw-Hill books are available at special quantity discounts to use as premiums and sales promotions, or for use in corporate training programs. For more information, please write to the Director of Special Sales, McGraw-Hill Professional, Two Penn Plaza, New York, NY 10121-2298. Or contact your local bookstore.

CFP and CERTIFIED FINANCIAL PLANNER are registered trademarks of the Certified Financial Planner Board of Standards, Inc.

Library of Congress Cataloging-in-Publication Data

Feigenbaum, Alan.
     The complete guide to protecting your financial security when getting
  a divorce / by Alan Feigenbaum and Heather Linton.
        p.   cm.
     ISBN 0-07-141032-5 (alk. paper)
     1. Divorce—Law and legislation—United States—Popular works.   2.
  Divorce—Economic aspects—Popular works.   3. Divorced people—Finance,
  Personal—Popular works.   I. Linton, Heather.   II. Title.

  KF535.Z9F448   2004
  346.7301'66—dc22   2003027002

To my wife, Janet Rose Levy, whose love and strength of character has been the ultimate navigator for 31 years in steering our marriage clear of our generation's countless detours to divorce. And to our almost-grown children, Carmela, Gibora, and Kelila, who provide a constant wonderful reminder of what marriage and family are all about.

To my parents, Richard Feigenbaum and the late Janet Feigenbaum who taught me nothing about divorce by providing a model of almost 49 years of marriage. And to my parents-in-law, Bettie Levy and the late Henri Levy whose 55-year marriage furthered the non-lesson.

—Alan Feigenbaum

I dedicate this book to my uncle, Jack S. Locher, who always believed in me. I want to be like him when I grow up: constantly engaged and engaging, interested and interesting, accomplished and always learning, a person who lives by the golden rule, someone who puts family and close friends first, someone who always maintains a positive outlook and good sense of humor. Thank you for all the lessons I have learned and am still learning.

To Uncle Jack's widow, Aunt Nancy, with whom I've shared the loss of Uncle Jack, and who teamed with him to become the reborn family that I lost so long ago. Your mother's love and caring sustain me as I continue "growing up."

—Heather Smith Linton

Finally and most importantly, we dedicate this book to the millions of divorced couples who've managed to remember enough about why they married in the first place to divorce with dignity and put the interests of any children as first and foremost. And to the millions of individuals who've survived destructive divorces and put their children first at great personal sacrifice.

Contents

Acknowledgments

Thanks to Tom Murphy, former managing editor of CBS MarketWatch, who gave me the opportunity to break into "bigtime" personal-finance publishing and later write a pair of articles about the female and male perspectives on divorce, planting the ultimate seeds that have grown into this book. And to all the AOL readers whose emails both blasted and blessed me in response to those divorce articles and taught me that divorce is 80 percent the husband's fault and 75 percent the wife's fault, except when it's 80 percent the wife's fault and 75 percent the husband's fault.

—Alan Feigenbaum

Thanks to all of my friends and family for the love and support you gave me while I was working on this book. I am looking forward to enjoying more quality time with all of you who make my life so rich, and appreciate your not divorcing me during this chapter of my life. My friends at Linton & Associates, PA, (Ann, Charlie, Gwen, Ginger, and Mary), deserve a special thank you for not only supporting me emotionally, but also for working harder in the office to meet the needs of our clients while I was spending time on "the book."

—Heather Smith Linton

Thanks to Jessica Faust—our agent at Bookends, LLC—and to Barry Neville, Mary Glenn, and Daina Penikas—our editors at McGraw-Hill—who did a great job of moving things along and keeping us on track. To John Bowman, Dan Caine, Lee Borden, and especially Craig Ross, who spent innumerable hours reading drafts, making important suggestions, and offering interesting and valuable quotes and anecdotes that we've included. Thank you all very much.

Introduction

Jackie Chan and Charlie's Angels aside, you're probably like most men or women who'd consider themselves fortunate to simply survive a brutal attack, let alone turn the tables on their attackers by pummeling them with a full arsenal of martial arts. For one thing, humiliating your attacker might invite later revenge. For another, if the attack occurred far from home, all the extra energy you'd expend turning the tables might leave you too depleted to make it back.

And so it should be with divorce. Rather than unleashing your own marital (ending) arts assault on a vindictive spouse, make your goal a mutually workable settlement. In other words, whether you're a man or woman, use the financial self-defense skills you'll learn in this book as a way to stay on your financial feet. Surely, that's better than overpowering or "overguilting" your soon-to-be ex-partner with a hollow victory that's likely to invite emotionally and financially costly reprisals both during the divorce process and long after.

But what if you think you've nothing to fear from a partner who purports to "just want to get it over with" in a "fair manner"? You might be right, but be vigilant about the possibility that your partner is planning to spring a nasty surprise, or that the wild emotional swings of divorce will result in a Jekyll-Hyde spousal change of mind that will leave you extremely vulnerable. More importantly, any children involved are totally vulnerable—largely lacking the legal standing to defend their own interests, which are often the most negatively affected by divorce. That's why financial self-defense is not only desirable but crucial in softening the devastating blow that divorce almost always delivers to children—and often to one or both spouses, as well.

Divorce Demands a Bodyguard's Wide-Open Eyes

Make no mistake, unless you're well prepared for what you're getting into when you file for divorce, you'll almost certainly be ambushed—by its process and mathematics if not by a wave of spousal fury. For starters, the total cost of maintaining the predivorce lifestyle after divorce for the members of the previously intact family is about 25 to 50 percent more than when everyone was together before divorce. That's true for several reasons, with the most significant being that after the divorce there are two separate expenses for housing and related items such as homeowner's or renter's insurance. In addition, health insurance is often much more expensive because a family policy can no longer cover everybody, and you might have to pay higher rates for purchasing individual insurance if you were under a spouse's group insurance. Furthermore, unless both spouses make nearly the same incomes, the sum of their separately filed tax liabilities usually exceeds their joint-filing liability. Other additional expenses include getting kids back and forth if the ex-spouses live in different towns, additional child-care expenses for young children because parents can no longer rely on each other as much, and often substantial adjustment expenses including family therapy to cope with psychological effects of the divorce.

Because money problems or disagreements are often a primary factor or symptom in divorce, a divorcing couple already lives under financial strain. So, with these additional divorce-induced expenses, there's no way everybody can continue their accustomed lifestyle. Thus, equitable divorce demands significant shared sacrifice. Resisting it only exacerbates the problem by draining limited resources to fund warring attorneys and expert testimony—often leaving *both* parties with less than they wanted.

For example, suppose you fight over splitting $500,000 of assets, with your spouse demanding 60 percent ($300,000) and you a 50-50 split of $250,000 each. Suppose it takes a combined $50,000 in attorney fees to wage the battle, and you ultimately compromise on a 55-45 split. Your spouse then gets $247,500 (55 percent of $450,000), and you get $202,500 (the balance). With all that expense, you're only $2500 better off than you would have been originally had you capitulated and settled for 40 percent of the original $500,000. And your spouse is $2500 worse off than he or she would have been at only 50 percent of the original $500,000.

If instead, you had agreed to a 55-45 split early on, and you had paid only $10,000 in legal expenses, you'd be dividing the remaining $490,000 into $269,500 and $220,5000—leaving you about $30,000 (each) short of the amounts you originally wanted, but about $20,000 each better off than if the other spouse had gotten what he or she wanted. Most importantly, you'd both end up far less bitter and angry—while avoiding some harmful resentment repercussions down the road.

Thinking self-defense rather than victory helps you avoid the typical fight spiral resulting from each combatant's wanting to get in the last blow—and essentially fighting to mutual divorce financial death. Instead, employing "divorce damage control" defensive techniques allows you to remain standing and in control of your rightful financial territory—instead of losing control to attorneys or your spouse. By fighting, you risk a knockdown that, accompanied by the following circumstances, might keep you from getting solidly back on your feet for years—if ever:

- *Financial disadvantage:* When low-wage or nonworking spouses in marriages with credit and other financial problems are surprised with divorce decrees, liquidity and credit problems can force them to accept highly unfavorable settlements.
- *Spousal support obligations:* Men have traditionally borne the spousal support burden, so until recently, it's been their exclusive franchise to feel that they're paying too much or for too many years. But with two-income marriages the norm—in which a significant minority of women earn the higher income—it's no longer unusual for higher-earning women to feel unfairly burdened by support obligations. Conversely, though, stay-at-home dads are often looked at unsympathetically and end up suffering the same fate as once commonly befell women—too little support after aggressive litigation by a more powerful spouse.
- *Credit problems:* Divorce can cause or intensify serious ongoing credit problems—adversely affecting your future ability to buy a house or car on credit, raising your cost of insurance, and potentially even ruining your prospects of getting good employment. These problems are often exacerbated by a spouse who has run up substantial debt with cards that are under both names or with a spousal card for which the other spouse is the primary card holder.
- *Looming bankruptcy:* Potential bankruptcy can be a factor in divorce cases, so it's critical to examine the likelihood of it eventually occurring before a divorce settlement. First, it sometimes works best for a couple to declare bankruptcy before the divorce. Second, when the settlement depends on a spouse who'll be under financial pressure to make sizable, long-term continuing payments, it's crucial to protect the receiving spouse from the paying spouse maneuvering to declare bankruptcy after the divorce, getting support obligations dissolved, and leaving the receiving spouse high and dry. Conversely, if assets and income are sufficient so that the couple shouldn't have to declare bankruptcy jointly, there's often a way to arrive at an equitable settlement that keeps both parties living a viable existence. Finally, if attorneys are heavily involved in your case, be up front about bankruptcy possibilities to avoid a

potential conflict of interest, or your case being dropped in midstream, due to their concern about being fully paid.

- *Foreclosure:* In addition to undesirable bankruptcy, failure to realize dire financial circumstances before coming to a settlement often leads to one party keeping the house and then being foreclosed upon later because the costs of upkeep prove too burdensome.
- *Rocky retirement:* Divorce is usually a serious setback to both spouses in their attempts to amass a sufficient nest egg for retirement. For a spouse who has been in and out of the workforce due to child-rearing responsibilities, it could mean little or no pension, thus dependence on paltry investment earnings from insufficient savings and an inadequate spousal share of Social Security.
- *Pension poverty:* When breadwinner spouses must split pensions, they have to work much harder and longer to retire than they originally planned. A combination of higher consumer debt, lower savings rates, and economic downturn has cracked most baby boomers' retirement nest eggs. They will have to work several years beyond normal retirement age, and many lucky enough to live far beyond life expectancy will spend their last years in dire poverty. It is therefore crucial that divorce preserve the maximum of the couple's wealth and distribute it fairly. Divorce settlements of long-term marriages must account for both the major blow to the primary breadwinner and the pensionless future of the child-rearing or secondary breadwinner.
- *Chilling children's reality:* Partly because they have no say in the divorce, children are usually the most injured of the divorce victims. For starters, twice as many children in divorced families live in poverty as compared to children who live in intact families. Furthermore, their ultimate economic well-being is lower than that of adults from intact families. Finally, they have more psychological problems before and throughout adulthood—including delayed and less successful marriage. These effects are most pronounced in acrimonious or inequitable divorces where money and custody are used as leverage by either or both spouses to hurt the other—setting the stage for continued postdivorce emotional and financial tensions.
- *Remarriage repercussions:* Financially inequitable divorce often negatively impacts a spouse's remarriage. A divorced person without adequate financial resources may hastily remarry to acquire a sense of security rather than carefully choosing a suitable partner. This can have both negative financial as well as emotional ramifications.

Asserting Yourself

By going into your divorce with your eyes wide open, you'll be more knowledgeable about the issues. That will make you more receptive to alternative paths to divorce such as mediation, arbitration, and collaborative divorce, which might be better for you ultimately than the results obtained by an adversarial attorney. You'll also be more flexible in considering a wide range of settlement possibilities. The key is your preparation for and willingness to assert yourself instead of relying on attorneys, "helpful" family members, or even (heaven forbid) your spouse to run the show.

Your assertiveness isn't certain to make your divorce financially equitable, and it definitely won't eliminate the disruptive effect that any divorce has on a family. But being assertive will likely help you avoid the foolhardy and destructive manner in which hundreds of thousands of this year's 1.1 million divorces will be conducted. Unless your spouse's behavior was criminal (abuse or serious drug and alcohol abuse, for example), you'll be able to rise above such emotions as feeling abandoned or being played for a fool—no matter how much they apply—and make the best of an expletive-deleted situation.

The key is to recognize that the most effective self-defense involves going on the diplomatic offense. Seize the small settlement window of opportunity that is usually available after the initial shock has worn off early in the divorce process. Then you'll be more likely to reach an agreement with your spouse that is truly fair. Although that doesn't always mean a 50-50 or better split—even if you think you "deserve it"—it will allow you to get on with your lives without undue obstacles. To best accomplish this, you must seek a proper balance of financial counseling, mediation, and legal help that maximally preserves the marital asset pie and results in a mutually (dis)agreeable settlement with which both parties can immediately live, and ultimately hope to thrive.

Equitable Means Never Having to Say You're Sorry

This book shows you how to achieve that balance by focusing on a recently introduced approach to equitable settlement that is not yet in the mainstream but is increasingly gaining favor with enlightened divorce professionals and the family court system. It is based on constructing a sound financial projection of what a given settlement proposal will offer each of the parties immediately, for the next few years, and—most importantly—in the long run.

Don't worry, you won't have to be a math whiz to understand this approach. But the fact that you've selected this book means you're able to become sufficiently conversant with the principles upon which divorce financial self-defense is based, including these:

- The actual designation of marital assets versus the way they're titled, the various forms of asset ownership, and the way your state treats them
- Why it's not necessarily best for either spouse to continue owning the marital home
- The surprisingly large reduction in income potential for a stay-at-home or part-time-employed spouse who's been in and out of the workforce
- Tax advantages of carefully crafted settlements
- Avoiding the pits or seeds when dividing a (cherry or apple) pension pie

By learning these principles, you'll stand a better chance of ending up in the black than do most of the 40 to 50 percent of couples who married the same year you did and will ultimately divorce. Read on to move to the head of the class and begin earning a coveted divorce self-defense black belt.

Part I

Preparing for Divorce

If the adage that "advice is worth what you pay for it" has any truth, it certainly applies to all the unsolicited suggestions you'll get for how to handle your divorce. We'd like to think our advice is worth more than what you paid for this book, but even if you don't agree, we're confident that what you'll get in Part I alone is better than all the free advice you may get elsewhere on the same subjects.

After all, what's a marital casualty to do when divorce planning becomes a daily, hourly, or minute-by-minute Stage-5 rapids ride through these waves of free, contradictory advice: Get revenge. Be nice. Be sneaky. Be open. Be aggressive. Be conciliatory. Take him or her for every last penny. Find a solution in which nobody truly loses. Get vicious Attorney X. Get mild-mannered Mediator Y. Get out now. Stay until you settle things. Don't even think of dating. Take care of yourself. And up and down ad nauseam.

If instead of trying to absorb and follow all that free-floating advice, you read Chapter 1, you'll find information and philosophy intended to help you make some sense—without losing too many dollars—of the thoughts and emotions that are swirling within you as a person who's either contemplating or pursuing divorce. Then in Chapter 2 you'll find overviews of the divorce process from a primarily legal perspective and descriptions of the many choices you have for initiating and carrying through the divorce, and their financial implications.

Together, these chapters get you started by distilling a small reservoir of sanity-saving guidance. Drink them in to keep yourself hydrated through-

1

out your divorce's most intense initial heated moments, and you won't find yourself gulping from the toxic river of rage and rhetoric fed by friends, family, and acquaintances.

Chapter 1

Divorce: So Money Things to Think About

I n seriously contemplating divorce, you naturally first focus on the heart-wrenching reality of ripping a family apart from its roots, particularly if you can justifiably say that it was mainly your spouse's doing. Violet Woodhouse, CFP and attorney, a nationally prominent financial advisor and author of *Divorce & Money: How to Make the Best Financial Decisions During Divorce, Sixth Edition*, warns against being guided by the "get" feelings you'll naturally have in those circumstances: the compulsion to get even if your spouse has either initiated the divorce or has acted in a way that gives you no other choice, the rush to get it over with by coming to a disadvantageous quick settlement, or the often-impossible desire to get back together. You must get over the "gets" by not letting the anticipated emotional pain and suffering, or the desire to escape it, obscure a sober view of divorce's economic realities. Then you will be able to come to grips with the full financial consequences that begin as soon as one of you begins packing—or have already begun if your spouse has long since anticipated the divorce and is already acting in self-interest.

The circumstances are different though if continued unhappiness or a desire to escape constant arguments and bickering has led either you or your spouse to initiate a divorce or both of you to mutually decide on one. Money considerations alone shouldn't change your mind, but don't act without the fullest appreciation for both the emotional and material consequences of a family unraveled. In self-reflection and communication with your estranged spouse concerning those consequences, you might discover a plausible basis to resuscitate your marriage.

Failing that, considering how and whether you can save your marriage might lead to a more constructive approach that tempers divorce's emotional pain and minimizes its financial deprivation. Emotional effects in divorced

3

families include a higher rate of child abuse, lower academic performance, and more drug use. Children of divorce commit more than 10 times as many criminal offenses that involve jail time. Two-parent families have a median income of almost $45,000, compared to $25,000 for custodial (one-parent) families after divorce—and that difference includes child and spousal support paid to the custodial spouse.

Speaking of financial deprivation, you might wonder why we're seemingly trying to talk you out of divorce; what if you don't read the rest of the book—and don't recommend it to others? It's precisely because of how much is at stake that we're willing to take that risk in order to emphasize the wisdom, in some marital situations, of easing up on the divorce throttle. It gives you time to turn back before taking the final deep descent through all the hair-raising twists and turns that often must be navigated in a divorce. After all, if a doctor told you that you had a spinal-disk condition that required major surgery, would you feel "cheated" if she canceled the surgery after the last-ditch experimental exercise program she had you try left you pain free?

Think Twice and Then Again

So unless your home and marriage are already irrevocably damaged, before breaking up your family, think about repairing your marriage versus repairing your home. Have you and your spouse been delaying an important home repair or improvement project for financial reasons? If so, imagine having to pay that amount now instead for a home demolition project otherwise known as divorce, with an average current cost ranging from $20,000 to $25,000—and that's strictly for attorney fees, court costs, and related services. However, with the more experienced divorce attorneys' fees typically ranging from $200 to $300 an hour but sometimes going as high as $500 an hour, bitter divorce battles involving couples of means can easily exceed an anything-but-grand $100 grand.

No doubt, some attorneys have high hourly rates and exploit your emotions so that you'll run up their hours in a take-no-prisoners pursuit of "victory." But even divorces conducted by good-faith attorneys are costly; he or she and the experts he or she engages, such as a CPA and certified divorce financial analyst (CDFA), can't afford to cut corners if they're to do the job right and fully protect your interests on matters you might not have realized were crucial—such as a spouse's stock options or the need for life insurance in case a support-paying spouse dies. That's particularly true when considerable assets, income, and the welfare of children are at stake.

The "Soft" Opportunity and Emotional Costs of Divorce

These divorce-process costs, covered in more detail in Chapter 2, are just the beginning though because regardless of the ultimate settlement, unless it's resoundingly one-sided, everyone will end up with a lower standard of living than before the divorce. That results from a combination of factors: The assets are drained to pay for the divorce, and the combined budgets for the average split family is 125 to 150 percent of what it was before the split. Furthermore, your energy and time sucked away in the divorce process will trigger indirect actual and opportunity costs of lost wages, retarded career advancement, less free quality time with the kids, and loss of some business connections who are either socially loyal to your spouse or were made through organizations or activities you can no longer afford. And if your finances are shaky now, consider that divorce is the fourth leading cause of bankruptcy.

It's also safe to say that divorce is the leading cause of emotional bankruptcy—particularly if it goes to court. In an article on AllLaw.com, Honorable Ann Kass, a district judge in New Mexico, says that when spouses focus on the past, it takes their energy from the present, where it really needs to be. She also suggests that by trying to place as much blame on the other party as possible, spouses avoid taking responsibility for their own lives, which also encourages them to fantasize everything magically working out. Yet avoiding responsibility leaves them feeling helpless to climb back up the several steps down they discover their lifestyles have taken when the dust clears from their divorces.

Children have no control over the divorce so they feel doubly helpless when their lifestyles must also take those financial steps down at the same time they've been emotionally let down. Making things worse, in their deteriorated financial situation, parents assuage their guilt by competing to give kids unnecessary gifts while being forced to stint them on things they need, or they make their kids feel guilty about asking for now-unaffordable things they'd normally expect.

The emotional costs of divorce also derive from missed opportunities. Bruce Derman, Ph.D., of the Coalition of Collaborative Divorce, suggests identifying and measuring missed-opportunity costs to determine their emotional toll. Here are a few (consolidated or restated) from his lengthy list:

- The opportunity for you and your spouse to work together, and not be at odds with each other, in raising your children
- The opportunity to jointly celebrate kids' college graduations, weddings, births, and other happy events in your children's lives

- The opportunity to avoid making kids feel responsible for your emotional well-being
- The opportunity to avoid exposing yourself and others to the worst you can be and instead be seen as constantly striving for the best you can be
- The opportunity to love more and hate less

Spending on Saving (Your Marriage)

And what if you didn't miss these opportunities and "spent" divorce's emotional costs on repairing your marriage instead? Some couples are astounded when in divorce mediation, normally intended to reduce friction and cost in coming to a settlement, they're so successful communicating about the financial and other heavy-stress issues that led them toward divorce that they apply their new ability to finding the solutions that enable them to stay married.

Think about it: If you and your spouse are considering divorce because you've been constantly butting heads about financial matters, the chances are pretty good that those financial problems will not go away when you get divorced. Divorce seems to hold the promise of allowing you the financial authority to manage your own money, but if your divorce is like most divorces, you will remain financially entwined with your ex-spouse for quite some time, even though you no longer sleep together. Furthermore, because of the money mess that you both helped create, you'll still both be sleeping with some shared financial nightmares.

Why not try to clean up the mess now by consulting a trusted, impartial friend or professional to help you, which might also possibly reduce the marital tensions enough to enable you to continue trying? According to attorney Craig Ross, a principal author of Michigan's spousal/child support guidelines, "at worst, you'll start constructive communication that could save you time, money, and aggravation if you should still divorce." Furthermore, couples who haven't attempted to clean up finances before filing divorce often never examine their own financial mistakes—instead, they carry their burden throughout their lives, which weighs them down like impossible-to-repay 50 percent interest loans.

When It's Time to Fold 'Em

Whether Kenny Rogers, no stranger to marital failure himself, was talking about poker or family stability when he sang, "You've got to know when to hold 'em, and know when to fold 'em," his lyrics certainly apply. Your relationship could well be beyond the point of no return, so asking yourself these financial questions will help you clarify just how good or bad things actually are. Rather than telling you how to score your answers, we want to get you thinking about things you might not have considered, help you assess your marriage's financial viability, and determine whether you might be able to make enough headway on financial problems to improve your marital fortunes.

- *Is there an imbalance of financial power and knowledge?* If one spouse is the primary earner, does he or she use that fact to control the other spouse—with a stingy allowance, for example? Even if he or she isn't stingy, does he or she deny the other spouse knowledge of the overall financial situation?
- *Are both spouses pulling nearly equal weight?* Are you both reliable and responsible employees with good work records, or does one spouse resent the other's chronic laziness, lack of ambition, or wanderlust—resulting in constantly losing or changing jobs?
- *Budget or can't be budged?* Are your financial lives based on some kind of budget that the two of you developed together, and do both of you make honest yet perhaps (thus far) inadequate attempts to stick to the budget? Or are one or both of you unwilling or unable to develop a budget or try sticking to one and you're in debt because of it?
- *Plenty isn't anymore?* If you're not in debt but don't live within a budget, is it because your incomes have always been enough, even lacking spending discipline? Are you finally starting to feel the financial pinch and realizing that your spending is out of control and your net worth is far less than it would have been if you had avoided such excesses?
- *Is there a financial communication gap or a disparity in competence?* Have you both contributed to your problems in managing money and are you both about equally responsible for a failure to communicate about it? Or is one of you a lovable but hopeless money moron? Is it likely you can do better because you were both better with money before your marriage?
- *My way or the highway?* Do you both have the knowledge and ability to manage money but you are totally at odds over how? Are the disagreements between you there because you truly have different money philosophies or because you're both using money as a proxy weapon for other marital conflicts?
- *Trying to buy happiness?* Are one or both of you overspending to compensate for general marital unhappiness but think you can curb spending if you solve other marital problems?

- *Programmed by parents?* Are one or both of you unable to avoid repeating destructive financial patterns ingrained from the roles money plays in your parents' marriages?

Indecision? Breaking the Tie on Breaking the Ties

Putting yourself through the preceding self-examination will most likely reconfirm your previous decision to divorce. But it might instead result in your firmly resolving to try and fix things. Occasionally, though, you'll remain seated on the fence, so here are some additional factors and strategies that might help you decide:

- *Can't count on spouse?* Perhaps you think your marriage can be saved if only your spouse would agree to abide by significant financial "rules"—and perhaps your spouse feels the same way—but neither of you has confidence in the other doing so. Instead of giving up, join the avant-garde by drafting a postnuptial agreement with an attorney that sets forth financial rules that apply to either or both of you, violations enforceable by civil law. If confidence in the viability of your marriage has been severely shaken, the postnuptial agreement can be expanded into a comprehensive document that can also serve as a basis for a divorce settlement, functioning much as a prenuptial agreement. Check out the Equalityinmarriage.org Web site for more about postnuptial agreements.
- *Can't take (or get) credit?* If your spouse has the financial power in your marriage, or if you're having credit problems, you'll have problems getting your own credit to provide crucial cash flow once you're divorced. So unless your spouse is pressing for the divorce, trying to fix things before making a divorce decision might be your best course of action.
- *Now's not a good time?* Divorce timing has significant financial ramifications. For example, passing the 10-year milestone in a marriage is a significant advantage for a spouse who has been mostly a homemaker or doesn't have a lucrative career. Although it's usually at a judge's discretion, Wisconsin, New York, Colorado, Texas, and California are among many states that define "long-term marriage" as lasting 10 or more years—thus qualifying such spouses for more than short-term "rehabilitative" alimony. And the Social Security system gives divorced persons at their retirement the option of basing their benefit payments on their own earnings or getting payments at retirement equal to one half of the payment to which their ex-spouses will be entitled. So think of being

married 10 years as "earning marriage tenure." If you're the one more inclined to divorce and your spouse is the primary earner, consider cooling your heels and zipping your lips until that milestone. And if your spouse is moving toward divorce, do whatever you can to stall it the necessary time.

- *(Perhaps) go your separation ways?* Trial separations were much more common before no-fault divorce laws became the norm, but they still have their place. If done correctly, they're to marriage what a yellow caution flag is in a NASCAR race: They provide a way to "suspend" the marriage without committing to end it and without either party being able to drain down accumulated marital assets. It can be quite expensive to draft a formal trial separation agreement, so one way to avoid that is to take mutually agreed protective measures such as closing joint credit accounts and changing joint asset accounts so that both parties have to give permission for any transactions. (See Chapter 4 for more details.)

Regardless of your decision, doing these exercises should make it clear that financial problems usually have a major communications failure component. In fact, overall communications problems are the number one cause of divorce. You will need to overcome those difficulties to reach an equitable divorce settlement. By communicating effectively about the divorce, regardless of the problems you think are leading to divorce, you might be able to rescue the marriage—or at least minimize the damage of divorce.

Don't even consider rescuing your marriage if spousal abuse is involved. Your life and mental health take priority over finances, and if you're in such a relationship, you're hardly alone—even if you're a man. About 4 million American women are estimated to be victims of violence at the hands of current or former partners (more than 1 million by the most conservative estimates). About one-tenth as many males are victims of female partners—although a substantial percentage of that is retaliatory. To find out how the legal system can help domestic-violence victims (free if you can't afford an attorney), check out the American Bar Association Commission on Domestic Violence at abanet.org/domviol/home.html.

With that thought, we'll move from possibly rescuing your marriage to the main theme of this book: how to rescue yourself from fatal financial attacks while running the divorce gauntlet.

The Divorce Battlefield: The Opening Salvos

Theodore Roosevelt, while serving as our twenty-fifth president, spoke frequently about the importance of motherhood and the need for federal divorce laws so that weaker state laws could not undermine family. But for our purposes, his most important statement was on his philosophy of diplomacy: "Speak softly but carry a big stick." During the divorce process, you should make it clear that you want equity, not victory, but the fact that you're not going for the jugular doesn't mean you'll allow yourself to be pushed around. Your aim is to demonstrate strength in order to avoid having to actually apply your fighting skills in an escalating conflict requiring heavy legal weaponry and correspondingly heavy expenses.

To accomplish this, strive for civil discourse with your estranged spouse from the moment the possibility of divorce becomes real. Lee Borden, a veteran Birmingham, Alabama, divorce attorney—who maintains an excellent Web site (www.divorceinfo.com) aimed at those who wish to divorce with minimal harm—cautions that this advice conflicts with what others might tell you: "Divorce lawyers often tell their clients not to talk to their spouse, and people involved in a divorce often want to follow this advice, at least at the beginning, because direct spousal communication is so painful. But if you and your spouse can't talk to each other, your only communication will be through your lawyers. This means you will be talking on your lawyers' timetables, about your lawyers' issues, and at your lawyers' hourly rates."

So make it a point to really listen to your spouse but also to clearly communicate what he or she needs to hear. Skip the recriminations about how horribly you've been treated because he or she is such a bad person. And skip the threats to deny custody, withhold child support, or make your spouse's new significant other wish he or she had never been born. Be prepared to back up unfighting words with whatever assertive actions are needed, and make sure your spouse knows you're ready to rumble—fairly but with ample firepower—for your economic rights.

Counter Counterproductive Reactions

By taking this tack of firm reasonableness, both husbands and wives can head off some of these common counterproductive reactions from their spouses:

- *Male guilt:* Men who are initiating divorce or those whose behavior has caused the wife to are quite likely to initially feel guilty and offer to give up the farm, only to later compensate for their moments of weakness by angrily trying to win at all costs.

- *Female anger:* Women served with divorce papers, or those who have filed because they felt they had no choice, are likely to be continually fueled by anger to get everything because they feel wronged.
- *He blames her.* Men who "had no clue" and were shocked by a wife's filing are likely to initially want to deny their wives their fair share because "the divorce is the wife's fault."
- *Two-way ratcheted rhetoric.* Both men and women sometimes respond to blustering inflammatory rhetoric by taking it at face value and escalating the conflict. Much like poker, this can lead to spiraling stakes in the form of hundreds of hours of attorney and other professional fees that neither party intended. So tone it down; the last thing you want to do is make your spouse feel that he or she has to call your bluff.

Deal with Dirty Fighting

Keep in mind, though, that one spouse's avoiding his or her own counterproductive reaction may not inspire his or her spouse to do the same. In fact, that spouse may resort to these types of all-out dirty fighting:

- Getting a restraining order and an order to abandon the marital home against a spouse who isn't actually abusive.
- Placing liens on marital assets when there are few assets in the spouse's own name, while maintaining access to assets in one's own name.
- Faking a job transfer and sending the spouse ahead to establish domicile in a state such as Texas, which does little for the powerless spouse, and then filing for divorce there.
- Using the discovery phase to launch a barrage of nuisance requests for files or requiring time-consuming paperwork and research.
- Filing just before the marriage is considered long term, thereby keeping it from qualifying for extended alimony. (Unfortunately, some judges refuse to see through such tactics and don't counteract them by deviating from the letter of the law.)
- Pretending there's a financial problem and cutting spending severely, way before filing, so that the marital lifestyle is viewed as less than it actually was and the dependent spouse doesn't get as much.
- Asking for last-minute continuances and schedule changes for meetings and court appearances, making it difficult for a resource-poor spouse who can't afford to miss work or hire babysitting help.

- Asking for full or even 50-50 custody with no real interest in having it, in order to gain a bargaining chip for the financial negotiations. Similarly, a spouse may ask for full custody in order to get the other spouse to capitulate because he or she has limited funds with which to fight the custody battle.
- Hiring a private detective to dig up apparent dirt on a spouse and cast doubt on that spouse's character during proceedings.

If your spouse does lower himself or herself to these tactics, you must resist the temptation to fight dirt with dirt for the sake of your children, and for the sake of your own integrity and sense of self-worth. Fighting dirty during divorce is like soiling a garment you'll be wearing for the rest of your life with a stain that will never wash out—not to mention rendering you so penniless that you'll struggle to afford detergent. If instead you fight dirty with clean, applying the tactical elbow grease we'll be covering in this book, things will be messy, but the grime of your spouse's sleazy tactics will come out afterward in the wash. Here's how to prepare for a clean fight even before the bell rings for the first round.

Line Up Your Financial and Legal Divorce Ducks

Your most vulnerable period during the divorce process is when you're only talking about divorce, when neither of you seems in a hurry to commit to that choice. You're attempting to keep the lines of communication open by taking a nonconfrontational attitude, but your spouse could see that as your lack of resolve to vigorously defend your interests. Although men and women do it in different ways, both are capable of playing their spouse's heartstrings with larceny in their own hearts—responding positively to their spouse's hopes for reconciliation while leading them down the primrose path to the poorhouse.

So while giving your spouse the public benefit of the doubt that you can work things out amicably, don't drop your guard—you may be seeing only the uncharacteristic kindness of a wolf in sheep's clothing. It is quite common for a spouse to seem to be negotiating fairly with you while he or she is actually preparing a full-scale attack through an aggressive divorce attorney. So don't put off getting an attorney. In fact, retain one now who is comfortable with only a protective role if you can work out an agreement with your spouse directly or through mediation. But make sure that attorney can protect you in the courtroom if called upon or can team up with an attorney who can.

Divorce Plans Are Need-to-Know Classified Info

To keep your spouse from ruining you, or at least trying to or threatening to, take these steps to avoid your spouse's finding out you're preparing for a possible divorce:

- *Keep your lips sealed.* Don't tell anyone other than the most trustworthy friends or blood family members (not children) that you are considering divorce; you don't want your spouse to inadvertently find out before you are ready to reveal it directly.
- *Divert your mail.* Rent a post office box where you can receive communications from your attorney, and books or other materials and documents you might order regarding divorce.
- *Keep a private cache.* Rent a safety deposit box for storing copies of important documents as well as jewelry and other valuables you don't want your spouse to grab and flee with. Use it also to keep an emergency supply of cash in case you're cut off from accounts.

Your Divorce Need-to-Know Portfolio

Now start amassing financial information and education. That means knowing what's going on in your family financially, and why, as well as collecting records, records, records—not to sound like a broken record. If you've been out of the loop regarding family finances, get the records first. Your spouse's antenna might start twitching if you suddenly start asking lots of questions about finances at a time that divorce seems possible, and records might soon disappear from sight.

In gathering records, don't limit yourself to copying those that are strictly financial. In case your spouse is hiding assets, you should make copies of address books and other lists of your spouse's contacts because they can prove useful in tracking down missing funds or records. Don't do this all at once, though, unless you're able to take a few days off when you know your spouse won't be around much. Amass your copy collection the way Clint Eastwood made a tunnel from his cell in *Escape from Alcatraz*—painstakingly digging a few inches (documents) a day, and surreptitiously unloading the dirt (copies) in the prison yard (your safe deposit box) without being noticed.

These records really are a kind of dirt—as many spouses play dirty tricks to hide or obscure accurate information about marital financial assets, income, and debts, particularly with regard to their own businesses. In addition to standard items such as tax returns, credit card and financial account statements, and insurance policy information, you're looking for other documents that might point to financial realms heretofore unknown:

- *Business records.* You might not have even known about the business or didn't know the full extent of it.
- *Conventional and cell phone itemized statements.* These could reveal calls related to a hidden business or other source of income or to other questionable financial transactions.
- *Employee benefit documentation:* These could reveal "golden-handshake agreements" regarding bonuses upon future separation from the employer, employee stock options, and other less common perks.

Your Divorce Financial Status

In Chapter 5, Figure 5-1, you'll find a detailed, annotated list of all the documents for which you should search. Once you have them, it's time to build your knowledge of what's actually going on financially in your marriage to enable you to answer questions such as these:

- *Marital assets.* Approximately how much is your own separate net worth of assets that can be proven to be yours, regardless of whose name they're actually in—and how much is your spouse's? What is your estimated joint net worth, not including the separate net worths you just determined?
- *Gross income and employment benefits.* How much is each of your gross incomes (not just take-home pay) from jobs in which you're employed by someone else? What paid-for (for example, medical) and vested (for example, pensions) benefits do those jobs provide?
- *Business income and value.* If one or both of you have businesses or are self-employed, what is the maximum potential income that could be taken from the businesses without impairing the viability of the businesses? How much more is that than the amount now being taken from them? How much would the businesses be worth if they were to be liquidated?
- *Family cash flow:* What have been your average or typical flows of money coming in (income and regular investment returns, for example) and going out (regular bills, taxes, and other expenditures) over the last year or two?
- *Debt and liquidity.* How much debt do you have, what interest rates are you paying on that debt, when is repayment due, and what is your

available credit line? How much of your assets are in cash or can readily be converted to cash to cover current debts and new expenses beyond normal expenses covered by your income?

Knowing What Constitutes a Fair Settlement

These figures provide you a general idea of what's at stake. Combine them with the documented details you've gathered, and you are in a far better position to begin figuring out what a fair settlement would be and to get help from whatever legal, financial, and mediation professionals you engage. Now that you are not at an informational disadvantage, you're ready to ask questions freely and tell your spouse honestly that you are prepared to do better in the marriage if things can be worked out or if not, to work together to reach a fair settlement.

Factors in a Fair Settlement

Assuming you go ahead with the divorce, you want to limit the professional services you must pay for by minimizing conflict with your spouse. You will need the help of some experts, though, because fair divorce settlements usually aren't a simple matter of dividing things 50-50. This is reflected in the Uniform Marriage and Divorce Act (UMDA), which many states use as a model. This act recommends that family courts consider the following factors:

- The value of separate and marital assets
- The income-producing capability of the assets
- The age, physical condition, emotional state, and financial condition of the person requesting alimony and the amount of time he or she would need for education or job training
- The ability of the prospective alimony provider to support both the recipient and himself or herself
- The length of the marriage and the couple's standard of living during it

A Fair Settlement Scenario

To illustrate how these factors might come into play, consider a fairly common scenario among younger couples with children. Both spouses had good jobs before the marriage, but once the children came, one of you continued climbing the career ladder working lots of (paid or unpaid) overtime, while the other took the "mommy track" or the "daddy track" and voluntarily took less outside career responsibility or worked only part-time hours to make the marriage and family work.

In this situation, an equal division of the equity in the home, retirement plans, IRAs, and any investment assets would generally not be enough to allow the home-oriented spouse to reenter the workforce at a meaningful level. However, with a few years of updated training, daycare, and hard work, the dependent spouse can get back on track to resume career advancement. But he or she will need help because he or she won't have the ability to take care of the children and pay monthly expenses while "retooling." This is a classic case for "rehabilitative spousal support," which the career spouse would pay for a few to several years until the dependent spouse is fully employed.

Other Fair Settlement Scenarios

We won't "resolve" this scenario now, but in Chapter 9 we'll show how "net worth" projections based on equal property splits often reveal enormous future financial disparities. Chapter 10 takes the fairness issue further with two full-blown examples—complete with incomes, value of personal property, and all other relevant details—of equitable, although not necessarily equal possible settlements. These along with additional cases we'll refer you to online, are drawn from these common divorce situations:

- *Long-term marriage, one main breadwinner.* When one spouse (more often the husband) is the primary breadwinner and the other (dependent) spouse is a homemaker, the dependent spouse has no hope at this point in life of ever supporting himself or herself in anything close to the lifestyle that he or she has led.
- *Medium-term marriage with child(ren), one spouse supports the other's education:* In these marriages, one spouse delays his or her own professional aspirations, working in a decent-paying grunt job for several years while supporting an aspiring doctor or similar professional during schooling and low-paid initial professional work. Then the supporting spouse quits work soon after the professional spouse becomes established and a child arrives.
- *Medium-term marriage without children, one spouse supports the other's education:* One spouse earns a professional degree with high pay potential while the other provides support in a stable and secure "job-job" with little career advancement potential. The divorce occurs shortly after the professional spouse gets the degree. The supporting spouse feels robbed of the future income potential of that degree and the loss of his or her own career opportunities that eroded while he or she supported the other's education.

- *Childless, two-career marriage:* Both spouses have been free to fully pursue their careers and other interests, neither having to act as the domestic spouse for the other's career.
- *Two-income, trailing-spouse marriage:* Marriage with no children in which one spouse has been a *trailing spouse*—that is, he or she has limited his or her career advancement, instead following the other spouse who continually chased career advancement.
- *Unequal entering financial status:* One spouse came into the marriage with considerable property, high income, and a high-status job, while the other lacked all of those. But the wealthier spouse didn't insist on a prenuptial agreement and wanted the other spouse to informally manage the couple's lives—made hectic by the affluent spouse's numerous business, social, and charitable endeavors.
- *Two serious professionals, decidedly different incomes and financial status:* One spouse has pursued a high-paying career while the other has pursued a lower-paying, service-oriented career. The couple has been living in an affluent lifestyle made possible by the higher-earning spouse.

The Unsettling Truth about Divorce Settlements

By now you've heard enough about the high stakes involved in divorce that you might be having some second thoughts about taking the plunge. This is a good time to think about it again. But if you are ready for the divorce games to begin, you need to formulate a detailed divorce self-defense strategy, which this book can help you do.

In Chapter 2, you'll learn about the different legal paths to getting a divorce, the typical steps involved, and the many ways in which divorce law and practices differ by state.

Be assured, though, that your state—of divorce trauma—is no different from that of all the other readers of this book. It might not give you much comfort now, but we've made it our job to put you in a more comfortable state of preparedness. Stay with us and learn how to split your nuclear family without being annihilated by the financial fallout.

Chapter 2

Setting the Legal Course for Financially Surviving Divorce

Y ou might think that your decision to divorce and the resolution of your divorce are between you and your spouse, but that would be like saying that a fight in middle school is strictly between Boy A and Boy B. Surely you remember how quickly after someone screamed "fight, fight" that a huge crowd gathered around the combatants, usually by the time the second punch was thrown. Perhaps that wasn't a bad way to resolve disputes before teens routinely started carrying guns and knives, but today virtually every middle school attempts to head off catastrophe with a dispute resolution peer process. And to head off catastrophe is why you should try for a level-headed resolution of your divorce battle, instead of risking the fatal financial and emotional consequences that can occur if you allow yourself to be goaded into an all-out divorce battle by the gathering crowd.

If your social graces demand it, smile politely and pretend to be seriously considering the advice of family, friends, and acquaintances who tell you how they or their acquaintances were the "shaftees" or "shafters" in their divorces. Meanwhile, use this book and other sources to learn as much as you can about the various and newer options—such as attorney-advised spouses' mutual settlements, arbitration, mediation, and collaborative divorce—and try to use one that best suits your situation. Furthermore, develop a basic understanding of how the process will work, so you won't be tempted to hire a hit man or a hit woman or resort to entering an insanity plea. This chapter will prep you on the legal process that leads to divorce, the choices you have in getting through that process, and how states differ in their legal treatment of divorce's procedural aspects and financial issues.

The Many Paths to an Executed Divorce

Just as most criminal cases end in plea bargains, 90 percent of divorce cases are resolved through bargaining rather than a trial—but they're no bargain either. That's because in up to 1 of 5 cases settled by "bargaining," the parties both hire attorneys and go through most or all of the process leading to court. But they stop short of the trial—often just short, of literally reaching a settlement on the courthouse steps on the day the trial is set to begin. This is one indication that some of the same attorneys who originally opposed no-fault divorce for fear it would dry up their business are now quite pleased with the no-fault adversarial process, which is different, but alive and well. While the issues at stake have changed, the process itself is not simpler than it was before. In fact, the opportunities attorneys now have to be funded to fight are more varied and lucrative than they were when their main job was proving a spouse's infidelity or other reasons that divorces were the fault of their client's spouse.

But perhaps no-fault is finally poised to realize its promise as a positive path to divorce resolution, now that a number of nonadversarial approaches are gaining in recognition and popularity. As the supply of experienced and well-qualified mediators increases, couples are discovering the time, emotional, and financial advantages of communicating through a "fair fight referee" who can be the hub of a three-way conversation. Contrast that with the three separate conversations—chest-thrusting Attorney A to chest-thrusting Attorney B, Attorney A to Client A, and Attorney B to Client B—that pass for communications in an adversarial process.

Mediation

The biggest advantage of using divorce mediators is that most are adept in calming the conversation to facilitate constructive dialogue that remains focused on the issues. Although some charge hourly rates that are almost on a par with attorneys' rates, they can often help couples reach a solution in a surprisingly small number of hours—and in a sense, couples get a 2-for-1 deal in both being able to talk to the mediator at the same time. However, mediation can be pennywise and pound foolish unless you do a good job in picking an appropriate mediator for your case and you understand the limitations of what the mediator can do.

Mediators' Legal Limitations

Even mediators who are qualified divorce attorneys are limited to answering questions of law. They are not allowed to serve as legal advisors for either party.

A question of law would be something like: "How long am I required to pay child support?" Mediators can answer this question based on state statutes, the ages of the children, who has custody, and so on.

Similarly, mediators can tell you about alimony, such as the difference between rehabilitative and long-term spousal support, and what your state considers a long-term marriage for the purpose of deciding which kind of spousal support should be awarded. They can also tell you whether the spousal support agreed to by you and your spouse seems to fall within your state's guidelines. But they can't give specific legal advice, such as whether a judge will or won't uphold it, or what a judge would be likely to decide if the case went to court. Even your own attorney can't be certain a judge will approve an agreement or predict a judge's decision in a court case, but unlike a mediator, he or she can tell you likely outcomes based on knowledge and experience.

In addition to relying on your own attorney for such advice, you should have him or her draw up complicated technical documents. For example, an attorney, after reading the plan documents, consulting the plan administrator, and perhaps consulting a benefits specialist, should draw up a *qualified domestic relations order* (QDRO), which is used to transfer qualified retirement plan assets. This helps ensure that the employer will honor the QDRO, and you won't have any unexpected nasty tax or other repercussions after the divorce is final. QDROs are not needed for individual retirement accounts (IRAs) or other nonqualified plans.

Mediators' Financial Limitations

While it might help if IRS agents were to use tax-savvy mediators as a first step in resolving tax disputes, they'd be hard-pressed to find many mediators with suitable qualifications. So don't expect your mediator to understand the tax ramifications of a proposed settlement. In fact, many mediators are generally short on financial expertise. So they usually don't know how to structure a settlement in a way that preserves the maximum amount of a couple's collective assets, and they don't know how to project what condition a proposed settlement will leave each spouse in several years down the line.

So be clear that the mediator's job is to help you come to an agreement with your soon-to-be ex-spouse—period. If you want that agreement to be financially equitable and legally valid, you and your spouse should expect to shell out significant fees to each consult with your own attorneys and financial experts. But you'll still be better off financially and especially emotionally by combining mediation with additional expert advice than if you become adversaries in a contested divorce.

Mediators Who Are Overcoming Their Shortcomings
You might be fortunate too in finding one of the many former adversarial attorneys who have become fed up with that way of life and are now becoming divorce mediators. Furthermore, mediators are increasingly recognizing the value of having more financial expertise and are acquiring additional training to lessen the amount of outside expertise that couples should seek. If you find a particularly good one, you might come out of mediation with an agreement to which each representing attorney and financial advisor will have only minor objections. Even with such a mediator, however, you should still each consult with your own attorneys and financial experts to ensure that the mediated solution is financially sound and legally valid, in which case, the bulk of your costs will be for mediation.

The Track Record for Mediation
When mediation is used, various studies show that it results in more equitable and more harmonious settlements. Although critics argue that these more equitable settlements usually come at a greater cost to men, usually the extra cost is often related to providing for better joint parenting and adequate child support. Furthermore, mediation has been found to substantially lower the cost of the divorce, which makes fairness to the dependent partner (which is more often the woman) more affordable. A study of about 200 mediated and 200 adversarial Connecticut divorces published in *Mediation Quarterly* ("To Mediate or Not to Mediate: Financial Outcomes in Mediated Versus Adversarial Divorces," Winter, 1999) illustrates these advantages vividly:

- *Mediation favored more father custody.* About two thirds of each group ended up with joint-legal/wife physical custody. Most of the remaining third of each group in mediation ended up in joint-legal/joint-physical arrangements. This contrasts sharply with the results of adversarial processes in which the usual outcome was wife-legal/wife-physical custody. Using mediation therefore has great potential for maintaining the husband's parenting role after the divorce.
- *Mediation resulted in more property, child support, and spousal support to women.* Because women more frequently face poverty and bankruptcy after divorce, this result is encouraging for them.
- *College education was more frequently provided for in mediation.* A victory for children; enough said.
- *Shorter time until divorce and fewer postdivorce modifications.* Mediation resulted in about an eight-month average time until divorce versus

almost a year for adversarial processes. And more than twice as many (about 20 versus 10 percent) adversarial cases went back to court post-divorce. These results show that mediation allows spouses to begin their separate lives sooner and more quickly put the divorce completely behind them—a victory for men and women.

Choosing Mediation

So why doesn't everyone use mediation? Unfortunately, mediation might not work in every case. However, the more of the following positive divorce mediation indicators that apply to your situation, the more likely mediation will work:

- *The mediation process was started early.* Mediation is much more likely to be agreed to and to work if it is initiated before the parties have drawn their respective lines in the sands about their positions and when neither party has done much to initiate an adversarial divorce—such as having paid an attorney a big retainer and having met more than once with the attorney. Mediators say that the biggest hurdle is to get both parties to come to at least a first meeting where they'll learn how the process actually works.
- *There is a balance of authority between the spouses.* Mediation results in a solution that has actually been worked out by the spouses, with direction and guidance from the mediator. Thus, mediation works best when both parties are capable of speaking up for themselves. When that is not the case, mediation becomes an arm-wrestling match in which the more forceful person pushes the settlement toward his or her desired outcome.

  But mediation can still work even when one partner feels uncomfortable by the other's hostility as long as the intimidating spouse is not abusive. After all, anger is a natural byproduct of initiating divorce, so a good mediator will expect it to some extent and sometimes will talk to the parties in separate rooms in order to soften it. The mediator will then bring them together to elucidate the issues.

  In addition, you can effect a balance of power by including your financial advisor and/or attorney at the mediation sessions. Although this strategy may appear to increase the cost of mediation, you may save money in the long run if you enter into a good legal and financial agreement that does not have to be reworked by these professionals after the mediation session. Mediation won't work, though, if one party has always dominated the marital discourse or, worse, has ruled by financial threat or physical and emotional abuse.

- *The couple has tried good-faith marital counseling.* The past proven willingness of both parties to resolve their marital differences bodes well for mediation working when saving the marriage is no longer realistic.

- *Both spouses are involved parents.* The more that the spouses have shared and enjoyed parental responsibility, the more likely it is that they'll be willing to mutually act in the best interests of the children. But even when one spouse has been the dominant breadwinner and the other the primary homemaker, success is still likely if the breadwinner has been supportive of the homemaker and has been involved as much as possible.

- *Trust exists.* Most divorces involve ill will and bitter feelings about the failure of the marriage and possible extramarital affairs. But a trained mediator can soothe these pains as long as the parties ultimately trust each other's basic fairness in not trying to put one over on the other financially. If the spouses see each other as having dealt honestly and fairly with others in financial affairs and business, then it should give them confidence that they'll abide by those ethics in divorce. However, because mediation generally doesn't involve the complete, expensive discovery process that's part of adversarial divorce, nagging doubts that each spouse has about the other's trustworthiness can undermine mediation.

Arbitration

Like mediation, arbitration involves using a neutral third party to reach a settlement. Mediation, though, allows either party to pull out of the process at any time or refuse to implement the final mediated settlement. In contrast, binding divorce arbitration requires parties to live with the arbitrator's decision. In arbitration, the parties meet together with their attorneys in front of the arbitrator, which is similar to mediation. But arbitration is unlike mediation in that it is more of an adversarial process in which attorneys play a central role—with the goal of taking less time and costing much less than going to court. While arbitration helps clean the toxic atmosphere of a lengthy battle, it does little to repair communications for the purpose of cooperative postdivorce parenting.

In considering arbitration you should know these additional facts about it:

- *Arbitrator selection.* Arbitrators are generally attorneys or former judges who act privately, not as agents of the government. They are generally chosen by agreement between both parties from a collective list compiled from both parties' suggestions. However, the judge in a divorce proceeding will appoint an arbitrator at the request of both parties.

- *Rules of evidence*: Although arbitration involves a hearing with all parties present, the parties can decide in advance on the rules for presentation, which can be less formal than a court proceeding. Parties can also decide whether or not to have attorneys present.
- *Settlements:* Arbitrators do not work with parties toward a settlement, but they will try to get the parties to settle before the hearing if the preliminary facts suggest a settlement can be reached.
- *Appeals:* Judges' decisions can be appealed for a variety of reasons, but an arbitrator's decision is rarely overturned by a court unless bias or an error in applying law can be proven.

PSEUDO-ARBITRATION?

Craig Ross, the divorce legal expert frequently cited in this book, presides over arbitrations. But he rarely ends up completing a hearing and writing a decision, despite the fact the cases come to him after the parties have reached a total impasse. "I rarely end up hearing the entire case and writing an opinion, though," says Ross. "Usually, about halfway through the evidence/testimonies I stop and ask if the parties would like to try to mediate since I now have some *ideas*! I try to adopt a facial expression and body posture as though something in their testimonies struck a miraculous chord. So long as the parties have had some opportunity to ventilate, I can usually move them towards constructive negotiation. I try to pick a spot where the parties seem a little tired/aggravated and then switch the nature of the process so that it ends up with the parties coming to a settlement. This almost always works, but I have no clue what to call it—as it's neither pure arbitration or mediation."

Collaborative Family Law and Collaborative Divorce

The chances for divorcing couples who want to give a nonfighting approach the fullest possible fighting chance have improved over the last 10 years with the emergence of collaborative family law and collaborative divorce. Picture the scene about 15 minutes before the start of a heavyweight boxing match. From opposite sides, the spotlights shine on each fighter and his entourage as he enters the ring, where various officials are already gathered in the center. The collaborative equivalent is that the spouses each enter the negotiation ring with their minientourage—an attorney and coach—and are met there by a shared family consultant and financial expert. No referee is in sight because the spouses and attorneys have agreed that they will throw no punches and they will not leave the ring until both have won a hard-fought end to their differences over finances and family sharing.

John Bowman, a family law attorney in Durham, North Carolina, draws a distinction between collaborative family law and collaborative divorce: the collaborative family law model starts with the parties and their attorneys with mutually agreed upon experts retained on an as-needed basis, while in the collaborative divorce model a team of professionals such as therapists, financial planners, CPAs, business valuators, and benefits experts is assembled at the beginning to aid in the process. Although the collaborative divorce model has the advantage of a team approach, it can also be very costly.

The Collaborative Contract

For many attorneys, to work together with another attorney whose client has seemingly opposing interests is to commit heresy. But collaborative law proponents claim that what makes it work is the fact that beforehand, they contractually agree that both attorneys lose their clients the moment either even acts as if he or she will throw a punch. That gives collaborative attorneys a powerful incentive to "put all the cards on the table" to reach a common goal rather than to hold back information and/or threaten litigation to force an inequitable settlement. Thus, collaborative divorce law has evolved as a conflict-resolution system intended to counter what's wrong with all the other approaches, in the following ways:

- *No motions:* Except for submitting the final judgment in order to get the divorce decree, the collaborative approach is the polar opposite of adversarial because everything is done out of court. There's no discovery: The parties pledge full disclosure, and each willingly provides all necessary financial information.
- *Limited emotions:* While it's impossible to separate powerful emotions from the divorce process, the collaborative process differs from the key focus of mediation, which is to defuse the emotional interaction between the parties in order for them to work things out. Instead, each spouse's attorney and/or coach helps channel his or her client's emotions

every step of the way so that the focus of the sessions can be a solution that is emotionally and financially satisfactory. Where mediation assumes the parties can work things out with the help of someone knowledgeable enough to help frame the issues, collaborative divorce assumes the need for input from several experts to help the parties understand and evaluate all viable alternatives.

• *No ruling:* Unlike going to court or relying on an arbitrator, the collaborative result is not a ruling in response to each side's presentation of facts, witnesses, and so on. Instead, it's more like a consensus decision made by a committee—in this case, of two people with a number of advisors. So you might think of it as an enhanced form of mediation with experts weighing in and advising you, with the goal an agreement that incorporates the issues and financial considerations that are important to the future of both spouses and their kids.

The Collaborative Catch

Collaborative divorce sounds too good to be true, so there must be a catch, which there is, and it's a big one: Although all parties agree to the process, that doesn't guarantee a solution. At some point, the parties might decide that a consensus will never be reached and terminate their involvement, resorting to arbitration or going to court. Nevertheless, the effort might still have been worthwhile in giving both spouses a better understanding of the issues and their legal, financial, and psychological ramifications. They might be able to agree on a number of points and then go to a narrow arbitration to settle the remainder. Or if they do go to court, they might have built up enough trust so that they can skip discovery and other parts of the process. Instead they can agree to provide both new opposing attorneys (because they can't use the collaborative attorneys) copies of the disclosed material used during collaboration.

Still, collaboration isn't cheap—although it is usually far less expensive than full-blown adversarial divorce litigation. And a lot of expense occurs early on. So if it fails and the parties emerge so disgruntled or embittered that no use can be made of what was done during collaboration, the divorce could end up costing more in time and money than a direct adversarial action.

The Caveat Emptor for Collaborative Divorce

While such failure doesn't seem to happen often, the current state of collaborative law is comparable to middle-stage clinical trials of a promising new drug. It clearly works well for some people, but caveat emptor (buyer beware) must be applied because the use of collaboration has begun taking off only in the last few years, so it's too early to tell how it will work in a larger population of divorcing couples and attorneys. Perhaps harmful side effects will emerge during more widely spread use, such as litigation against the professionals involved if one or both spouses feel the process betrayed them. For example, what if many cases emerge in which one spouse later discovers that the other held out during full disclosure and that the attorney or financial expert should have picked up on it?

Unlike clinical trials, however, no government agency can prevent you from trying collaborative divorce. So it's up to you to do the quality control of checking out both attorneys and the other professionals that will be involved to be sure that they are qualified, successful, and experienced in the process. Chances are that a little effort will result in you and your spouse being able to find a good collaborative team if you live in Minnesota (where it originated), California, or a few other states. But don't be surprised at a "huh, what's that?" reaction in some smaller population states not known for progressive approaches to social issues.

Litigated Divorce

While nonadversarial (couple-only, mediated, and collaborative) or minimally adversarial (arbitration) solutions are usually preferable, sometimes the gloves must come off—either because no technique is likely to work or your spouse is unwilling to go any other route. Here are the situations most likely to get you to court:

- *Fugitive spouse:* He or she has absconded with significant assets and left no forwarding address.
- *Abusive spouse:* The relationship has been abusive or your spouse is now making threats.
- *Prenuptial preemption:* You or your spouse challenge an existing prenuptial agreement.
- *Controlling spouse:* Considerable assets are at stake and your spouse has either kept you out of the financial loop or has frequently demonstrated a willingness to engage in questionable, if not dishonest, business practices.
- *Secretive spouse:* You find out that your spouse has secretly been planning a divorce and you need to take action to prevent the assets from being drained or to not end up being liable for considerable new marital debts.
- *Spouse is successful divorce attorney:* For chuckle effect, but true!

- *Negotiation breakdown:* Attempts at mediation or a collaborative approach have failed.
- *Stakes too high:* There's too much at stake to rely on an arbitrator's decision that can probably not be appealed.
- *Need leverage:* You really want a fair settlement, but you know the only way your spouse will agree to one is for you to show that you mean business by filing and making fighting noises.
- *Greed:* You want everything you can get, regardless of who gets hurt in the process.

Take the Vengeful Fight Outside

Let's start with that last and easiest reason. If your anger is a 500-gallon cauldron boiling over but you haven't yet crumpled some pages or thrown this book across the room (or at your spouse), then read no further; take it back now, and ask for a refund. This book is about fairness and fair fighting in defending yourself. It is not the kind of "husband get wife" or "wife get husband" tome that you'd want to hide from your spouse once he or she knows that you're planning divorce. In fact, you'd want to encourage your spouse to read this book so that you'll have at least a partially shared framework for the issues you're facing.

Of course, offering this book to your spouse won't help if domestic violence is an issue in your divorce. In that case, you must regard your spouse as the worst kind of adversary and you must litigate accordingly, including getting protective orders and possibly physical protection. Make sure you get an attorney who is extensively experienced in that area and who will help you line up the other professionals you'll need to protect you physically, as well as financially—including recovering the costs of necessary protection for which you had to pay. How to do that goes beyond the scope of this book, but we can say this: Even if your abusive spouse suddenly acts repentant, you still need to get legal protection for yourself and any children in your home.

Indoor Fighting Rules

This book will help you prepare for any heavy-duty divorce fight that can't be avoided. Although the path to court should be a last resort, it's still a road often traveled. So here's an overview of the basic litigation steps that you, your spouse, or your attorneys will take—who does it depends on your choices regarding representation and what your state allows or requires—from filing to final judgment:

1. *Summons or waiver:* If you and your spouse have agreed to proceed with divorce, then one of you should file a *waiver of service of process.* Otherwise, the divorce must start with a *summons* that states an intent to serve divorce papers no sooner than the number of days specified in the state statute (often 21, 28, or 30).

2. *Petition/complaint and (proposed) marital settlement agreement:* Either spouse can file this document, known as either a petition or complaint, which includes rudimentary information about the spouses such as age, place of residence, and date of marriage. It also states the grounds for the divorce, which are generally *irreconcilable differences* because most states have no-fault divorce. The proposed marital settlement agreement addresses custody, and financial issues such as child support, spousal support, property division and attorney's fees. According to family law attorney, John Bowman, most litigation follows a failed attempt to resolve these issues by agreement. However, if the spouse has no way of knowing financial details, the marital settlement agreement might be expressed in either general terms, such as "half of . . . ," or it might deliberately overreach to make sure enough is being requested pending discovery (see step 5).

   2a. *Related documents:* When the complaint is served, a document sometimes called a *return of service* is filed. Depending on your state's procedures, if you have a simple divorce that incorporates a settlement agreement, you might also have to file the following minor documents: an *affidavit, verified statement,* and *record of divorce.*

   2b. *Acknowledgement of settlement agreement:* If the spouse who has been served the divorce petition doesn't contest it, he or she then files an *appearance, consent, and waiver form* (sometimes referred to by other names in different states) that permits the marital settlement agreement to be converted to the *final divorce decree.* This is the classic *uncontested divorce* that requires no more than a few hundred dollars in court fees and possibly a few hundred more in attorney's fees if an attorney drafts and files the official documents.

3. *Response to divorce petition/complaint:* In a contested divorce, this paperwork officially expresses a spouse's refusal to accept the terms of the complaint—or to the marital settlement agreement, if it is set forth in it. It amounts to a counteroffer, although like the petition, the response might be stated in general or overreaching terms pending discovery.

4. *Temporary orders and injunctions, separation agreement, court-ordered mediation:*

4a. *Formal separation agreement contract:* In many cases, couples begin separations with verbal agreements as to childcare, custody, and financial support. But sometimes it's better to formalize it into one of three types of separation agreements. The first is when you've agreed to a trial separation for a period of a few months while deciding whether to continue the marriage or divorce. Unless you'd be in dire circumstances if your spouse didn't live up to the agreement, though, it's usually better to simply rely on a verbal agreement because the period is so short. The third is when the marriage is definitely dead but you've agreed to defer a divorce indefinitely or have reasons that it will take a long time. In either event, recognize that a separation agreement under these circumstances could become tantamount to a divorce settlement; many people have discovered to their dismay that all or parts of an open-ended separation agreement could not be overridden by the ultimate divorce agreement. So you should definitely get good legal advice and assistance in drafting it, before deciding on such an agreement or its terms.

It's the possibility of reaching the second type of separation agreement that concerns most divorcing couples, however. If you know that you want to divorce as quickly as possible, but that it will take some time due to the complexity of the case, then you might want to have a separation agreement that covers a clearly designated specific period of time. By doing that, you'll avoid the trap of being stuck with that agreement in a final settlement while meeting your needs, even if imperfectly, during the twilight-zone period of your pending divorce. To ensure escaping this trap, have an attorney draft the agreement.

4b. *Court orders, temporary orders, and injunctions:* One advantage of a formal separation agreement occurs if your spouse violates it. You can then use it to obtain a court order that will put your spouse in contempt of court upon continued violation. Also, when filing a divorce petition or response, you might also ask the court to issue orders or injunctions if you have concerns about assets being drained, marital debt being incurred, or the children being kidnapped. These might include a personal protection order (in a case of domestic violence), an injunction that freezes accounts, an order asserting responsibility for paying bills, an order to vacate the marital home, and a temporary custody order.

4c. *Court-ordered mediation:* Even if you've considered or explored mediation and have decided not to pursue it, many states require that you meet with a mediator or counselor before proceeding with the litigation. However, you can probably get the requirement waived if you present evidence that you've been through failed mediation, there are allegations of domestic violence, or the parties live far apart.

5. *Discovery, conferences, and motions:* To prepare for trial, each side needs complete financial information that usually includes documents and records that the other party has. In addition, especially when custody and spousal support are involved, each side might want detailed information about the other spouse's past and current lifestyle and future plans

   The discovery phase involves providing documents, data, responses, and deposition testimony on these issues, including the following:
   • Net worth statements
   • Pension and business valuation
   • Real estate and other property appraisal
   • Employee benefits and insurance coverage
   • Oral depositions (examinations by opposing attorneys before trial), written responses to opposing attorneys' interrogatories, requests for admissions, or requests for production of documents.

   During this phase, the spouses and their attorneys jointly attend one or more pretrial conferences to clarify issues and procedures regarding the case. Just as portrayed in TV criminal trials, each side might file motions with the judge dealing with witnesses, evidence, and possible problems with complying with discovery.

6. *Negotiated settlement or trial:* Although settlements can be negotiated at any juncture in this process, they often occur after most or all of the financial disclosure, pretrial testimony, and document exchanges have taken place. Negotiations occur then because both sides have a better sense of how long the trial might take and the probable outcome of the case. That enables them to better weigh the potential gains or losses that are apt to occur in court in addition to the certain losses they will have from the additional hours they'll be billed for attorney courtroom time and expert witness testimony. They may also realize the extent of public embarrassment, loss of privacy, and trauma they would experience in the course of a trial.

7. *Final judgment and modifications:* Whether by settlement or court verdict, the final judgment details the disposition of the case. It is subject to appeal if it is reached by verdict, which is one more reason that a settlement is desirable for the party that has the most to lose on successful appeal or cannot afford the expenses of defending an

appeal. Nevertheless, any final judgment is subject to later modification by the court for changed circumstances regarding either ex-spouse. All states allow changes regarding child support and custody issues, many regarding spousal support, but very few regarding property division.

When a Prenuptial Is Not Enough

One special form of divorce litigation is used when a marital settlement agreement already exists in the form of a *prenuptial or antenuptial* (before marriage) or a *postnuptial* (during marriage) *contract.* The bad news or good news, depending on whether you had one done to protect your assets or to insure certain assets, is that many judges don't view such agreements favorably—one key reason being that they're often found to have been made under one party's perception of duress. Nevertheless, getting an agreement broken in court, or defending against that happening, can be an expensive process that often leads to a settlement other than what the contract states.

So, whether you're the "out spouse" trying to get more or the spouse of means trying to plug the leak in the marital dike, you must weigh your willingness to settle or fully litigate against the chance the agreement will be upheld. The better that the following circumstances describe your prenuptial, the more likely it will be broken in court:

- *Last minute:* The out spouse was presented with it and signed it as the wedding came down to the wire, rather than having several months or more to digest and negotiate it.
- *Insufficient representation:* The out spouse didn't retain an attorney to thoroughly review it or retained an attorney who wasn't fully competent to deal with the complex issues involved.
- *Coercion:* The out spouse can prove that there was a pattern of threats that the wedding would be cancelled or there was continued urging (bordering on harassment) to sign it.
- *Rotten in Denmark:* The agreement isn't in the interest of public policy, was drawn in violation of family law, or is just plain unfair to the out spouse, even allowing for considerable differences in economic circumstances entering the marriage.
- *Hidden information:* The out spouse can prove that he or she was given less than full disclosure and thus was led to believe that the wealthier spouse's financial circumstances were far less favorable than they actually were.

Most of these circumstances shouldn't have applied if you and your spouse signed a postnuptial agreement, in which case, it is likely, but not guaranteed, to be upheld.

Do-It-Yourself Divorce (Almost Anyway)

Perhaps all this litigation talk makes you think you should stay as far away from court or attorneys as possible. So why not do it yourself (pro-se divorce), as many infomercials and print or Web ads urge you to do. Divorce-expert Craig Ross, who is not a litigator, urges caution: "If (a) there are no kids and (b) no pensions and (c) not much in the way of assets and (d) it is a short marriage then pro-se is fine. Otherwise, the odds of screwing up are about 99%."

So step carefully if you do it yourself and separate the wheat from the chaff among divorce-aid products. Find do-it-yourself books, kits, or software packages that are specific to your state and available from Nolo and other reputable legal products distributors. You might also check out some of the online services (such as www.LegalZoom.com and www.CompleteCase.com) that purport to completely prepare the documents you'll need to file for divorce in your state, which you then download and print, based on information that you provide in a secure-server online questionnaire.

Whether by online "lawyer" or kit, however, don't trust the result to be legally pure. Instead, regard it as a polished draft of your final divorce agreement. You should be able to find many competent divorce attorneys who charge reasonable hourly fees, who will take no more than a few hours to review your draft and make sure everything is in order and that you're not missing anything obvious that makes your agreement unfair or invalid.

For longer-term marriages, those involving considerable assets or disparities in income, or any in which kids are involved, you can still start with the do-it-yourself (DIY) approach. If you're able to agree on the result, you're well on your way to finalizing the divorce quickly and efficiently. But don't rush; regard the initial do-it-yourself product as no more than a first rough draft of an ultimate marital settlement agreement. You should each definitely consult your own attorneys to carefully evaluate the draft agreement: first to determine whether it protects your interests; second to ensure that it conforms to your state's divorce laws and will likely be accepted by the court; and finally to suggest substantive changes that would correct any imbalances and put it in legal conformance.

After you and your spouse reconcile any differences, you can have one of your attorneys put the document in final form and have the other attorney review it, but both of them do not need to separately redraft it. It's possible that you might have trouble resolving these differences, but don't rush into court. Instead, finalize the points on which you agree and perhaps hire a mediator for one or two sessions to resolve your differences.

Extending this logic, if do-it-yourself doesn't produce something on which you initially agree, it still might help you come to agreement on certain aspects and then go to full mediation with a good chance of success because you've already communicated positively. But even if your spouse is not willing to work with you initially on a do-it-yourself approach, you might find such tools useful for developing a solution that you think makes sense, provided that you know enough about the marital finances. As long as you don't regard do-it-yourself as an all-or-nothing proposition, it can help save you time, money, and emotional turmoil in your divorce. Think of it the way you think of doing part of the work in finishing a basement—sheet-rocking, final painting, and so on—while hiring a carpenter, plumber, and electrician to do the more skilled parts of the job.

With the understanding that we don't endorse these or recommend their use totally independent of an attorney, here are some do-it-yourself divorce kits to consider:

- Divorce Yourself: The National No-Fault Divorce Kit (www.smartdivorce.com/selfhelp.htm)
- INFOAMERICA No-Fault Divorce Kit (www.divorcekit.com/)

Divorcing a Missing or Nonresponding Spouse

If your spouse has gone missing with a lot of assets, then you might consider first calling *Court TV* or *Lifetime TV*; perhaps they'll offer a fat sum for rights to the eventual TV movie, which should help compensate for what you might not get in the courts. Seriously, though, you have an obvious problem. The good news is that states do allow unilateral divorces to proceed after you've demonstrated a good-faith effort to find your spouse. Or if your spouse isn't missing but hasn't responded to the divorce petition, you're simply required to prove that you did serve the papers. Furthermore, if a forensic accountant can help you trace your spouse's accounts, you might be able to get an injunction that freezes those accounts, so that a lien might later be put on them to award you part or all of the judgment you obtain.

In most cases, though, missing spouses are the same sort that might have hidden or drained assets and might pay child support only if confined to a torture chamber. If that describes your spouse, you can at least be assured that it will be relatively cheap and easy to obtain a divorce in which you're not asking for anything from the spouse. However, if considerable assets are involved or you're worried about the possibility that your spouse might later attempt to get custody of the children or kidnap them, you should retain an attorney experienced with such divorces to protect your interests.

Comparing Your Divorce Options

Figure 2-1 compares the key features and costs of each type of divorce (do-it-yourself, litigated, mediated, arbitrated, and collaborative).

Divorce Differences among States

Your best choice of divorce options might vary depending on where you live because of state laws concerning support and property division, as well as the legal process itself. For example, in some states, the old-fashioned fault-based divorce remains as the only option. But increasingly, states have adopted no-fault divorce, which usually requires only that the grounds be "irreconcilable differences"— or separation for the statutorily required time—with no favorable financial judgments for spouses who are victims of multiple-offender marital cheating or even domestic violence. And a number of states have compromised by offering both options. Here's a closer look at how divorce grounds and other aspects of divorce differ by state statute.

Divorce Grounds, Residency Requirements, and Timing

The grounds for a fault divorce include cruelty, infidelity, desertion, imprisonment, mental incapacity, and lack of sexual consortium. These grounds are most often used to simply justify a divorce. But in states that allow both fault and no-fault, cruelty and infidelity are sometimes used to try and obtain a more favorable financial disposition. So if you're being sued for divorce on grounds of fault but it's clear your spouse simply wants a divorce and is not trying to get additional financial leverage, it often isn't worth the additional attorney preparation and court time to contest the grounds; seek a fair settlement instead.

If you're trying to get divorced in Idaho, you're in for a five-year separation before a divorce will be granted. And you'll have to wait three years in Texas, Utah, and Rhode Island. However, most other states require either no separa-

	Contested	Mediated	Collaborative	DIY/Uncontested	Comments
Client/Attorney Consultation	Expensive billed time often wasted using attorney to vent, offer solace, or provide counseling. Much information gathering and dialogue provides strategic background that isn't needed in other approaches. Generally requires advance retainer of several-thousand dollars.	Attorney can sit in on sessions, and you meet to determine needs and objectives, and whether agreement satisfies them. Generally requires 6 to 12 two-hour sessions at about $200 to $300 each.	Requires the most attorney/client time, but it's mainly devoted to determining your needs and objectives, and in meeting together with your spouse and attorneys. This approach is probably overkill when not that much is at stake and issues aren't complex.	Do-it-yourself (DIY) consultation with the attorney is critical to ensure the agreement is legally valid and protects each spouse by assuring that the other is not taking undue advantage. Uncontested enforcement is a key issue also, so a consult is similarly needed. Some attorneys offer a package deal to cover meetings, document prep, etc.	Contested approaches sometimes necessary; save billed time by first cooling off, getting emotional support elsewhere, and gathering information for attorney offline, etc. In this table, DIY/uncontested is either just consulting an attorney but working with your spouse toward resolution, or divorcing a spouse who doesn't respond or can't be located. Attorney hourly fees generally same for all methods of resolution. Phone: Flat per-call charge plus prorated hourly rate.
Opposing Attorneys Communication	Most spousal contact is through attorneys, which is inefficient and expensive.	Still needed but less because spouses communicate directly in sessions.	More than other methods, but totally focused on problem resolution rather than serving as overpaid communication conduits.	In DIY, attorneys briefly communicate to make sure agreement reflects both parties' wishes.	When selecting an attorney, make sure to ask how much billable time generally goes into this for cases like yours.
Research and Case Prep	Heavy attorney time here to prepare winning case.	Sometimes needed on points of law. Mediator can't give legal advice.	Focused on points of law intended to find win/win solutions.	Research sometimes needed (DIY) and case prep sometimes needed for a court hearing when spouse is unresponsive.	Make sure that you're billed according to who's doing the work. Attorneys often have their paralegals of junior staff do most of work.

FIGURE 2-1 Comparison of Divorce Option Features and Costs

	Contested	Mediated	Collaborative	DIY/Uncontested	Comments
Document Prep	Wasted time when attorneys play document ping-pong in reaching an agreement.	Bulk of attorney's time here.	Limited to those needed for legally complete, valid agreement.	Usually the biggest expense in these divorces. Can save by having a paralegal prepare documents and an attorney check them.	A marital settlement agreement generally costs from $500 to $1500. QDRO about $1000. These costs are for preparation when the agreement has already been made and the facts gathered.
Discovery	Can be the most expensive in bitterly contested cases. Most of billing should be at clerical (not attorney) rates.	Generally defeats the purpose, but some limited discovery might still make sense.	Generally not needed in atmosphere of trust, full disclosure, respect.	Usually Not Applicable	Save substantial money by gathering and copying family financial records before separation.
Filing Motions	Often used to bury spouse in paperwork, intimidate, or embarrass.	Sometimes needed, but compromise encouraged by mediation mindset.	Generally not needed because custody, etc. are agreed collaboratively.	Sometimes needed in uncontested cases with non-responsive spouse.	Attorney costs involve both time to draft the motions and appearances in court.
Court Time and Court Costs	Can get out of control with appearances for series of motions, etc.	Generally doesn't require appearances, only court filing fees.	Generally doesn't require appearances, only court filing fees, which might exceed mediation or DIY because of more complex issues.	Court appearance sometimes necessary in non-responsive cases.	Most jurisdictions post a schedule of court costs on their government Web sites.
Mediation and Counseling	Courts often require either or both before a case can be heard.	Resistance to trying to reach a mediated settlement is often reduced by starting with counseling and continuing it throughout mediation.	Counseling before or during collaboration process can help assure it doesn t break down.	Counseling before or during the DIY process can help assure it doesn t break down.	Mediation and counseling have excellent track records in limiting both the financial and emotional damage of divorce. Even if mediation doesn't lead to a resolution it can slow down the escalation in a contested case.
Other Expert Professionals Services	See comments for financial experts. Experts for custody and forensic	See comments for financial experts. Prudent to still use forensic accountant	See comments for financial experts. Can save with collaborative by exploiting good	See comments for financial experts. Only others are those needed to ensure that	Financial experts (financial planners, accountants, benefit experts, etc.) play a key role in all approaches so that spouses

38

	accounting can cost tens of thousands of dollars.	if trust is shaky and lots at stake. Mediation could lead to agreeing to jointly consulting custody expert on what's best for child.	faith of spouses to consider jointly using some experts.	QDRO and other documents prepared properly. Should consider different method if it seems you need custody consult or forensic accounting.	can understand what's at stake, how various settlements translate into future financial health, and to prepare pension QDROs. They generally charge from $150 to $300 hourly. Full valuations of closely held businesses can range from $7500 to $10,000.
Expert Court Testimony	Can be extremely expensive because billing generally by day rather than court time, and can include travel, etc. Beware of unexpected costs when the court appoints an expert even if you hadn't planned on one.	Generally not applicable	Generally not applicable	Might be needed or wise when spouse is in absentia to solidify custody decision or resolution of other matters against future challenge.	Just because expert opinion might be critical to resolving a case doesn't mean that experts have to testify. When it's an issue of financial valuation, consider compromising on opposing experts figures rather than spending thousands more to have them appear in court.
Indirect Expenses	Difficult to plan for in this approach. Find out if you can do some tasks on your own or provide information in a way to minimize costs.	Successful mediation avoids a lot of these.	Attorneys should be able to provide a reasonable estimate	A major area of saving for this approach.	Can include various clerical and paraprofessional costs for scanning, copying, number crunching, etc. by paralegals, secretaries, clerks, law students, etc. usually at 1/2 attorney's rate.
TOTAL Typical Costs	$25,000 to $75,000 but protracted, escalated litigation can easily drive it over $100,000	$5000 to $15,000 when mediation is successful and the case not overly complex. But fees are often wasted when parties are too contentious or the case too complex.	$5000 to $30,000 (usually in the higher range), including counseling and financial experts, but can partly pay for itself in most efficient settlement that least damages both sides finances in long run.	$2500 to $7500 depending on complexity for DIY.	All fee ranges here depend on case complexity and prevailing area fees for attorneys and other experts.

FIGURE 2-1 Continued.

tion, or various durations of one year or less. In addition, most states require a minimum period of residency, usually six months or less—although a few require a year.

If your state does require separation, don't just assume you know what that means, because separation is defined differently in different states. Its definition ranges from merely telling your spouse your intention to file to the date papers are filed to the date you actually physically separate. The most obvious importance of the separation date is how it might affect the way you choose to file federal taxes. But it comes into play even more regarding its use in your state's treatment of debt, valuation of retirement funds and businesses, and determination of spousal support. By the time you've completed your divorce, you might end up regarding the family law judge's job as similar to that of an athletic event timekeeper, who must be obsessively concerned about when "the clock starts" and when "the clock stops."

Figure 2-2 summarizes the grounds and residency requirements for, and the timing of, divorce in each state.

Titling and Ownership of Property

Possession might be nine tenths of the law, but don't mistake the name your property is in with possession because all but one state disregards the actual name in which property is held. Instead, they rely on evidence of whose property it really is. So don't panic if you've put a bunch of your own money from before marriage, or money given specifically to you during marriage, into a joint account. If you can trace how you obtained it and it got into that account, it might still be considered your separate property. From here on, though, avoiding commingling of separate property with joint property is the safest way to make sure inheritances, gifts, or property you owned before the marriage remain your separate property.

You might think the same is true if you and your spouse have always treated all your money as belonging to whoever earned it, but you'd be wrong! In community property states, all property earned during the marriage, or not specifically gifted to or inherited by one spouse, is treated as half-owned by each spouse, so the smaller earner gets a windfall and the big earner is out of luck. And even in most of the states without community property laws, part of the earnings of one spouse can still be considered as belonging to the other spouse. That's particularly true when the other spouse helped earn it. For example, the wife of a business executive whose social activities have helped the executive perform the job better and rise in the ranks can be considered to have helped earn the

STATE	No Fault Sole Ground	No Fault Added to Traditional	Incompatibility	Living Separate and Apart	Judicial Separation[5]	Durational Requirements[6]
Alabama		x	x	2 years	x	6 months
Alaska	x		x	2 years	x	6 months
Arizona	x	x[1]			x	90 days
Arkansas		x		18 mos.	x	60 days
California	x				x	6 months*
Colorado	x				x	90 days
Connecticut		x		18 mos.	x	1 year
Delaware		x	x	6 mos.		6 months
District of Columbia	x			1 year	x	6 months
Florida	x					6 months
Georgia		x				6 months
Hawaii				2 years[3]	x	6 months[4]
Idaho		x			x	6 weeks
Illinois		x		2 years	x	90 days
Indiana			x		x	60 days
Iowa	x				x	1 year
Kansas			x		x	60 days
Kentucky	x			60 days	x	180 days
Louisiana		x[1]		6 months[2]	x	6 months

FIGURE 2-2   Grounds for Divorce and Residency Requirements in Each State

41

Maine		x			x	6 months
Maryland		x		1 year	x	1 year
Massachusetts		x			x	None
Michigan	x				x	6 months
Minnesota	x				x	180 days
Mississippi		x				6 months
Missouri		x		1–2 years	x	90 days
Montana	x		x	180 days	x	90 days
Nebraska	x				x	1 year
Nevada			x	1 year	x	6 weeks
New Hampshire		x		2 years		1 year
New Jersey		x		18 mos.		1 year
New Mexico		x	x		x	6 months
New York		x		1 year	x	1 year
North Carolina		x		1 year	x	6 months
North Dakota		x			x	6 months
Ohio		x	x	1 year	x	6 months
Oklahoma			x		x	6 months
Oregon	x				x	6 months
Pennsylvania		x		2 years	x	6 months
Rhode Island		x		3 years	x	1 year
South Carolina		x		1 year	x	3 months (both residents)

South Dakota			x	None
Tennessee	x	2 years	x	6 months
Texas	x	3 years		6 months
Utah	x	3 years	x	90 days
Vermont	x	6 months		6 months
Virginia	x	1 year	x	6 months
Washington	x			1 year
West Virginia	x	1 year	x	1 year
Wisconsin	x		x	6 months
Wyoming	x	x	x	60 days

* California requires domicile as distinguished from residency for jurisdictional purposes.

1. Covenant marriage statutes establish specific grounds for divorce for covenant marriages (thus limiting the circumstances in which no-fault divorce can be used).

2. Two years for covenant marriages.

3. Grounds are either marriage irretrievably broken or two years separation.

4. Six months in state and three months in circuit waiting for divorce itself, but can file as soon as residency established.

5. A judicial separation is a court-authorized separation agreement under which the parties live separate and apart indefinitely, without terminating the marriage.

6. Durational Requirements are the duration of residency required before eligibility to file for divorce.

©The American Bar Association. This chart used with permission of the American Bar Association and footnotes have been expanded for clarification. It can be found at this location on its web site: http://www.abanet.org/family/familylaw/Chart4_GroundsDivorce.pdf

FIGURE 2-2   Continued.

43

executive's salary. Or if a husband has lent significant marketing support to a wife's successful entrepreneurial public relation's firm, then he might be entitled to a greater portion of the firm's income or value than he would have received otherwise. To the extent that one spouse develops his or her own business during the marriage, it is still considered marital property subject to equitable distribution, whether or not the other spouse helped build the business.

Furthermore, in equitable distribution states, once it's been determined who owns what property separately, the remainder of the marital property is subject to equitable distribution, which usually doesn't mean 50-50. Instead, in a long-term marriage, that distribution is intended to maintain equity between the lives each spouse had during the marriage and their lives going forward—taking into consideration the fact that divorce costs leave less to be divided. Thus, consider a couple with two young children in which the wife had a high-paying, high-powered job involving frequent travel, and the husband gave up a long-hours job as a chemist to gain the parenting flexibility of being a chemistry professor at a local community college. If the divorce resulted in joint custody, that might free up the husband to return to a higher-earning chemist's job, with both spouses relying more on third-party care of the children. But the husband's detour from the chemistry profession left a considerable salary gap, so equitable distribution would also imply that the property division be tilted to the husband to allow him to maintain a semblance of the lifestyle he enjoyed during the marriage, or the wife may be required to pay spousal support to achieve the same result.

In some states too—such as Alaska, Connecticut, Kansas, and Oregon—equitable distribution can extend even to property determined to belong specifically to one or the other spouse. And in most states, equitable distribution takes into account factors that affected the acquisition or consumption of property during the marriage. For example, most states consider economic misconduct, so if one spouse was a compulsive gambler or spent a lot of money having affairs, that spouse's share could be negatively impacted. Similarly, if a husband did most of the maintenance on the cars or the wife did a lot of needed home maintenance, those nonmonetary contributions might be reason for them to get higher shares.

Finally, in dividing property, two key questions are "as of when?" and "before or after taxes?" Again, states differ, with some "freezing" the value as of the separation date, while others adjust the value as of the date of signing the settlement agreement. Most states value property at its market value, while some take into account what the property will actually net if sold—after capital-gains taxes are paid. The tax issue is particularly critical because the total property held by a couple can stretch further if it's divided in a way that maximizes its net value after the respective spouses liquidate it. So if your state doesn't do that, it's all the more reason to try to reach a settlement out of court that minimizes taxes in ways discussed in later chapters.

Figure 2-3 shows the key aspects of how each state handles property division in divorce.

Treatment of Debt

Dealing with marital debt can be trickier than many other divorce issues, yet is often dealt with as an afterthought—which Attorney Lee Borden finds unrealistic: "Our image of divorce from movies and television is of couples fighting over the vast wealth they've accumulated during their marriage," says Borden. "That's not what I see, though. Most of my folks are trying to figure out who gets stuck with what debt." We hope that's not your situation, but because it might be, we're going to cover some divorce debt difficulties.

In community property states, all debt incurred by either party, regardless of how accounts are titled, is considered the responsibility of both parties. In many of the other states, even though the spouses or court might allocate debt as part of the settlement, creditors will ignore that allocation and regard any debt not specifically incurred by one party (credit card or loan only in that person's name) during the marriage as the responsibility of both parties. Thus, if one spouse defaults on marital debt after the divorce, creditors can go after the other spouse.

Similarly, the IRS will ignore how you divide up federal tax debt and hold both spouses liable if a joint return is filed. Fortunately, though, federal law does protect an "innocent spouse" who's been misled or deliberately kept out of the tax loop regarding the other spouse's illegal or fraudulent tax filings. Even so, this federal law is not uniformly applicable because of state differences in such areas as community property laws.

Therefore, to simplify your life and avoid being hounded by both creditors and "revenooers" after divorce, a good settlement will involve fully dealing with all debt and tax liability before divorce—liquidating property as needed to pay off the debt. If assets aren't sufficient, the couple should consider joint bankruptcy; however, bankruptcy laws differ considerably among states if they don't totally conform to uniform federal law. For example, different states vary in which property is exempt from bankruptcy litigation.

But where debt remains and bankruptcy isn't jointly filed, the spouse left without debt should make sure that the one carrying debt has refinanced it in his or her own name coincident with divorce, thus preventing creditors from pursuing the debtor's ex-spouse.

STATE	Community Property	Only Marital Divided	Statutory List of Factors	Nonmonetary Contributions	Economic Misconduct	Contribution to Education
Alabama		x		x	x	x
Alaska	x^1			x	x	
Arizona	x				x	x
Arkansas		x	x	x		
California	x	x	x	x	x	x
Colorado		x	x	x	x	
Connecticut			x	x	x	x
Delaware		x	x	x	x	x
District of Columbia		x	x	x	x	
Florida		x	x	x	x	x
Georgia		x				
Hawaii		x^4	x^5	x^2	x^3	
Idaho	x		x			
Illinois		x	x	x	x	x
Indiana		x	x	x	x	x
Iowa			x	x	x	
Kansas			x		x	
Kentucky		x	x	x	x	x
Louisiana	x					
Maine		x	x	x	x	
Maryland		x	x	x	x	
Massachusetts				x	x	x
Michigan		x		x	x	x
Minnesota		x		x	x	
Mississippi		x	x	x	x	x
Missouri		x	x	x	x	x
Montana			x	x	x	
Nebraska		x		x	x	

46

State	1	2	3	4	5
Nevada	x		x	x	x
New Hampshire		x	x	x	x
New Jersey		x	x	x	x
New Mexico	x			x	x
New York		x	x	x	x
North Carolina		x	x	x	x
North Dakota			x	x	x
Ohio		x	x	x	x
Oklahoma		x	x	x	x
Oregon			x	x	x
Pennsylvania		x	x	x	x
Rhode Island		x	x	x	x
South Carolina		x	x	x	x
South Dakota			x	x	
Tennessee		x	x	x	x
Texas	x			x	
Utah				x	
Vermont		x	x	x	x
Virginia		x	x	x	x
Washington	x		x	x	
West Virginia		x	x	x	x
Wisconsin	x	x	x	x	x
Wyoming		x	x	x	

1. The parties by contract can agree to make some or all of their marital property community property.
2. During marriage nonmonetary contributions do not affect property division nor does the lack of them.
3. No statutory provision apply; case law is mixed.
4. During marriage nonmonetary contributions do not affect property division, nor does the lack of them.
5. No statutory provisions; case law is mixed.

© The American Bar Association. This chart used with permission of the American Bar Association and can be found at this location on its web site:
http://www.abanet.org/family/familylaw/Chart5_PropertyDivision.pdf

FIGURE 2-3   How States Treat Property Ownership and Division in Divorce

47

To get to that point, though, requires assigning responsibility for the debt, and states differ on this point just as they do on property—not surprising because debt can be thought of as "negative property." Thus, equitable division of debt might not be 50-50 either. But for starters, most states treat property acquired in both names as being the equal responsibility of both spouses, and debt incurred by either party alone as that spouse's responsibility. However, different states allow various adjustments for proof that a debt incurred only by one party was for marital property used by both parties. Similarly, if a debt incurred in both names can be shown as existing only for the benefit of one spouse, then some states allow judges to reallocate it to that spouse.

States also differ considerably on what constitutes marital debt. In some states, any debt incurred right up to the time of the divorce is considered marital, while other states regard all debts as separate after a designated key date—such as the date of filing, separation date, or the date a settlement agreement is signed.

Spousal Support Guidelines

Strictly legally, spousal support is determined separately, but in practice it's closely tied to the division of property and debt. Increasingly, updated state laws and/or the evolution of judges' attitudes have resulted in the family court seeing its task as coming to an equitable settlement. Consequently, tradeoffs are frequently made between property and support awards. However, because very few states allow postdivorce modifications of the property division, you should tend to regard property as a bird in hand because in some circumstances a support award is subject to later modification.

For examples of tradeoffs, if significant spousal support is warranted but would severely strain the paying spouse, then the judge might instead reduce the support payment and tilt an otherwise equal division of property toward the supported spouse. Or if the paying spouse wanted an expensive marital home constituting most of the property, while the other spouse didn't, then the "house keeper" might be assessed higher-than-normal spousal support payments. Most commonly, tradeoffs are based on what would be most tax advantageous overall between the parties, thus preserving more assets to be divided.

Despite the interrelationship of support determination and property division, each state has its own specific guidelines pertaining to the determination of amount and duration of spousal support. These guidelines are either specific formulas, rules of thumb based on case law, or a combination of the two. Virtually all take into account the marital standard of living and the relative standard of living at which each spouse would live in the absence of spousal support.

Many consider marital fault in general or specifically related to dissipation of assets while about an equal number don't consider marital fault. And a majority of states consider the needs of a spouse, beyond pure child support (see the following section), related to being the custodial parent.

These spousal support guidelines are summarized in Figure 2-4.

Child Support Guidelines

All states have their own guidelines for child support, but most are based on the standard of living the child has had while the marriage was active, the ongoing and special needs of the child, and the parents' relative ability to pay. Each state's specific guidelines have been incorporated into formulas that you can use to estimate what your or your spouse's obligation will be. However, high-income earners are usually "off the charts" so if you are in this situation, you will have to interpret the guidelines and develop a case for your own child support proposal.

Every state's child support formula takes into account the paying spouse's income, the number of children, the amount the custodial spouse is paying for child care (net of any child care tax break), and medical insurance for the children. Most states also factor in the custodial spouse's income. Beyond that, states differ widely in using other variables such as these: FICA and federal, state, and local income taxes paid by the paying spouse; alimony paid by the paying spouse; age of the children; the paying spouse's other child support obligations; the percentage split of custody; cost to medically insure the paying spouse; and mandatory pension payments and union dues.

Although the actual child support awarded often equals the formula calculation, the judge has discretion to override the formula results to take extraordinary expenses and other factors into account. In addition, many states now consider college education to be a formal part of the support obligation, although it's usually determined separately and not reflected in the child support award. Because the formulas or judge's determination of the non-college child support often don't mesh with the reality of what it costs to raise children, many couples work out arrangements on their own as part of the overall settlement. But they must be careful because if spousal support is reduced at a time that coincides with "a child-related" life event such as high-school graduation, the IRS might later recharacterize these previously deductible spousal support payments as nondeductible child support. (However, a Section 71 payment, covered in Chapter 8, can be used in some complex circumstances to redefine portions of what would otherwise be considered nondeductible child support as tax-deductible.) The states' child support guidelines are summarized in Figure 2-5.

STATE	Statutory List*	Marital Fault Not Considered	Marital Fault Relevant	Standard of Living	Status as Custodial Parent Considered
Alabama			x	x	
Alaska	x	x		x	x
Arizona	x	x		x	x
Arkansas		x			
California	x	x		x	
Colorado	x	x		x	x
Connecticut	x		x	x	x
Delaware	x	x		x	x
District of Columbia			x	x	
Florida	x		x	x	
Georgia	x		x	x	
Hawaii	x	x		x	x
Idaho	x		x		
Illinois	x	x		x	x
Indiana	x	x			
Iowa	x	x		x	x
Kansas		x			
Kentucky	x		x^1	x	
Louisiana	x		x		x
Maine	x	x			
Maryland	x		x	x	
Massachusetts	x		x	x	
Michigan			x	x	
Minnesota	x	x		x	x
Mississippi			x		
Missouri	x		x	x	x
Montana	x	x		x	x

Nebraska	X			X		X
Nevada				X	X	X
New Hampshire	X			X	X	X
New Jersey	X			X	X	X
New Mexico	X	X		X		
New York	X			X	X	X
North Carolina	X			X	X	
North Dakota				X	X	
Ohio	X	X		X		X
Oklahoma		X		X		X
Oregon	X	X		X		X
Pennsylvania	X			X	X	
Rhode Island	X			X	X	X
South Carolina	X			X	X	X
South Dakota				X	X	
Tennessee	X			X	X	X
Texas	X			X	X	X
Utah	X			X	X	X
Vermont	X	X		X	X	X
Virginia	X			X	X	
Washington	X	X		X		
West Virginia	X	X			X	X
Wisconsin	X	X		X		X
Wyoming			X			

* Although there is a statutory list of factors, the judge (court) may in its discretion consider other factors under the particular circumstances of the case.

1. Only fault on the part of the party seeking alimony.

©The American Bar Association. This chart used with permission of the American Bar Association and can be found at this location on its web site:
http://www.abanet.org/family/familylaw/Chart1_AlimonySpousalSupport.pdf

FIGURE 2-4   Spousal Support (Alimony) Guidelines in Each State

51

STATE	Income Share	Percent of Income	Extraordinary Medical Deduction	Child-care Deduction	College Support	Shared Parenting Time Offset
Alabama	x	x	x p	x m	x	
Alaska	x	x	x m	x	x	x
Arizona	x		x m	x p		
Arkansas	x	x	x d	x d		
California	x		x m	x m		x
Colorado	x		x m	x m		x
Connecticut	x		x d		x	
Delaware			x m	x m		x*
District of Columbia		x	x d	x	x	x
Florida	x		x d	x m		
Georgia		x	x p	x m		
Hawaii	x	x	x m³	x	x	x
Idaho	x		x m	x p		x
Illinois		x			x	
Indiana	x		x p	x m	x	
Iowa	x			x m	x	x
Kansas	x			x m		x
Kentucky	x		x m	x p		
Louisiana	x		x m	x m		
Maine	x		x m	x m		
Maryland	x		x m	x m		x
Massachusetts		x	x m	x	x	
Michigan	x		x m	x m	x	x
Minnesota		x		x m		x
Mississippi		x	x d	x d		
Missouri	x		x	x	x	x
Montana			x m	x m		
Nebraska	x		x d	x m		x
Nevada		x	x m	x d		x
New Hampshire		x	x d		x	
New Jersey	x	x	x m	x m	x	x

New Mexico	x		x p		x m	x
New York	x	x	x m		x m	x
North Carolina	x	x	x p		x m	
North Dakota	x	x			x d	
Ohio	x		x p		x m	x p
Oklahoma	x		x a		x m	x
Oregon	x		x p		x m	x
Pennsylvania	x		x m/d		x m	
Rhode Island	x		x d		x m	
South Carolina	x		x d		x m	x
South Dakota	x		x d		x d	
Tennessee	x	x	x m	x^1		x^2
Texas	x	x	x d		x d	
Utah	x		x m		x m/p	x
Vermont	x		x m		x m	x
Virginia	x		x a		x a	x
Washington	x		x m	x	x m	x
West Virginia	x		x m		x m	x
Wisconsin	x	x	x m		x d	
Wyoming	x		x d		x d	x

* by case law
a mandatory add-ons
m mandatory deduction
p permissive deduction
d deviation factor

1. May be voluntarily agreed by the parties, in which case it is contractually enforceable thereafter, but otherwise may not be imposed by the court. However, an obligor parent may be required to contribute during a child's minority to an educational trust fund which would be used for college costs post-minority.

2. Support may be increased or decreased it the obligor spends more or less than 80 days (the putative normal amount of time) with a child.

3. Credit given for actual cost of health care insurance premium paid for children.

©The American Bar Association. This chart used with permission of the American Bar Association and can be found at this location on its web site:
http://www.abanet.org/family/familylaw/Chart3_ChildSupportGuidelines.pdf

FIGURE 2-5 Child Support Guidelines in Each State

Child Custody and Visitation

A court's child custody ruling is totally separate from its child support determination. Although "the best interests of the child" are the universal criteria, these criteria are never met in most custody fights. More than any other area, if you end up in a court fight about custody, you and your children will lose, even if you win—so mediating is a far better way to come to this decision if you, your spouse, and your children can't work it out among yourselves.

Nevertheless, you should know what factors courts consider, which should come as no surprise. Almost all consider a history of domestic violence, and most consider the children's wishes. Many consider the health and health care needs of the children—such as whether either parent smokes. A number also factor in a child's living pattern, such as activities and religious practice—but especially what schools the child would attend and how the home environment would facilitate education. Other factors include the children's ages, the parents' lifestyles and mental and/or physical health, the marital history of the parental care-giving, where the parents will be living, and the appropriateness of various joint and shared custody possibilities.

The states' child custody guidelines are summarized in Figure 2-6.

State versus Couple Differences

We hope we've succeeded in convincing you of the importance of understanding your state's laws and guidelines regarding divorce decisions, as there are marked differences. The best way to learn about the rules that pertain to you is to consult a competent family law attorney in your area. You should be able to do this on an hourly rate basis without paying a retainer or making a commitment to work together in the future. Except for the major difference between community property states and equitable division states, however, chances are that you and your spouse will have more differences regarding what you think is a fair settlement than any two states do. In the next part, we'll explore how to start dealing with those differences and reach a state of equity, if not harmony.

STATE	Statutory Guidelines	Children's Wishes	Joint Custody	Cooperative Parent	Domestic Violence	Health	Attorney or GAL
Alabama	x	x	x		x		
Alaska	x	x	x		x		x
Arizona	x	x	x	x	x	x	x
Arkansas					x		
California	x	x		x	x	x	x
Colorado	x	x	x^1	x	x	x	x
Connecticut		x	x				x
Delaware	x	x	x	x	x	x	x
District of Columbia	x	x	x	x	x	x	x
Florida	x	x	x	x	x	x	x
Georgia	x	x^8	x^7		x		x^9
Hawaii	x^2				x		
Idaho	x	x	x		x	x	
Illinois	x	x	x	x	x	x	x
Indiana	x	x	x	x	x	x	x
Iowa	x	x	x	x	x	x	
Kansas	x	x	x	x	x	x	
Kentucky	x	x	x	x	x	x	x
Louisiana	x	x	x		x		
Maine	x	x	x		x		
Maryland		x	x	x	x		x
Massachusetts			x		x		x
Michigan	x	x	x	x	x	x	x
Minnesota	x	x	x		x	x	x
Mississippi	x		x			x	x^2
Missouri	x	x	x	x	x	x	x
Montana	x	x	x		x	x	x
Nebraska	x	x	x		x		x
Nevada	x	x	x	x	x	x	x
New Hampshire	x	x	x		x		x
New Jersey	x	x	x	x	x	x	x

FIGURE 2-6 Child Custody Guidelines in Each State

55

New Mexico	x	x	x	x	x	x	x
New York		x^2	x		x^2	x	x
North Carolina		x	x^3	x	x	x	
North Dakota	x	x^5		x	x	x	
Ohio	x^2	x	x	x	x		x^4
Oklahoma	x	x	x	x	x		x^3
Oregon	x	x	x	x	x		x
Pennsylvania	x	x	x	x	x	x	x
Rhode Island		x	x	x	x	x	x
South Carolina		x	x	x	x	x	
South Dakota	x^5	x^6	x	x			
Tennessee	x	x	x	x	x	x	x
Texas	x	x	x	x		x	
Utah	x	x		x	x	x	x^4
Vermont	x^2	x^2	x	x	x	x	x
Virginia	x	x		x	x		
Washington	x	x	x	x	x	x	
West Virginia	x	x	x	x	x	x	
Wisconsin	x	x	x	x	x	x	
Wyoming	x	x	x	x	x		

1. Now uses term "parental rights and responsibilities."
2. Considered if child is old enough.
3. By case law.
4. Not mandatory.
5. The court must listen to the reasonable preferences of a child twelve or older, giving greater weight to the preferences of older children. The court may at its discretion hear the reasonable preference of children under the age of twelve.
6. In divorce, the courts no longer use "custody" terminology, instead, separately allocating between the parents (1) residential time; and, (2) parental responsibility in specific areas such as nonemergency health care, religion, education and extra-curricular activities.
7. Emphasizes "best interest of child."
8. If child is of sufficient age and capacity to reason and form intelligent preference.
9. Appointment of custody evaluators and guardians ad litem authorized by administrative rule.

©The American Bar Association. This chart used with permission of the American Bar Association and can be found at this location on its web site:
http//www.abanet.org/family/familylaw/Chart2_CustodyCriteria.pdf

FIGURE 2-6 Continued

Part II

A Strategic Course for Financially Successful Divorce

*O*nce you or your spouse files for divorce or announce that you want a *divorce, events can spin quickly out of control, and with them, your chance to minimize the financial damage that is always part of divorce. Your spouse, with a few clicks of a mouse, can transfer from hundreds to hundreds of thousands of dollars that might really be yours, forcing you to either spend untold amounts of money to prove in court that they're yours or to settle for less than you should have coming to you. Financial moves made in dividing up property without planning can cost tens of thousands of dollars in unnecessary taxes. Separating on immediate emotion, without considering the impact of the separation date on the legal process and eventual financial outcome, can be similarly costly. Like a boxer heading into the ring, you must be fully alert and armed with a carefully constructed divorce plan, so that one momentary lapse won't permanently flatten your financial future.*

So get ready to rumble, even though you probably find divorce distasteful and offensive. To counter your revulsion, take a lesson from boxers and defend yourself in a way that minimizes the punishment you must absorb to score a better payday. In fact, as either the initiator or receiver of a divorce action, you'll feel like a boxer who's just been put on the canvas by either your sense of guilt and loss, your outrage, or a defeatist attitude about marital failure.

Assuming you haven't been knocked out, though, imitate the way savvy pugilists react to being decked. The best boxers resist the temptation to spring right back up and even the score. Instead, they neutralize their opponent's tem-porary advantage by rising just before the full knockout count, getting balanced, eluding damaging blows, and regrouping to take the offensive. Otherwise, in a wobbly state, they could quickly end up back down for the full count.

Similarly, you must counter the wobbly state that accompanies divorce ini-tiation by keeping your balance in the unsettling early stages. By gearing your strategy specifically to your spousal opponent, you can thwart any financially lethal moves he or she might make. For example, if your spouse intends to try for an early knockout by using threats, intimidation, and shelling out a bun-dle on high-powered legal warriors, you must get in a neutralizing clinch by filing orders that will require your spouse to provide you ample funds to hire equally powerful help. If your spouse intends to annoy you by dancing around the ropes with a teasing insincere offer, hoping to lure you in and catch you flatfooted, you must remain on your toes near the middle, staying centered on your own life. By cutting off the ring, you'll eventually force your spouse to confront the issues and either fight it out or resolve things with a draw. And if your spouse's continued bothersome jabs, in the form of legal motions, bury you in paperwork, you mustn't succumb to the temptation of swinging wildly back. Eventually your spouse's arms will tire, and you'll both tell your corner cut-men to put away the bandages and help you cut a deal instead.

But why enter the ring at all if you can convince your spouse that just as in boxing, the attorneys (promoters) will walk away with the bulk of the cash? Meanwhile the two of you will be left stripped down to the almost-bare fash-ion and financial essentials—and, unlike your attorneys, bloody and bat-tered. Worse, your children had to watch the gory spectacle from ringside seats, and they'll likely see plenty of impromptu rematches over the next several years.

So try doing something that's taboo in boxing but encouraged in divorce: mutually agree to "take a dive" by throwing the fight—into a conference room instead of a courtroom. In Part II, you'll learn to assess your situation and develop a winning "lose-lose minimally" strategy that won't add any jewel-studded championship belts to your valuables but might save them from the pawn shop. We'll do that with a set of strategic steps that should be followed in every divorce—which we present in the following four "rounds"—Chap-ters 3 through 6.

Chapter 3

(Round 1): Prepare for Prosperity: Your Head, Heart, and Money

I n boxing, what separates the champions is not the best punch but the most heart and the use of one's head—figuratively, that is—in the heat of battle. That's also how to win financially in divorce, but it's hard, considering how much it messes with your head and pains your heart.

To fight for your financial rights, get your head on straight and your heart emptied of hate. You must overcome hurt, anger, and similar emotions that, if left unchecked, will have you seeing red and color your checking account red too. This part will help you keep things in balance by taking your spouse's viewpoint into account, keeping yourself stable and on a steady course, and being clear on what matters most financially and otherwise.

Take Your Spouse's Viewpoint into Account

We've started this part and chapter with a boxing analogy both because it fits into the self-defense theme and it emphasizes that this is not your typical poor-unfortunate-spouse divorce book. We are taking a different tack because we have not seen either self-absorption or self-pity work to anyone's advantage. Instead, we have found that women are better able to stand up for themselves if they demonstrate the capacity to see the stereotypical male view of divorce, in which the man is either the aggressor because of initiating the divorce or by reacting to it as a challenge to his manhood—hence our use of a boxing metaphor. Similarly, men are better able to make genuine progress toward their true goals if they demonstrate the capacity to see the typical female view of divorce, in which women initiate or respond to it in a passive/aggressive manner—think Muhammed Ali's "rope-a-dope" of alternately taking a lot of punishment and then lashing out—to protect their sense of self. Of course, these are only stereotypes but we use them to emphasize that in a typical couple, the husband and wife will see the divorce in distinctly different ways.

Whether you're the husband or wife, you must understand what your spouse is saying or doing, and why. Instead of reacting viscerally to your spouse's words and actions, understand what's behind them in terms of both your spouse's own feelings and the influence of gender and marital role. With the goal of better divorce from better mutual understanding of where each is coming from, let's look at each gender's major traditional beliefs and biggest concerns surrounding a number of key divorce issues.

Whose Fault?

Men feel that they're blamed for divorce far more often than the facts support, citing numerous studies such as Brinig's and Allen's "These Boots Are Made for Walking: Why Most Divorce Filers Are Women" (American Law and Economics Review). Yet women counter that they're often left with no choice but to initiate divorce after years of repeated attempts to communicate their dissatisfaction fall on their husbands' deaf ears. And this happens more frequently today than in the past because initiating divorce wasn't a choice available to them without the undue ugliness of public character assassination, which frequently occurred in the days before no-fault divorce.

But men who are primary breadwinners feel that wives who leave them shouldn't be entitled to as much because the women chose to put themselves in that situation. They also think that where financial pressures have been a major problem, wives who they perceive as engaging in stereotypical female overspending on designer clothes and jewelry, home decorating, and excessive socializing shouldn't be rewarded for it with what men see as excessive support and an unfairly large share of property and assets. Meanwhile, women often feel short-changed when they view their husbands as guilty of stereotypical male overspending on gambling, bar-hopping, and other women. They also point to controlling husbands whose beliefs in traditional roles hindered or prevented wives from further education, well-paid work, or career advancement.

All of these things are sometimes true—which often makes either the husband or wife more at fault and seemingly less deserving of a fair share. However, both men and women benefit from seeing things clearly and recognizing that fault should come into play only when the behavior of either party has damaged the couple's overall finances or the other party's future financial prospects—or when serving in a tennis match. In fact, they should take a lesson from tennis, which grants a second chance (serve), and deal with their anger over fault by including an item in the settlement that provides each a punching bag and an indelible marker, so that they can label them "His Fault" or "Her Fault" and whale away.

Who Gets Custody?

"Why can't we all just get along?" Those immortal words of Rodney King, whose videotaped beating by the LA Police was nationally televised, certainly apply to the beating everyone endures in the typical custody battle. Men say women use implied threats to hold out for sole custody and limited visitation as a way to squeeze them for better settlements.

Even more men, though, feel that their role as father is trivialized or that they're cast as the marital villain whose involvement after divorce will be toxic. They cite a far higher percentage of claims of child abuse, particularly sexual, lodged in custody hearings than statistics on actual abuse suggest could be possible, and they are livid about such gutter tactics being used to deprive them of access to their children. In fact, they cite statistics showing that 80 percent of child abuse is committed by women. (It is true that women commit more child abuse, including neglect, than men—although the bulk of studies suggest 60 to 70 percent. But that statistic is grossly misleading because women hold the lion's share of childcare jobs, married women spend much more time with children than their husbands, and never-married mothers commit the highest rate of abuse.) Finally, men say that some laws still are based on anachronistic beliefs that mothers are the caretaker of choice and that even in states where the law is modernized, too many family court judges are older men out of step with today's times who are biased in favor of the mother's natural role

In countering, women say that men who never showed any real interest in the kids are advised by their attorneys to fight for joint or even full custody, as a standard tactic to soften a wife's stance on the financial settlement. They complain that just as in politics, money has come to rule the awarding of custody; they say judges are unduly influenced by men's claims that they can provide better for children, and that many men are able to win sole custody by spending lavishly on experts who will testify to the wife's unfitness and the husband's superior financial position. (Of course, the increasing role of women as the primary marital breadwinner has led to many more men claiming the flip side—getting flattened in court by their wives' financial steamroller.)

Women whose midlife husbands have traded them in for younger models are also driven to reduce the influence of the "other woman" on their kids. And they say that many seemingly "out of the blue" charges of men abusing children are consistent with the reality that women who feared reporting abuse during marriage finally get the courage to do so when custody is at stake.

Unfortunately, courage is in short supply in the vast majority of divorces that don't involve true child abuse but do feature bitter custody battles. Men and women lack the courage to admit that they're both flawed parents. In fact, it's nothing short of arrogant to hold a partner to a higher parenting standard after marriage than standards most parents uphold during marriage. Because divorce forces many children to grow up prematurely, the least parents can do is grow up also and recognize that their children come first and that their children want both parents, warts and all.

Financial (Un)Fairness

"It's only money" ranks right down there with "let's be adults about this" as among the least-used phrases uttered by divorcing couples. That's because "it's only about money" is the unintended impression they too often give. Wives resent husbands who balk at paying even the stingy child support calculated by some states' formulas—especially when they argue that the ex-wives are just spending it on themselves. Men chafe at women's citation of statistics showing the millions of men whose child support payments are late or never arrive, and they counter by citing statistics showing more than 75 percent of unpaid child support occurs when men are denied any form of custody.

Men are also furious at wives' being motivated to get all they can by inflated statistics about how much better men do than women after divorce. For example, a continually cited but grossly inaccurate statistic is that after divorce, wives' average standard of living drops by 73 percent, while husbands' goes up an average 42 percent. However, women are angry at men motivated by men's groups to portray themselves as the overwhelming victims of divorce. For example, after Lenore Weitzman admitted her 73/42 statistic was in error, men's rights groups continue to tout a widely criticized study by Sanford Braver, who did correctly debunk Weitzman's findings. Based on his data collection from only 400 families, he found that although women initially suffer a drop, after a few years, ex-husbands and ex-wives have approximately the same standard of living, when you take into account taxes. (Most experts take the middle road: ex-wives' standard of living goes down between 20 and 30 percent, while ex-husbands see an average rise of between 10 and 20 percent.)

Other Divorce Financial Grievances

The following areas of divorce contention are only a few of the far too many attempts both men and women make at sabotaging settlement negotiations.

- *Spousal support:* Men say that women are unrealistic about their spousal support needs and that the women's true needs are not as high as they claim. Men believe women are being told by their attorneys to pick up the pace of spending before filing so that they'll have documented financials to support their claims. Women say that men do just the opposite upon the advice of attorneys, that men get stingier about family spending before filing so they can justify less support. Craig Ross says these strategies point out a key spousal-support determination problem in our overspending society: "Need should not be measured according to 'what I need to spend'—although it's a common practice in divorce litigation. Need should mainly be based on family income and composition. Looking primarily to 'budgets' to define spousal support is highly problematic."
- *Earning capacity:* Women say that they deserve to be compensated when their husbands have cited the needs of the family as the reason to not take good jobs, advance their careers, or further their education to increase their earning potential. This is also an argument for paying more attention to 'needs' independent of both budget and income, because the budget was limited by the wife's lower (or lack of) earnings. Men say that wives often themselves cite the needs of the family as justification for not doing those things, which held back the family's accumulation of wealth or increased its debt.
- *Homemaker handicaps:* Women who have been in and out of the workforce say that men and the courts make unrealistically high assumptions about how much they will be able to earn when they return to full-time work. Women also feel that men and the courts fail to take into account the damage to the women's retirement savings accumulation because of those breaks in service. Men say that they base those claims on wives' inadequate efforts to get the best-paying job possible and their unwillingness to expedite their progress in going back to school and acquiring updated and new skills.
- *Pension envy:* Mediators and attorneys involved in divorce negotiations say that some men get irrationally attached to their pensions and refuse to acknowledge that women are entitled to a proportionate share of their ultimate value, based on the length of the marriage. Men say that

giving ex-wives a share of their ultimate pensions, possibly in combination with long-term spousal support, leaves them financially unemancipated for years after the divorce, if not for the rest of their lives. Justified or not, that long-term financial tie to the ex-spouse is a source of white-hot rage for these men.

Spouses' Viewpoints: Should Right Make Fight?

So who's right? Let's just say that you are, but we're also whispering the same thing to your spouse. What truly matters is that you accept that your spouse is likely to be at least partially motivated by a stereotyped perspective of who wins and loses in divorce—and that you will be too! To successfully travel the road to reasonable resolution, each of you must be willing to look at both sides of the divorce highway—even if it takes sitting on a few telephone books so that you can see over the gender-difference road divider.

Furthermore, you must fit these biases into your own circumstances, such as the increasingly common role reversal in which the woman is financially dominant. If that applies to your marriage, you might want to reread this section after mentally editing it to selectively substitute "wealthier" or "higher income" for "man"—and "less well off" or "lower income" for "woman." Regardless of who has or earns more, though, expect to deal with a perception gap between you and your spouse.

Take Your Own Viewpoint and Feelings into Account

It should be clear how understanding your spouse's viewpoint could help financially by reducing the cost of the divorce and possibly "winning" on the financial issues that matter most to you. But it might be harder to see how understanding your own viewpoint can do the same. Yet, how can you deal rationally with financial decisions if you don't really know what you want emotionally, or if what you want is destructive or self-defeating? Through counseling or other healthy forms of support, you can vent your hostilities and frustrations and sort out your thoughts.

Common Financially Destructive Divorce Behaviors

Counseling is not a cure-all, but it can be particularly valuable in helping you take the following preventive measures to avoid financially destructive divorce behaviors.

- *Not letting bad feelings get you bad results:* While nobody wins, you can lose big, so make "remember what's at stake" your mantra by weighing the consequences of acting on your feelings instead of your finances.
- *Overcoming denial and paralysis:* To make your divorce work, you must be able to act in a timely, logical fashion. But depression, rage, self-pity, and related emotions can literally paralyze you. You might start missing work, ignoring the phone and mail, sleeping most of the day and night, anaesthetizing yourself with liquor or drugs, or letting your work performance suffer because you spend your time fantasizing about revenge. These (in)actions could allow your spouse to take control of the divorce financially and give you a permanent reason for perpetuating such behavior. Or they could lead to detrimental, even criminal actions that will deny you custody. Or your spouse may cite such behavior in arguments to decrease spousal support or property division arrangements, which could hurt you financially because you would be deemed unreliable.
- *Avoiding panic-manic behavior:* Divorce can also create panic that drives you into a frenzy of unhealthy activity such as seeking comfort from excessive spending and eating, using illegal stimulants, making a habit of acting impulsively, stalking, becoming promiscuous, and wearing out your welcome with even the best of friends when they finally realize that they're unable to comfort you or you just don't want to be comforted. The financial problem with excessive spending is obvious, but generally being impulsive also often leads to excessive spending—such as making a last-minute reservation for an unplanned trip that suddenly sounds good. Excessive eating, drug use, and promiscuity can lead to eating disorders and addictions that can be very expensive to treat.
- *Easing self-imposed financial pressures:* It's natural to want to make extravagant financially related promises to children, but you must resist those temptations, and do so by understanding the emotions behind such a promise. Similarly, if you're in another relationship, you might be concerned with living up to your part of the new bargain financially if you don't achieve your financial goals in the divorce—or worried that you won't be able to find the kind of new relationship you want because of reduced financial status. Such guilt feelings or insecurities can undermine your reaction to a fair settlement offer if you feel it will damage a relationship with your child or a new partner.
- *Coping with divorce changing everything:* You've probably taken that quiz in which you indicate which life events you've experienced in the last year, and then added up the points to determine your level of stress as it relates to your health. While you're getting divorced, your

point total might be high enough to put you in the "how can you be reading this, you're already dead" category. Divorce has a huge point total because it comes with so many of those experiences built in. According to divorce attorney and mediator Lee Borden, "Sometimes you have to change where you live, how you spend your day, what you can afford to do, how much time you spend with your children and on what schedule, and how you can plan for the future—all while you're trying to deal with a whole new world of lawyers, judges, pleadings, and court dates."

Filtering Out Destructive Emotionally Triggered Behavior

In a particularly memorable 1980s commercial for Fram Oil Filters, which provides a great lesson for divorce, a mechanic holds up a cheap clogged oil filter and says, "You can pay me now or pay me later." Think of divorce counseling as an automobile oil filter that keeps the emotions running freely through your system instead of your feelings being clogged up inside and later causing dangerous behavioral backfires. By unclogging your feelings through immediate counseling or participation in support groups, you might save yourself the cost of a major emotional-engine overhaul. Here are some sources that answer some common questions or provide information on finding a therapist or group for support during and after your divorce:

- Divorce Central, "FAQ on Surviving the Emotional Trauma of Divorce," www.divorcecentral.com/lifeline/lifefaq.html
- Divorce HQ, "Divorce Dos and Don'ts, " www.divorcehq.com/dodont.html
- Divorce Source, "Surviving Separation and Divorce: Coping Skills," www.divorcesource.com/info/surviving/coping.shtml
- Divorce HQ Support Groups Listing, www.divorcehq.com/spprt-groups.html, and www.smartdivorce.com/support.htm
- Parents Without Partners organization, www.parentswithoutpartners.org/
- Better Divorce Family Counseling Page, www.betterdivorce.com/info/mcounseling.shtml
- Divorce HQ Directory of Divorce Services, www.divorcehq.com /servicedir.html

Keep Your Eye on the Prize

Understanding your spouse and yourself are both key ingredients in avoiding a destructive divorce. But knowing what you want and need emotionally and psychologically is the best way to ensure that you steer clear of destructive hazards and get to your goals. So before you set a single financial (quantitative) objective, determine a desired outcome that consists of qualitative (quality of life) objectives. By doing that, you might find creative ways to achieve those goals and reduce the overall cost of the divorce, leaving you in a financial position to have your desired postdivorce quality of life. Here are some common objectives and ways that you might be able to achieve them more economically.

Children

If you have them, they're undoubtedly your most important consideration. You want them to be emotionally and physically healthy, and if not happy (near term), at least coping as well as possible. If it means giving up on getting everything you "deserve" from the settlement, shouldn't you do it if you know how much more likely it will be that your child will have a better future? Statistics show that children whose parents have divorced are more likely to get divorced themselves, which means they're more likely to suffer the same financial setback with which you're now dealing. Furthermore, children of divorce are more likely to have academic problems, which can translate into a disrupted or abbreviated education and a reduction in their adult earning power. In general, troubled kids are more likely to become troubled adults whom you might feel compelled to rescue financially by your choice or their request.

So, for example, in considering custody, you should factor in with whom your child should live to get the best possible public school education. That might mean more or less child support depending on where the child will be, but so what: In the long run, you'll both save on bills for tutors and by making it more likely your child will qualify for merit-based scholarships for college. Similarly, your child needs the support of loyal friends now more than ever. By arranging custody and visitation so that he or she has plentiful access to friends, you'll ultimately save on excessive mental health and other expenses that could result from a poor postdivorce adjustment. For articulate expert advice, see Judith Wallerstein's book, *What About the Kids: Raising Your Children Before, During, and After Divorce* (Hyperion Books, New York, 2003).

Living Accommodations

It's sometimes best for children to remain in the family home, but that must be weighed against other factors that will affect everyone's health and well-being. Your main consideration should be living in a reasonably safe neighborhood in a residence that's in good condition and not too cramped. If saving money by selling the house puts you in acceptable but less luxurious living circumstances, isn't it worth it if it makes money more plentiful for going back to school to pursue a career that will give you more life satisfaction or greater earning power? Or perhaps it will let you keep up a part of your lifestyle that is expensive but vital to your or your child(ren)'s happiness—such as traveling yearly to do social-service projects in impoverished communities or participating in high-cost sports or activities such as skiing or earning your pilot's license.

Social Life

It's vital for you to keep as many of your good connections as possible and to make new ones that might lead to a new partner if that's what you eventually want. You'll be more able to do that if you and your spouse make living and financial decisions that include babysitting for each other to minimize the cost of caring for your children while either of you goes out. And if that's not possible, saving money in other ways can make more available to pay for babysitters. For women in particular, who often have custody, getting social relief might be the deciding factor in avoiding possible child abuse, which is highest among single and divorced mothers.

Your child's social life is also critical. While it's likely that you'll have to cut back some on your children's expensive pastimes, you do want to make sure that such cutbacks don't worsen an already disrupted social life. You or your spouse might think it's crucial that your child continue expensive private athletics coaching or time-consuming piano or horse-riding lessons. However, unless that's really what your child wants and you can afford it, isn't it better to save the money so that it can be used on activities that maximize your children's exposure to peers?

From Strategic Preparation to Strategy Formulation

In this chapter's Round 1, we've been in "shrink" mode—getting psychologically and emotionally prepared to develop a clear-headed strategy. We'll do that in Round 2 (Chapter 4) by going into a logical and tactical "think" mode. It's only by being able to view the divorce in terms of actions that will produce logical, desired consequences that you can escape your current unbearable lightness of being without the unbearable lightness of wallet or pocketbook.

Chapter 4

(Round 2): Prepare Your Financial Fight Strategically

I n developing a sound divorce strategy that will leave you financially solvent, you must take into account timing, logistics of separation, immediate and postdivorce family-related and financial goals and objectives, overall method of resolution, and how much and how you'll pay. This chapter will cover these topics beginning with some broad strategic analysis to gauge how complex and difficult your divorce will be in light of your desired goals and objectives and compromise alternatives. We'll then look at the specific strategic decisions you must make within the following categories: property division and (re)titling, immediate and postdivorce living arrangements, immediate and postdivorce financial arrangements, divorce-specific and divorce-related paperwork and arrangements.

Strategic Divorce Analysis

By the time you've completed the divorce process, you might feel like you've spent the preceding year or more in a lion's den. So in determining where the lion's share of your divorce planning efforts should be directed, it seems appropriate to consider how a lion tamer earns the lion's share of a circus audience's applause. Spectators step up their response according to how many hoops the lion jumps through, how many are ringed with fire, how narrow the hoops are, what sorts of chairs and other protective props the trainer uses, and a number of other factors that determine how dangerous and complex the act is.

Likewise, the way you strategically respond to your divorce should be based on similar factors that affect how difficult it will be to defend your interests: the number and types of natural hoops you and your spouse have to jump through due to the complexity of your marriage's finances, how financially powerful and dangerous your spousal lion is, and the number of hoops your spouse makes you jump through with the stunts he or she devises to break down your defenses. Here's how to evaluate factors that determine whether you need a lion-taming lawyer, a mild-mannered mediator, a tenacious team of advocates, or just a couple of chairs to seat you and your spouse at the kitchen table.

Family Composition and Financial Condition

If your collective incomes and net worth are modest at best, then you can't afford an expensive divorce. So if you don't have children and there are no complex financial issues such as business ownership or unusual employee benefits, you should make every effort to mutually reach an agreement on your own. Then pay an attorney only to draft it and process it through the family court system.

However, if you have significant debt, primarily due to your spouse, you need more outside help to make sure that you don't get stuck with it. Or if you're not in debt but have young children, even if you agree on custody, you'll need years of help supporting the children. Even if your children are older, with only a few years of child support eligibility left, supporting more than two will almost always require significant contributions from both parents. So if you need child support help and your spouse won't agree to something like the amount your state formula calculates, you might have to resort to court or, preferably, arbitration.

If your children are nearing 18, few potential child support years remain. So you should do everything possible to minimize the cost of paying for the divorce itself. However, don't forget college education, which has become a legal support responsibility of both ex-spouses in an increasing number of states. Once again, minimal fees for a mediator or arbitrator might best resolve this if you and your spouse can't agree.

Finally, if one spouse earns significantly more than the other, or you collectively have substantial assets and income, then you'll probably need expert financial planning and tax accounting help to work out an equitable agreement that minimizes taxes—thus minimizing your respective drops in standard of living. Part III, Chapters 7 and 8, covers the many potential complexities of dividing property.

Postdivorce Parenting

Although the majority of couples battling over child custody tie it to child support and other financial settlement issues, the law views it separately, and so should you. So if you and your spouse can agree on everything but custody, then you've significantly reduced your divorce's degree of difficulty. Unless you're truly callous, that means you've significantly reduced the cost of litigating custody because you'll be far less inclined to get hired-gun mental health professionals who'll testify to the numerous parallels between your spouse and Charles Manson or Susan Smith.

Even so, you might find it hard to come to an agreement if your spouse will be living in a different state, which would also make enforcement trickier and necessitate more work through your attorney to do what you consider necessary to protect your child. More likely, your adamant custody positions might be due to a spouse who is abusive, a substance abuser, or otherwise emotionally unstable, so you might feel you have to battle over custody in court. However, you might still simplify things by coming to a temporary custody agreement with a provision that you'll revisit it in a year. Meanwhile the money saved might be applied for spousal mental health treatment that will help allay your concerns about your spouse's parental fitness and make it possible to negotiate some form of joint custody outside of court.

Spouses' Personalities and Relationship

You're getting divorced, so your marriage obviously had big problems, but the degree of difficulty you'll have reaching a divorce agreement depends on which areas of your relationship were the biggest failures. If you had a power imbalance due to one spouse needing to assert superiority, you're unlikely to reach a settlement without expert mediation or collaborative divorce lawyers, and you'll be lucky to avoid litigation.

If the superiority was expressed in terms of one spouse's controlling the finances in a secretive manner, the other will almost surely have to involve a forensic accountant to ensure knowing the true and full story about your marital finances.

What if, in contrast, you verbally fought frequently over finances and other aspects of the marriage, and both spouses effectively managed to get in their licks? Well, you were communicating! That bodes well for relying on each other for disclosure and successfully bridging your differences with mediation. If there was physical and/or verbal abuse, however, the abused spouse will probably have to use the adversarial attorney route, with additional legal moves to assure his or her protection and safety. (Yes, although men are responsible for 98 percent of serious injury physical abuse, that leaves more than a handful of women who present a continuing danger to their ex-husbands.)

If either or both spouses relied almost exclusively on their parental roles to derive self-esteem, then expect an extensive, possibly expensive custody battle. And if the children have clearly suffered from their parents' individual and relationship dysfunction, the divorce resolution must allow for significant financial resources to try and head off severe behavior problems that might manifest in serious outcomes or conditions such as outright suicide, eating disorders, delinquency, and academic failure.

In addition to these more abstract psychological problems and consequences, you must also consider whether psychological problems or moral turpitude have led you or your spouse to cause severe financial damage in your marriage. If so, to recover damages via an adjusted property settlement, the nondamaging spouse might have to hire a private investigator to compile a comprehensive report that documents these behaviors and associated financial losses. For example, if one spouse's midlife crisis over his or her employer's downsizing led to losing several hundred thousand dollars day-trading while he or she was presumed to be job hunting, then the other spouse might be entitled to compensation. Similarly, one spouse might be due compensation for the other's day-trysting if it included shelling out tens of thousands of dollars for housing and lavishing gifts on a mistress or (very!) personal hunky trainer.

Double-Standard on Double-or-Nothing?

"It isn't necessarily fair to penalize the day-trading gambler, because what if it had worked," says Craig Ross, half-seriously. "Then the risk-taker's gains would be subject to equitable division. I have actually heard this argument in many forms." A dead-serious litigant once told Craig, "I stole that property and since I took all the risk I should keep it!"

Breadth and Depth of Divorce Issues

Even if your family and its individual members are as psychologically sound as you could hope for in a divorce situation, your divorce could still prove quite complex and costly due to the sheer number of issues to be resolved and the difficulty of those issues. For example, you might have a special-needs child, high income, or other circumstances that don't fit the child support formulas. Or you could be disabled yourself and require continuing care that's currently paid for through your spouse's insurance but now will require insurance and benefit experts to help make other arrangements and fund them. Your investments might be an eclectic collection that includes real estate, limited partnerships, and other ownership interests that are difficult to value and have complex tax ramifications.

You can be sure that your divorce will be financially messy if one of you owns a business with substantial value or is an executive. You'll almost certainly need a team of professionals because of how businesses complicate family finances: closely held stock, stock options, executive perks, taxes keyed to form of incorporation, buy-sell life insurance agreements, corporate defined-benefit and defined-contribution pensions, self-employed pensions, employee stock ownership plans (ESOPs), deferred compensation, and business valuation. Don't worry if you don't know about most of these, but do worry if you don't get the expert help to determine their part in an equitable settlement.

And what if you've been a long-term homemaker who's been master of your family's domestic but not its financial affairs, at your high-income spouse's behest or encouragement? Like presidential candidates who've been governors but not members of Congress or Senators, you'll be forced into the world of foreign-to-you (financial) affairs. To help you understand quickly where things stand, you'll need a "cabinet." Your cabinet of advisors should include a *certified divorce financial analyst* (CDFA), formerly known as a *certified divorce planner* (CDP) or a *certified divorce specialist* (CDS). Both are from a new breed of expert trained in complex divorce financial issues such as making the economic case for lifetime spousal support that at least comes close to continuing your accustomed standard of living.

If your divorce must address many of these or related issues, then you're dealing with heavy-duty complexity. You might want to start by consulting professionals who call themselves *divorce coaches.* They're often attorneys, financial advisors, or mental health professionals who are well versed in divorce and the professional services that come into play. Rather than seeking to represent you, they offer a service that evaluates your situation and helps you choose a course and build the team you'll need. It might seem like just one more in an endless series of fees that you'll be paying, but consider the option anyway because investing a few to several hundred dollars up front could save you thousands down the line, and it should definitely facilitate the process.

Understand Your Spouse's Strategic Analysis

If allowed to unfold naturally, the way your divorce proceeds will depend on your spouse's strategic strengths and weaknesses as much as yours. But if you anticipate how he or she might act, then you might be able to make things go more efficiently, cheaply, and fairly than they otherwise would by making an initial proposal or response that negates the need for aggressive and expensive strategies. Here are a few areas to analyze in anticipating your spouse's likely strategy:

- *Balance of power:* Does your spouse have a much higher paying job, many more separate assets, and good connections for legal and financial advice? Did your spouse hire an "alpha-attorney?" Or are these factors relatively equal or in your favor? If your spouse is hiring the big guns, with a powerful financial arsenal to back them up, he or she could be poised to litigate you to the death, both to protect wealth and wear you down.
- *Sense of urgency:* Is your spouse eager to terminate the marriage because he or she is involved in a new relationship? Or does he or she see you as a growing problem for reasons such as serial infidelity, gambling, or substance abuse? Conversely, have you dumped him or her because of your urgency in that regard? If your spouse wants out quickly, then he or she is less likely to pursue aggressive litigation. But if you have dumped your spouse, he or she might try to hang on through litigation for as long as it takes to take you for all he or she can get.
- *Emotional stability:* If your spouse has always been emotionally unstable, or has become so as your marriage has deteriorated, then his or her actions in the divorce will be the least predictable. If you want certainty, then you'll want to treat the situation much as you would in bidding on a house during a seller's market, when you expect to pay somewhere near the asking price. So by preemptively setting an asking price that seems reasonable to your spouse, you might be able to get out quickly and avoid a roller-coaster divorce involving multiple strategies and associated excessive expenses, even if the settlement is less than you really "deserve."
- *Personality type:* Have you ever heard of the Meyers-Briggs Type Inventory (MBTI)? Your spouse's strategy might be predicated on how he or she deals with life issues overall. Many counselors use the MBTI in marital counseling to get an idea of where each spouse falls on the following scales:

- Introverted to Extroverted
- Sensor (relies on concrete data) to Intuitive
- Thinker (uses hard logic) to Feeler (emotion plays part in reasoning)
- Judgers (organizes and plans) to Perceivers (thinks in immediate terms)

To take an extreme hypothetical example, if your spouse is an Extroverted-Intuitive-Feeler-Perceiver (EIFP), then you might expect a strategy consistent with an impulsive, abstract nature—so he or she might prefer a quick negotiation between the two of you that will be settled when something sounds good, rather than litigation, mediation, or collaborative process. In contrast, if your spouse is an Introverted-Sensor-Thinker-Judger (ISTJ), then collaborative law might appeal because an attorney will be there to protect the introverted nature, everything is highly logical, and you can expect things to be done in a painfully tedious manner with excruciating detail.

Divorce Financial Strategy Decisions

Unlike one infamous military nemesis, you don't want to end up living in a spider hole. So in strategically preparing for your divorce battle, think of what we've just covered as though you're a field general who has looked at the troops and weapons at your disposal, the battlefield conditions, and the threat your adversary presents. Now you're ready to deploy your resources and launch your offensive, but to do so, you must first plan the specific strategic financial and logistical steps described in this part.

Make Immediate Financial Arrangements

Do you feel like using all that you've learned from mystery movies and novels and doing away with your spouse? Assuming yours is only a harmless fantasy, it serves our purpose in envisioning the immediate financial consequences of starting the divorce process. Suppose that like Harrison Ford as Richard Kimble in *The Fugitive*, you were wrongly convicted of killing your spouse and have just escaped on the way to the death house, with nothing but a torn, prison-issue outfit on your back. How would you immediately survive, and how would you finance the legal process that you'll hope to go through at some point to end your fugitive status and be exonerated?

Even without Tommie Lee Jones as Lt. Gerard chasing you, it won't be easy. What you must do to successfully escape this saga of your life is described in the following paragraphs.

Financial Resources Snapshot

To fund this interim period, you must determine what's available to you in liquid assets, available credit, and any expected one-time payments. You should also determine the approximate after-tax value of other assets you might either liquidate or use as collateral for a loan. Include what's available in shared marital and spousal assets, as well as spousal income, because you might either be able to arrange a support order from your spouse or get a court order allowing you to tap the joint assets if they've been frozen. Or you might have to pay interim support.

Don't worry about having this information absolutely complete or exact; that will come later when you're preparing to mediate, negotiate, or litigate a settlement. Right now you're looking for a reasonable sense of what financial resources you have available in order to stay afloat while the divorce proceeds, but you'll also be getting a head start toward compiling the complete information.

Until-Divorce Budget

Determine what it will take to stay afloat by preparing separate predivorce and after-divorce budgets that list all of your monthly income and expenses. In addition, prepare a sheet of one-time transitional expenses you anticipate due to the divorce, as well as current bills and credit balances that aren't already listed in the budgets as monthly loan payments. The before-divorce budget will help you determine your cash flow; if it's negative (more expenses than income), you'll know whether and how much you'll have to tap the resources you listed in the previous step in order to stay afloat.

Use the worksheet in Figure 4-1 as a simplified model to prepare your own more detailed budget.

Tax Filing during Divorce

Beyond dealing with your spouse's attacks, you'll have to deal with your spouse about taxes. If your spouse has always been the family tax-filer, and you've filed jointly and will continue doing so until the divorce, you'll want to be extra careful in checking the current and recent-past form(s) in case your spouse is deliberately underreporting income. Furthermore, even if you choose one of two filing options that don't seem to involve your spouse—married filing separately

Balancing income and expenses

Step 1 — Your monthly income (take-home)

	Before Divorce	During Divorce	After Divorce
Salary, wages	$	$	$
Unemployment compensation	$	$	$
Child support	$	$	$
FIP	$	$	$
Food stamps	$	$	$
Spousal maintenance	$	$	$
Other	$	$	$
A. *Total monthly income*	$	$	$ (A)

Step 2 — Monthly expenses

	Before Divorce	During Divorce	After Divorce
Housing (mortgage or rent)	$	$	$
Utilities (electric, gas, phone, etc.)	$	$	$
Food (at home and away)	$	$	$
Transportation (gas, car repairs)	$	$	$
Medical care (doctor, dentist, hospital, prescriptions)	$	$	$
Credit payments (loans, credit cards)	$	$	$
Insurance (life, health, disability, car, property, house)	$	$	$
Household operations and maintenance (repairs, cleaning, laundry supplies, etc.)	$	$	$
Clothing and personal care (clothes, laundry, toiletries, etc.)	$	$	$
Child care	$	$	$
Education and recreation	$	$	$
Miscellaneous (gifts, allowances)	$	$	$
Funds set aside for seasonal and occasional expenses	$	$	$
B. *Total monthly expenses*	$	$	$ (B)

Step 3 — Balance Income and expenses

Total monthly income (A) $ _____ − $ _____ = $ _____ *Total monthly expenses* (B)

FIGURE 4-1 Divorce Budget Worksheet *Courtesy of the Iowa State University Cooperative Extension*

79

and head of household—you must still coordinate with your spouse to make sure you've combined all the necessary information.

And if your goal is to jointly save as much money as possible, then you will have cooperate even more closely to determine which of the three filing choices would be collectively more advantageous. You should consider eligibility for the child tax credit and dependent care benefits as well as who should claim the children as dependents. These determinations must be made on a case-by-case basis. Consider getting help from a tax professional because each of these provisions is subject to phase-outs based on income as well as changing tax laws. The following information provided by the American Institute of Certified Public Accountants, summarizes the pros and cons of your choices:

- *Joint return:* This status generally offers the lowest tax bracket, but each spouse is then liable for the other's tax liability. The innocent-spouse provisions of tax law offer some protection to spouses who don't know about certain income and thus some relief from the responsibility for the other's taxes.
- *Married filing separately:* This status helps you avoid responsibility for your spouse's tax liability, but tax rates are higher, several potential credits and other tax benefits are lost, and if one spouse itemizes, both must.
- *Head of household and married filing separately:* You can choose this combination by mutual agreement only if you have children but you and your spouse haven't lived together the last six months of the tax year. The spouse who pays the majority of household costs for a home that is also the child's home for more than half the year can file as *head of household* (HOH). The HOH status offers several additional credits over married filing separately, and it lowers certain marginal tax rates. The HOH filer can take the standard deduction, which is higher than it is for married filing separately, even if the other spouse itemizes. The custodial parent is always entitled to the dependency exemption and child credit for each child unless that parent specifically waives the right. The dependency exemption provides an income deduction worth $3050 for 2003 returns and will be adjusted for inflation in subsequent years, while the child credit currently reduces tax liability by $1000. If you have two or more children, you might be able to work it out so that both of you can file with the HOH status by each of you having at least one of the children living with you for more than half the year (six months and one day).

Insurance Changes for Separation

Don't make the mistake of assuming that you need be concerned about insurance changes only after the divorce. Your separation has the potential to affect all of your insurance policies immediately, and you might need to formalize responsibility for insurance payments in a written separation agreement. We'll cover after-divorce insurance changes later, but here's a rundown of potential insurance concerns during separation:

- *Health insurance:* If you, your spouse, and kids are all covered under the same health insurance, you're probably OK as long as that insurance is kept in force during the separation. However, check with the provider because some policies don't allow marital coverage to continue when the dependents don't live in the same residence as the primary insured. In that case, most employer plans allow the employee's spouse to continue coverage on or after the date of legal separation (or the date of divorce for those not offering it as of separation) under the Consolidated Omnibus Budget Reconciliation Act [COBRA]. The COBRA coverage is offered at 102 percent of the rate that the insurer charges the employer to provide that group coverage, a lot more expensive than the employee's cost but often more attractive than buying new insurance on the open market. If the employee's spouse can't get COBRA until the divorce, or has other reasons such as anticipation of a new employer's coverage, short-term coverage can be obtained from select providers (see www.consumerbenefits.net) such as Fortis. Also, beware that even when the employee family coverage continues during the divorce process without COBRA, some spouses with employer coverage, in a fit of pique, cut off dependent-spouse coverage, so it might be necessary to get a court order to maintain or restore the coverage.

  When both spouses have their own employer's coverage available, they might agree to rearrange coverage so that the custodial spouse provides his or her own coverage and includes the kids, while the other spouse has only self-coverage. But be careful about any preexisting conditions when switching insurance because there might be a waiting period before the conditions are covered. Is all this confusing? You bet, so you might want to check this more detailed explanation (http://hrcenter.bna.com/pic2/hr2pic.nsf/id/BNAP-5HLTVD?Open-Document) or check with a benefits expert to be sure of what to do.

- *Automobile insurance:* The news is bad, financially, but at least your insurance agent should be able to tell you exactly what to do. In many states, once spouses live in different households, they must carry separate insurance policies, and any child drivers must be insured either under the custodial spouse's policy or under their own policies. Rules differ, though, so ask your agent. Furthermore, even if you can stay under the same policy, you again must be sure that the policy is maintained for both of the spouses and child drivers. This is also a good time to review your liability limits and buy an umbrella policy if you don't have one. Consider buying or increasing your umbrella coverage to $2-$3 million to protect against lawsuits arising from incidents such as auto accidents where someone is hurt or killed.

- *Homeowner's insurance:* If you and your spouse physically separate into different households, the one who moves must definitely get either renter's or home insurance to cover the second home, depending on whether the property has been leased or purchased. But because the household in the original property has changed, and some property might have been moved out, that policy will have to be updated as well. Again, check with the agent.

- *Life insurance:* Certainly, spouses who have insured themselves and made their spouses and children beneficiaries will want to make changes effective upon divorce—almost certainly cutting out or changing the amount that would go to an ex-spouse. But during divorce, the dependent spouse still needs the protection for which the original policy was purchased, so the separation agreement might dictate the continuation of the coverage and who must pay for it. This also might be the time for a spouse to purchase insurance on a (soon-to-be) ex-spouse, while he or she still maintains a legal "economic" interest in that spouse. For example, the new insurance might replace the payments stipulated in the divorce agreement in the event the ex-spouse (support payer) dies. This is a complex area that we'll revisit later when covering how estate plans should be revised in light of divorce.

Access to Funds and Credit

Despite advances in genetic engineering, you still can't get blood from a turnip. Similarly, you can't turn up money from a debt-laden marriage, but you can take actions to protect yourself against debts that are the fault of your spouse. Furthermore, if your spouse is hoarding whatever cash crops your marriage does have, you're entitled to harvest enough of it to effectively make your divorce case. Later in this chapter you'll learn how to level the divorce-proceeding playing field and plant seeds to grow your nest egg after divorce by preventing your spouse from draining accounts, filing a motion to have your spouse pay legal fees, and protecting and improving your credit.

Expenditure Tracking, Temporary Support, and Bill Payment Responsibility

Although the money is gone when you spend it, the amounts you and your spouse spend during separation can play a part in the ultimate divorce settlement. If the two of you aren't homicidal, then try to agree at least informally on who is responsible for what bills, and possibly for temporary support to be paid by one to the other. We'll later discuss the pros and cons of informal and formal separation agreements, but for now you should know that any amounts spent, charged, or borrowed that weren't specifically stipulated as being the responsibility of one spouse or the other are up for grabs in terms of counting as original marital assets to be divided. And in some circumstances, even the amounts agreed to might play a part in the settlement and could definitely affect taxes (for example, temporary support paid could be deductible as alimony). Therefore, it's crucial that you track every dime you spend during the separation period, and you should try to get your spouse to agree to do that as well. In fact, communicating about this and agreeing on it could go a long way toward creating a spirit of cooperation that will aid in the reaching of a settlement without undue antagonism.

Prepare to Propose or Evaluate a Financial Settlement Offer

While dealing with those issues to make it through the divorce financially alive, you must also be concerned with addressing the issues that will determine the financial verdict. Continuing our fantasy, let's assume that you either actually did commit the crime and need to cop the best plea you can, or that you're completely innocent and have been railroaded, so that you're now settling a suit for damages. In either case, you need to formulate a proposal that is most likely to lead to an agreement and avoid the courtroom.

In Chapters 7 and 8, we'll do an in-depth exploration of the financial elements that go into your proposal, but to set the stage, here's a brief overview of them.

Dividing Property and Debt

Your divorce decree must stipulate who gets and who must pay for every single thing that either of you own, owe, or are owed. This includes cash, stock, residential and commercial real estate, value of a business, personal property, and amounts owed to either of you, and even amounts that will be owed to either of you in the form of deferred payments from completed work for an employer, payment for contracts, and trusts. Even if these payments are owed due to events that took place before the marriage or that will take place after the marriage, it is possible that they should be included in the property to be divided. For example, if an employer were to pay an incentive bonus a few years down the road based on your or your spouse's performance over a period of years that included time during the marriage, part of that amount could be considered marital property.

Spousal and Child Support

Although custodial spouses have historically had trouble collecting it, child support is usually awarded because regardless of how much the custodial spouse makes, both parents are legally responsible for supporting children as much as possible in the manner to which were accustomed. In addition, legislative action and specific judicial rulings are steadily increasing the number of states in which child support obligations extend beyond the age of 18, usually only for children with special needs or those enrolled in college or other postsecondary education. And such support increasingly includes sharing in the cost of providing a college education. All states have formulas that are applied in standard cases, but the formulas aren't used in special circumstances or when the parties agree to something different that is acceptable to the court.

In contrast, while spousal support is awarded according to different conditions depending on state law, it doesn't follow formulas. It's sometimes either forgone in favor of a more favorable property settlement, or it is increased to compensate for a smaller property settlement. In short-term marriages, it's generally awarded based on the need to provide a bridge to self-sufficiency, usually for just a few years. Or it's awarded permanently to maintain a lifestyle to which a homemaker spouse had become accustomed in long-term marriages. Your divorce decree should specify exactly under what conditions spousal support is awarded and terminated—for example, it's sometimes ended upon remarriage—and what systems have been put in place to assure its continued payment upon the payer's death, disability, or unilateral suspension.

Share of Spousal Social Security and Pension

If either spouse has the best bargaining attorney in the world, and the other the worst, it shouldn't affect one aspect of a divorce settlement—namely, the right of one spouse to a Social Security payment based on the other spouse's payment. That right is determined by U.S. law, which entitles ex-Spouse A to a payment starting at age 62 that is 50 percent of ex-Spouse B's payment if the marriage lasted at least 10 years and that amount is greater than what ex-Spouse A is entitled to based on his or her own earnings. However, if ex-Spouse A starts payments early (before age 65) based on the ex-Spouse B's earnings, then those payments will be less than they would be if they weren't started until age 65, so starting early is usually a bad idea unless it's absolutely necessary for financial survival. Spouse A's payment doesn't cost Spouse B a dime, but Spouse A might be entitled to recourse if Spouse B deliberately sabotages future earnings just to spite Spouse A. Unfortunately, though, the law doesn't give Spouse A recourse against congress for sabotaging future payments.

Pensions are not as straightforward, however. For one thing, many companies have been doing their best to deny all or part of future pensions to those anticipating them; they've phased out traditional pensions in favor of 401(k) and cash balance plans. So if you've been married more than a few years and there is a significant potential pension at stake, you'd be wise to involve a pension expert to determine what the employer's plan document and your state's law generally says you should be entitled to and how to translate that into formulas from which your share would be calculated.

We'll cover pensions and other retirement plans in some detail in Chapters 7 and 8, but in general, you're entitled to half of your spouse's retirement benefit if you were married the entire time during which it was earned, and proportionately less the more years that it was partially earned outside the marriage. Because future pension amounts are uncertain or most spouses who expect to receive them don't want them diluted by a share being subtracted for an ex-spouse, settlements are often structured to award additional property now in lieu of a future pension. Or a future balloon payment backed by life insurance or a trust might be arranged if paying a lump sum now would be prohibitive. Regardless of what arrangement you make, if it involves one spouse receiving a portion of the other's pension, it's critical that you have a qualified domestic relations order (QDRO) drawn up by a knowledgeable attorney (possibly in conjunction with a benefits expert) and filed with the pension-paying employer in compliance with that employer's specified procedure.

Taxes and Other Considerations in Structuring the Settlement

As if hammering out agreements on these points wasn't hard enough, settlements are further complicated by the tax consequences of various forms of regular payments or current property transfers. But taking taxes into account often is a win-win for both spouses. That's because a higher-income spouse making spousal support payments can save more money with those payments deducted at a higher tax rate, while the receiving spouse won't owe that much tax on payments received at a lower tax rate. Furthermore, appreciated property such as stocks with significant built-in gains can be given to the spouse with the lower tax rate who could then cash them in for more after-tax dollars than they would have been worth had they been cashed in by the higher-bracket spouse.

Timing of transfers, payments, and investment liquidations can also make a huge difference in total taxation. Tax balancing a sizeable settlement is a delicate process that should always involve CPAs or other tax experts. It's well worth your paying the fees, however, because it could preserve tens of thousands of additional dollars of marital assets.

Taxes, though, are only one leg of the wobbly legs of the divorce settlement stool. Appropriate financial assumptions about interest rates, future tax rates, and other economic factors must be made in determining the equivalency of a stream of continuing payments to a current lump-sum settlement. Because nobody can accurately forecast future rates, you should have a financial expert compare different scenarios based on varying rate assumptions to see what assumptions are least sensitive to small changes. However, if you're number-savvy, you can use the *Split-Up* divorce-software product—referenced in the Resource Appendix and the basis for examples presented in Chapters 9 and 10—to estimate the outcomes of various scenarios you'd like to compare.

That expert should also help determine whether and how to use life insurance, as well as, or in conjunction with, trusts that provide funds for education or special-needs children. In addition, provisions for transferring a minority portion of a family business require thoughtful structuring to avoid potential negative tax consequences. Finally, couples with considerable means might want to involve an estate attorney to find tax-saving creative approaches to include in the settlement.

In general, the more that's at stake, the more likely that a settlement derived without appropriate legal and financial expertise will yield far less collectively than it could have. But even if your assets are modest, it's worth a brief consultation with an unbiased financial and/or divorce planner to make sure you won't make a costly mistake.

Immediate and Postdivorce Custody and Domicile

When Paul Simon cited the 50 ways to leave your lover, the housing market must not have been as tight and kids probably weren't involved, and he likely had a more substantial stash of ready cash than most of us. Because you don't want to sleep under the Ferris wheel at Scarborough Fair, nor enrage your spouse if you don't have to, it's crucial to line up some alternatives for either you or your spouse; a little good-will in exchange for doing some homework might go a long way. Furthermore, unless you have reason to fear abuse, you shouldn't necessarily have to have a physical split right away. For example, Massachusetts is among a few states that doesn't require physical separation in order to divorce. But even if your state requires it, you could lose the right to return to your house if you impulsively leave, so don't until you check your state's rules—which you can do on any one of the general divorce Web sites, such as divorce-source.com, listed in the Resource Appendix.

The more difficult issue involves your children. If there's any one thing that's likely to sabotage a constructive approach to your divorce, or to make it more likely, it's how well you're able to communicate with your spouse and kids to ease the pain and assure them and each other that you're restructuring the family but not destroying it. Unless there's an overwhelmingly compelling reason, such as a legitimate concern that your spouse might disappear with your kids, you should bend over backward to arrange some form of joint custody or liberal visitation. The alternative is expensive child custody litigation. Consider what Mai Mai Ginsburg, LSW, a Chapel Hill, North Carolina, therapist heard: glee in the voice of a prominent psychiatrist when he said that he had paid for a full year of his child's Ivy League education with the fees from just one child custody case in which he was an expert witness.

Chapter 5 contains specifics on domicile and child-related issues connected with separation, but to emphasize how crucial your children are in this process, we suggest you read the poignant "Children's Bill of Rights" in the Supplementary Materials section of the Resource Appendix.

Line Up Your Logistical Divorce Ducks

At the risk of overdoing the crime metaphor, let's now think of divorce as the crime and you as the detective. So far you've given considerable thought to two of the three components of solving the crime: the motive you have for the divorce and the means to go through with it. But before you file, you must have the opportunity to see it through, and keep your co-perpetrator spouse from preventing your appearance at the "trial." Here are the elements of your witness protection program:

- *Method:* Although the divorce action might change, you should know how you hope to pursue it once you or your spouse have filed it, and you should have also given thought to the alternatives. For example, will you propose or agree to mediation or collaborative law, and are you prepared to go to court if need be?

- *Team:* At a minimum, have you consulted attorneys for initial advice and lined up several you might potentially retain depending on the divorce method? Have you met with your financial advisor to help determine where you stand and what the major issues might be, or have you lined up potential advisors if you don't already have one or will need a different one to avoid a conflict of interest with your spouse? Have you compiled a list of mediators, and thought about therapists, family mental health professionals, forensic accountants, and other professionals you might need depending on your case's circumstances?
- *Timing:* All times are not equal when it comes to filing, for both family and financial reasons. Keep in mind that bad family timing could prove financially costly. For example, do you really want to risk overburdening a spouse who is particularly stressed out over a major work project—risking that he or she will lose a job or advancement opportunity? Do you want to risk getting your kids' school year off to a horrible start and then spending thousands for tutors and mental health professionals to repair the damage? There's no good time, but there are definitely some really bad ones, and even if you sense your spouse is getting ready to file, you might hint that you're ready to talk about that possibility and then agree to delay it until what both of you consider to be the best time. All family considerations being equal, a financial advisor might help you determine the best financial timing for tax or other reasons.
- *Work arrangements and support network:* Prepare for your divorce as though it was a second full-time job because the more you do, the more you can keep down the cost and help keep the process under control. So try to arrange the possibility of taking some time off on a spur-of-the moment basis so that you won't have to delay various meetings or court appearances. And line up a solid string of child care providers so that you'll be able to quickly find someone when you do need to have those meetings, as well as to allow some blowing-off-steam time with friends and family.
- *Handling the divorce-process and divorce-related paperwork and arrangements:* If you've always been tempted to grab the Yellow Pages and hire one of those entrepreneurs who've started household-organization businesses, then divorce is going to be an even worse nightmare of paperwork for you. It's no coincidence that some mental health professionals liken divorce recovery to a postmortem grieving period—and attorneys do too, but for a more relevant reason: The need for well-organized paperwork in divorce is similar in complexity to the need for it in administering a deceased's estate. So now's the time to get things in

order, no matter what it takes, and enlist help for the ongoing paperwork from someone other than one of the minority of attorneys who would be just as willing to charge hundreds for an hour of filling out forms as for an hour of meeting with you. For example, consider using an independent paralegal.

Sum Up Your Strategy

Before you do any official paperwork, however, take a little time to summarize your strategic position on paper, including the various resources, contacts, and professional possibilities you've identified. Your strategy will evolve as you proceed, but putting it in writing now gives you a point of reference for your subsequent efforts. Also consider purchasing *The Divorce Record Keeper* (www.divorcefind.com/a/divorcehelpbooks/recordkeeper.shtml) or other divorce-organizing products listed in the Resource Appendix. Armed with a documented strategy and the tools and materials you'll need to implement it, you're ready for Round 3 in Chapter 5, where we'll give you a blow-by-blow description of what happens when the divorce action officially begins.

Chapter 5

(Round 3): Initiate Divorce and Negotiate a Moneywise Marital Settlement

Rounds 1 and 2 are just shadow boxing in comparison to Round 3, when you'll be fighting for your postfiling financial life. If you've done everything discussed so far, you're as ready as you'll ever be to defend your interests vigorously, whether it involves knuckles or negotiating. We've touched briefly on some of this chapter's material, but it's covered more thoroughly here in the form of a specific, detailed combination of steps to take when you stop pulling punches and start pulling out all the stops to achieve a successful divorce.

Prepare to File or Respond, and Separate

This book primarily concerns divorce's financial aspects, so we skip filing-and-responding legal details. Your state's rules, available either at libraries or on general-divorce and state-specific listed in the Resource Appendix, cover the specific filing procedures you'll need to use. In the filing-and-responding stage, we recommend that you hire qualified legal counsel to make sure all the *i*'s are dotted and the *t*'s are crossed. But before you or your spouse file—assuming you can anticipate when he or she will do so—here's what to do to ease the financial transition.

Pay Current Bills and Make Needed Marital Expenditures

Pay as many marital bills as possible using marital assets. If you use credit to pay for anything, make sure it's on a credit account for which you're both responsible.

Rather than arguing later with your spouse about needed child support and spousal support expenditures, make those expenditures now. Use marital assets to purchase products and services that are generally considered marital—such as home repairs, automobile maintenance, or buying a new or late-model used car to replace one that is long past seeing its best days. Get your kids started with an orthodontist or with contact lenses if they're close to being ready anyway. Also take care of any medical matters that you've been delaying due to lack of time.

This could also be the time to resume your education and career planning if you've worked part-time or sporadically, or have a dead-end job. Don't hesitate to spend on tuition, related educational expenses, career counseling, and a work and/or interview wardrobe upgrade. It's much easier to justify rehabilitative spousal support if you've already started "rehabilitation." If you've been a long-term full-time homemaker, though, check with an attorney, because doing this before the settlement could work against your receiving as much spousal support as you deserve.

Don't spend unnecessarily, though, because if you spend money frivolously at this time, you'll have less credibility later defending your expenditures. You might have heard elsewhere that you should spend as much as you can while you have the chance. But that assumes an adversarial approach, while you're trying to avoid unnecessary conflict and its associated excessive litigation expense.

Get a Job and Establish Your Own Credit

Because you should close all joint accounts to prevent your spouse from using them, you'll need a separate account for your own credit. If you've been a homemaker, it won't be easy. So try to get at least part-time work and establish store and gas credit in your own name well before you divorce so that you'll be able to qualify for a significant line of credit by the time you file.

But don't increase spending with the additional money you're earning. Instead, save it in a separate account that isn't linked to your checking account, so that you'll have it available later if you need it. Although putting money in a separate account before separation guarantees you access to the funds, doing so does not make them separate property. Again, some advice you'll read differs on this point, suggesting that you up your spending across the board as you approach divorce because it will be easier to justify asking for more child support or spousal support. More likely, though, suddenly increasing your spending will just add to the financial distress that you'll all suffer through during and after the divorce.

Get More Involved in Family Life

It's natural to detach from family life when marriage goes sour, but it only make things worse upon separation and divorce—possibly resulting in an expensive and bitter custody battle. If you've succeeded in working with horrible teachers, work colleagues, and supervisors, you can certainly manage to coexist with your spouse in order to keep your family company running. Think of this period as preparation for successful joint custody after the divorce. The Resource Appendix lists several books concerning family issues surrounding divorce, such as effects on children, custody arrangements, and co-parenting with your soon-to-be ex-spouse.

Compile a Marital History

Any aspect of your marriage could become fair game once you file, so start spending some time every day compiling a history of your marriage. Start with estimated budgets for different phases of your marriage and major expenditures that were made over the course of your marriage. Estimate the proportional contributions that each of you made to each major expense, the ongoing expenses, and savings and/or investments. Then detail money-saving and non-monetary ways you've contributed to the family overall, to child rearing, and to your spouse's career. Also include explanations for behaviors and situations that might be brought up in a negative light.

Treat your marital history like a school report in the sense that it includes photographic, documentary, and other materials that support your story. Use an informal and concise outline style, because it might be something your attorney will use later. And, because you might be relying on this document for your own purposes in later negotiation, make this a confidential document that isn't subject to legal discovery by your spouse's attorney. You could think of it as a master document from which you can pull information quickly as you need it throughout the divorce process. Having a thorough history will make it much easier later should you have to produce such a document for legal discovery by your spouse's attorney. In that case, you would make "how to do that" one of the many questions you'll ask the attorney you'll consult for initial divorce advice.

By keeping this version of your marital history confidential, you can freely mention your spouse, without concern that positive comments about his or her contributions will work against you in a formal setting. And in private, such positive comments might instead work helpfully against your negative emotional impulses, facilitating your objective assessment of both the financial and nonmonetary contributions you've each made. Here are some attorneys' Web pages where you can find more information on marital histories:

- An attorney's online marital history form
  (www.sherridonovan.com/marital.htm)
- An attorney's list of what to include in a marital history
  (www.vuotto.com/pendentelite.htm) Page down to paragraph
- An attorney's explanation of a marital history
  (www.moriartydee.com/divorce/) See Item 7

Start a Divorce Ledger

To minimize "he said, she said" (or "did") arguments during the divorce process, start compiling a day-by-day accounting of events and expenditures related in any way to the divorce. (Check out the *Divorce Record Keeper*–at divorcefind.com/products/recordkeeper.shtml). In addition to facts, you might make a daily closing comment on where things stand, how you feel, and what comes next. It will make it easier to keep track of what has and has not been done, and it can give you a sense of progress toward the goal. In fact, it might help you see counterproductive actions you've taken so that you can possibly correct them and do better moving forward. Again, protect this from discovery.

Witness Divorce Suffering Firsthand

If you need further encouragement to take a nonadversarial approach to divorce, or you want to know what to expect if your spouse takes you to court, why not get up close and personal with the legal process. Find out when and where cases are being heard, and take off a few mornings or afternoons to view the proceedings. It will be a dose of reality far more potent than Reality TV, *Court TV*, or *Divorce Court*. And the few hours of forgone wages might be compensated by avoiding hundreds of hours of attorney fees, while helping you formulate questions that will allow you to deal more efficiently and effectively with an attorney.

Report for Dirty-Trick Guard Duty

Even if you're planning to file and you don't think your spouse has a clue, he or she might have much better radar than you think. So be on the lookout for potentially harmful financial and family moves such as large discretionary expenditures, money moves between accounts, opening and closing accounts, secretive communication with your children or others, and cutting off communication with you. If you're the primary breadwinner, think twice before following the often-advised but often questionable strategy of drastically decreasing family spending in order to justify paying less child support or spousal support. That will only inspire your spouse's righteous indignation about unfairness and might lead to requesting more-than-reasonable support. Besides, some judges are wise to this tactic and will look back to expenditures during happier times

Your spouse certainly has the right to do the same ethical things you're doing to prepare for divorce, but you want to be sure that your kids aren't spirited away and that you're not left without financial resources. Consider hiring a private investigator if you suspect that your spouse's behavior is leading to either of these things or that your spouse is expending considerable marital resources on an affair.

Engage and Consult Divorce Professionals

Now's the time to put the earlier "intelligence" you've gathered to work by consulting or retaining the (team of) various professionals you'll need. Consult the "Directories and Web Sites of Divorce Professionals and Organizations" section of the Resource Appendix for Web sites, addresses, and phone numbers of directories, organizations, and professionals. But first read the following section for brief descriptions of each type of professional you might engage.

Legal and Related Professionals

Attorneys fill a wide variety of roles during divorce—ranging from planning consultant who doesn't represent you, to the person who fights your battle from the opening gun until the court decision. And sometimes paralegals can do most of what you need. The following are the different divorce roles played by legal and related professionals such as custody evaluators.

Consulting Attorneys

Before you're ready to commit to a specific course of action in your divorce, it could be well worth your time and money to consult an attorney experienced in family law. Perhaps you'll end up hiring that attorney on retainer or as your representative in a collaborative divorce, but he or she also might advise you to negotiate a settlement via mediation or directly with your spouse. You may want the consulting attorney to be your divorce-closing attorney (see below) by representing you in a nonadversarial capacity and advising you about signing documents. He or she might agree to this role or might refer you to a paralegal or another attorney for those purposes. If you do engage someone to officially represent you, be prepared to sign a representation agreement and a sizable retainer check.

Traditional (Adversarial) Retained Attorneys

You'll want to retain an attorney if there's a lot at stake, you want a settlement that you don't think can be negotiated directly or through mediation or collaboration, or if it looks like your case will end up in court—especially if your spouse has hired an attorney known for being highly adversarial. Ideally, your attorney should be equally adept at enticing the other side to settle and fighting for your rights if needed in the courtroom. By retaining an attorney when you feel you can't trust your spouse, you'll be much more likely to deal with sticky legal issues such as child custody, long-term spousal support, the discovery of hidden assets, the value of a professional practice or other business, and extensive compensation in the form of corporate benefits.

Before putting an attorney on retainer, make sure you interview at least a few that come highly recommended. You should ask about their training; it's a plus if any are certified family law specialists. Then ask about experience in general and on your type of case: How savvy are they on the complex tax and other financial issues that could come into play? What strategy do they think they'll use, and what do they think the case outcome will be? How will communication work during the case, and what circumstances do they consider to be valid emergencies when they should be reachable during a meeting or off-hours? Will they or their subordinates do most of the work, and how qualified are those subordinates? Perhaps most importantly, Craig Ross suggests finding an attorney who works well with other attorneys, regardless of how contentious the case, while vigorously representing you. "Ideally, if your spouse has already hired an attorney, find a good one who has a history of working well with that attorney," suggests Ross.

Furthermore, it's critical that you get full details on billing rates for the multitude of services that could be used during the divorce and for any professionals that they consult on the case. Ask for a very rough ballpark figure for what they think your case will cost and whether they have good suggestions for reducing costs. Also, find out their comfort level in working with professionals that you might involve, such as your financial or tax advisor, and with your continuing discussions with your spouse that could help toward resolution. Just as you don't need the very best surgeon if surgery can be avoided, you don't need an alpha courtroom gladiator if you can resolve things without "bloodshed." Finally, make sure that the attorney isn't among the one third who don't carry malpractice insurance.

Collaborative Divorce Attorneys

Collaborative attorneys specializing in divorce are every bit as competent to deal with complex issues as traditional adversarial divorce attorneys. You and your spouse might want them because you really don't know what's fair, or you share a sense of what's fair but aren't sure you know how to put together a settlement that matches your intentions or preserves the most of your mutual assets. So you might think of the difference the way you'd distinguish between someone who wants to pay the lowest amount of taxes period, and someone who accepts the responsibility to pay taxes but wants the breaks to which he or she is clearly entitled. The rock-bottom taxpayer is willing to push the envelope in every way with an extremely aggressive tax advisor (comparable to the gladiator divorce trial attorney). In contrast, the prudent taxpayer uses a skilled CPA to avoid paying more taxes than dictated by the spirit and intent of the tax laws (comparable to the "do best what's right for all" approach of collaborative attorneys).

When the collaborative divorce "play" works the way it's drawn up on the chalkboard, the opponent doesn't steal or intercept the ball, so there's no need for offsetting legal maneuvers. The open and full disclosure of information by both parties means there is little need for the attorneys to do extensive research and investigate the financial situation of the marital estate. They don't have to charge for discovery or court time, which reduces legal costs and the time it takes to complete the divorce.

Divorce-Closing Attorneys

Many divorce attorneys will handle cases the way that real estate attorneys handle closings—they charge for a package of services that includes limited consultation, composing the marital settlement agreement and other relevant documents, and processing everything through the family court system. Use this type of attorney if you and your spouse agree on what you want but want to make sure that everything is done right. You and your spouse can share an attorney to close your divorce, but if you do, you might also want to each spend a few hours having separate consulting attorneys review the agreement drafted by the closing attorney to make sure you're getting what you expected, and it is reasonable given all the circumstances.

Divorce Paralegals

Paralegals aren't licensed attorneys, so they can't give you legal advice. However, they can help you save a bundle of time or money preparing divorce forms that you want filled out based on the prior consultations with an attorney or for an attorney's review of the settlement you and your spouse have reached, perhaps through a mediator. Your attorney's paralegal might be a good choice, assuming the rate charged isn't that much higher than the typical independent paralegal rate in your area. If you decide to hire an independent, carefully check out the paralegal for specific divorce qualifications and experience because the courts will often reject error-laden forms.

Bankruptcy Attorneys

You might want to consult a bankruptcy attorney under three possible circumstances. The first is a constructive use of bankruptcy. It would be a situation in which a mutual bankruptcy would allow you and your spouse to get out from under overwhelming debt before divorcing and starting anew—with a settlement in place that will make sure to take care of the children and a spouse who has much lower income.

The second is the possibility your spouse might use bankruptcy to avoid support obligations or even a property settlement, despite having assets and being capable of providing the support. So if you have an inkling that your spouse will try abusing bankruptcy in that way, make sure your attorney is sufficiently versed in bankruptcy procedures, or consults a bankruptcy attorney, to fully explain how your spouse's bankruptcy would work, how it would affect you, and your spouse's likelihood of success. That knowledge will help your attorney ensure you get the best possible settlement to which you should be entitled based on the true financial situation—which might also involve filing for a judge's temporary order that blocks your spouse from filing bankruptcy until the divorce is final. It might also affect how to structure the divorce settlement; for example, you might want to protect yourself from such bankruptcy manipulation, which could occur even after the divorce, by rejecting spousal support in favor of a more favorable property division. Or under the third set of circumstances, you're the higher-income spouse, and the combination of existing bills and excessive demands by your spouse means that you simply won't be able to provide the support, still eat, and not be homeless. It might be cheaper in the long run, in terms of minimizing your divorce attorney's time spent countering your spouse's demands, to plan a legitimate bankruptcy that won't be blocked by a favorable ruling on a spouse's motion filed in family court.

Your divorce attorney might be knowledgeable enough so that you don't have to go to a bankruptcy attorney to assess the threat of your spouse's abusive bankruptcy or your need to file because of a spouse's abusive demands. But if you and your spouse are planning bankruptcy together, consider using a specialist unless your divorce attorney has considerable experience in that area. Think of legitimate bankruptcy as the jaws of life used to get a severely injured passenger out of a crushed vehicle; it gets you out from under the debt but doesn't completely remove you from the debt obligation. So make sure you're pulled from the crushed car delicately so you will have the best chance of long-term recovery.

Mediators

Chapter 2 included extensive coverage of advantages, disadvantages, and favorable and unfavorable circumstances regarding divorce mediation. It's important to understand that mediators are hired by both spouses together. However, some will agree to talk with you in an exploratory interview if you're not ready to broach the subject with your spouse and are trying to decide whether to use mediation or you are compiling a list of qualified mediators to present to your spouse.

Although your mediator can't practice law by giving specific legal advice, you should prefer a mediator who is an attorney—particularly one who no longer practices adversarial divorce law because he or she has "had it." Such an attorney will be trained in conflict resolution but will also be highly conversant with the legal and financial issues—as opposed to some mediators who are expert counselors, therapists, social workers, clergy, or related professionals but have less divorce-specific experience. Nevertheless, you and your spouse might prefer the less technical and more "touchy-feely" mediator if you both have a pretty good grip on the issues but simply can't come to an agreement. It's an added plus to find a mediator who is qualified to compose the marital settlement agreement if your state allows mediators to do that.

If you're going to mediation because your state or locality requires it, and you and your spouse have attorneys, some jurisdictions will allow them to attend mediation to provide the legal advice the mediator can't give you. But if you've chosen mediation on your own, if you and your spouse prefer, you can definitely agree on both having attorneys present at mediation sessions—or you might want to start without them but bring them to the last one or two when you'll hopefully be close to forging an agreement. If you plan to mediate, look for an attorney with similar philosophy and traits to those you'd find in a collaborative divorce attorney.

Arbitrators

When mediation and collaborative law approaches lack the backbone to force a settlement, and divorce court provides too many bones to pick, arbitration might be your best bet. Unlike mediators who often aren't attorneys, most arbitrators are attorneys—many are actually retired judges. However, a number of arbitrators are actually also mediators, and it's possible to start using a mediator-arbitrator in mediation and then go to arbitration if mediation isn't progressing sufficiently.

Arbitrators preside in a "courtroom" that is actually a conference room, where each spouse sits—often accompanied by his or her attorney. Proceedings are often less formal than they would be in court, and testimony isn't public record—although the ultimate binding judgment is. Arbitrators set the rules on how each side presents its case—usually having more leeway to dismiss "nuisance" witnesses, and just get the facts out—without having them obscured with countless motions and countermotions.

Arbitration will probably prove more expensive than mediation because you are paying the arbitrator for his or her "court" and decision time—usually about the hourly rate of a competent divorce attorney—while possibly also paying your attorney to help prepare your case and appear with you. But because the arbitrator's decision is final and the process is more streamlined than it would be in a court case, you'll save considerably over standard litigation and the appeals that often follow—especially if you arbitrate without attorneys.

You can find an arbitrator through the American Arbitration Association (AAA) on their Web site at adr.org or, in some states, have one (called a *special master*) appointed by the court. You can also find them in various Internet and attorney listings, and through local and state bar associations.

Private Investigators

When you think of divorce and private investigators (PIs), perhaps you picture the opening scene in the Coen Brothers' first and best movie, *Blood Simple*—and indeed many judges view private detectives to be as trustworthy as the seedy PI who got tangled up in murder. But credible, quality PIs do have their place in divorce cases, even though adultery is no longer a consideration in most no-fault divorce states. For one thing, proving adultery still matters in fault states, and the nature of the adultery can matter in no-fault states if it has systematically damaged the marriage in a way that has financial impacts—such as money lavished on a lover or additional expenses due to the adulterous spouse not pulling weight in the household.

Furthermore, you might need a PI to prove stalking, other criminal behavior that might include fraud and use of drugs and alcohol, and/or to locate missing assets. And the PI today is more brainy than brawny—and more savvy than sexy (a la Kinsey Milhone of *A is for Alibi*). He or she is often a technology expert who collects evidence by computer tracking and (legal) hacking, and electronic and/or video surveillance.

So look for those qualities if you need a PI, and make sure he or she is properly (state) licensed, has a clean record, isn't a fired ex-cop or the subject of litigation, and has no conflict of interest regarding work for the law firm representing your spouse. Also, make sure your PI is adequately bonded and insured and that the contract ensures that you and your law firm are indemnified against damages from any investigative misconduct. And try to use a hiring arrangement that shields the work product from legal discovery by your spouse by virtue of its being an attorney-client work product.

Custody Evaluators and Other Mental Health Professionals

While these are not legal professionals, they're often hired by attorneys to testify or provide information to support a legal strategy. You might need a child psychologist or other mental health professionals to evaluate you, your spouse, and your children and then submit a report concerning the fitness of either or both spouses to have custody, and to give an opinion on what would be in the best interests of the children.

In addition, consider counseling for yourself or your children to make it through the divorce process and begin adjusting to postdivorce life. Most divorcing individuals can benefit from at least a couple of sessions with a therapist to help them get in touch with their feelings and help them move forward in a positive way—including making sound decisions about the divorce that are minimally clouded by emotions. If one spouse doesn't have the means to pay for this but the other does, then the lower-income spouse might file a temporary order to have the higher-income spouse pay for the counseling.

Financial Advisors and Specialists

In addition to a good attorney and other legal professionals, you might need financial and other nonlegal specialists, depending on the issues in your case. Win, lose, or draw, divorce causes decisive changes in your financial circumstances. So it's a good time to at least consult a financial advisor for postdivorce planning if you've never used one before, and in Chapter 6, we'll cover how that advisor should help you. Meanwhile, though, we'll devote this section to how various financial professionals can help you during the divorce process.

Financial Advisors

Many people call themselves "financial advisors," but few of them are experienced and qualified in handling divorce situations. To help you make the best financial decisions during the divorce process, you want someone trained and experienced to deal with your overall financial picture and how it's affected by various key life events. So that excludes those stockbrokers, insurance agents, and other financial sales professionals whose main training is on what financial products can do for you. Instead, you need someone who can advise and guide you regarding budgeting, debt and credit management, college funding, tax considerations, revised insurance needs, cash flow and net worth analysis, and related issues—preferably with specific training on the role those issues play in divorce.

Your best bet is somebody who has one of several long-recognized certifications for financial planning and also one of the newer certifications for divorce planning. These are the professionals on whom you should focus your search:

- *Certified financial planner* (CFP): This certification is the oldest and most widely recognized in the relatively new field of financial planning that began in the late 1960s. To become a CFP, a person must take an approved course of study to prepare for and pass the comprehensive two-day, 10-hour CFP Certification Examination that tests the ability to apply financial planning knowledge in an integrated format—covering the financial planning process, tax planning, employee benefits and retirement planning, estate planning, investment management and insurance, and other issues for which the typical person might need guidance and advice. The certification also requires three years of financial services experience and adherence to a detailed code of ethics as well as continuing professional education to periodically renew certification.
- *Certified public accountant and/or personal financial specialist (CPA and/or PFS):* If your finances are complex, you might prefer using a certified public accountant who also holds the CPA professional organization's designation as a personal financial specialist (PFS). That's because a typical CPA has far more tax training than a typical CFP, and as we've indicated, tax issues can play a major part in structuring optimal divorce settlements. However, the PFS is a newer designation than the CFP so

it's not as easy to find a CPA who has more than 10 years of experience doing broad financial planning, while there are many veteran CFPs with 20 or more years of planning experience.

- *Divorce financial advisors (CDFA and CDS):* The certification of financial advisors with expertise in divorce was introduced in the midnineties with the certified divorce planner (CDP)—which morphed into the certified divorce financial analyst (CDFA)—and now also includes the new certified divorce specialist (CDS) designation (see the Resource Appendix for information on finding one). These divorce-finance professional designations typically augment the most common financial planner designations, the CFP or CPA/PFS.

    The divorce-finance specialty resulted from the realization by some financial planners that divorce finances were becoming increasingly complex and were not sufficiently addressed. Their divorcing clients were not being adequately advised by attorneys because those attorneys had insufficient financial expertise. In addition, their clients' financial advisors, whose certification process didn't include sufficient divorce finance training, were more helpful but still operating by the seat of their pants. So divorce-planning certification curricula were devised to better prepare financial advisors help their divorcing clients gain a clear understanding of their current and potential future financial pictures. The goal was to get their clients more focused on reaching a fair and workable settlement, more able to negotiate effectively, and better prepared to achieve an equitable settlement. These steps would maximize marital assets to be divided, by minimizing taxes and attorney fees.

    The specific ways that divorce-finance professionals can help include determining the current and postmarital budgets, estimating likely child support, quantifying the value of the spouses' nonmonetary contributions to the marriage, estimating the value of employee benefits, pensions, and client-owned businesses, showing the effect of different scenarios for front-loaded versus uniform long-term spousal support, and seeing the immediate and long-term impact of different asset and debt divisions—especially including what happens if either or neither party winds up with the marital home.

- *Accountants:* As just mentioned, the typical accountant doesn't have financial planning training and also differs from financial planners in perspective—accountants generally deal with historical financial data rather than forward-going financial projections. But an accountant, particularly a certified public accountant (CPA) who must pass a rigorous exam and complete 40 hours of continuing professional education each year, is a very useful consultant on your divorce team for financial issues with complex tax ramifications, such as extremely tricky employer stock options that a spouse might hold.

If you or your spouse own a business, any good CPA can estimate its value, but a CPA with a certified valuation analyst (CVA) designation is a bona fide business-valuation expert. You might also want a CPA with special training to trace or identify hidden, shifted, and understated assets using forensic accounting techniques. Generally, a CPA would be brought in by the adversarial or collaborative attorney, or the financial advisor, but you might bring one in on your own if you're resolving your divorce through mediation or direct negotiation.

Other Financial Specialists

Either you, your attorney, or your financial advisor might need or find it advantageous to engage the services of the following financial professionals who specialize in pensions and insurance, other benefit matters, property and business appraisal, career assessment and counseling, and debt management:

- *Benefits and/or insurance specialists:* If a spouse has a traditional (defined-benefit pension) that is projected to provide sizeable payments during retirement, then it might be prudent to obtain the services of a certified actuary [an associate (ASA) of the Society of Actuaries or a fellow (FSA) of the Society of Actuaries] who specializes in pension valuation. The actuary can arrive at a very close estimate of the current value for that future pension under various retirement scenarios and even look into the soundness of the pension plan and whether the company is likely to make changes that would devalue it because of financial difficulties.

  Whether you use an actuary or not, once a value of the pension is agreed on and alternatives for splitting it up are determined, you should consider consulting a a certified employee benefits specialist (CEBS) to help your attorney draw up the qualified domestic relations order in a way that fully complies with the IRS and employer's rules for transferring pension assets in a divorce situation. In Chapter 8, we'll examine why it's so critical to write a QDRO correctly and the mistakes that are commonly made in drawing one up that can cost a spouse a share of the pension.

  A CEBS might also be consulted to put a value on the employee benefits that one spouse gets from the other spouse's employer, to help ensure that the cost of replacing them is considered in the settlement. And the CEBS can definitely help plan the transition to new insurance if a spouse or child has a serious and expensive medical condition, and he or she can help set up life insurance that guarantees support payments should the paying spouse die.

- *Property appraisers:* Depending on whether property will be liquidated or transferred, you might need to engage the services of one or more appraisers to determine the market value or replacement value of expensive property. Consult a gemologist for expensive jewelry and appropriate professionals for collections, a personal property appraiser for recreational equipment such as boats and household furniture and furnishings—particularly grand pianos, antiques, and similar items—and a certified real estate appraiser (not an agent) for the family residence and vacation or investment property.

- *Business valuators:* Closely held businesses, by definition, are not traded on the public securities markets so it is not easy to determine their value. This is where professional business valuation analysts and appraisers who are trained and certified to determine the value of such companies enter the picture. Under the accountant heading, we've already mentioned the certified valuation analyst (CVA), but others include accredited senior appraiser (ASA), certified business appraiser (CBA), or certified public accountant accredited in business valuation (CPA/ABV).

- *Career and debt counselors:* Well-qualified career counselors can establish the cost of education and the earning potential of a spouse who is either returning to the workforce or planning to get new training—in addition to helping explore alternatives. And if your biggest problem is what to do about debt rather than assets, then you might do better with a trained debt counselor from a reputable nonprofit credit counseling firm. They charge either nothing or modest fees on a sliding scale, and they can help you formulate a budget and manage your debt and finances.

Based on your income and debts, credit counselors will negotiate with major creditors such as banks, credit card companies, and department stores to determine how much and how often to pay on your debt. Payments are made directly to the credit counselor, who in turn transfers the monies to the proper creditors. A credit counselor is often able to secure a cancellation of wage garnishment or he or she can sometimes have interest and late charges dropped entirely.

Be extremely cautious, though, because many questionable credit counseling firms with national TV and radio ad campaigns have sprung up in the last few years. Don't be fooled by the label, "nonprofit"—which has been severely abused in recent years by some such organizations. Instead, look for long-established nonprofit organizations such as those affiliated with the Consumer Credit Counseling Service, the United Way, or the YMCA.

Practice Money-Conscious Management of Your Divorce Professionals

If you've ever had a home built, or even contracted for a major home-improvement project, you know that it's up to you to deal with all the professionals, suppliers, neighbors, local government officials, and other parties involved to get the most for what you pay for and to save as much money as possible. The same is true in having to deal with all involved parties effectively and efficiently in order to get the best result in your divorce. Here are suggestions for saving money and managing the divorce process:

- *Compatibility:* Find an attorney or mediator with whom you are comfortable in both communication and qualifications. Make sure he or she is experienced in the type of divorce situation you are facing and the way you want it conducted—including the way he or she communicates with opposing counsel. Be leery of any attorney who excessively schmoozes with you or projects a "Don't worry, I'll take care of everything" attitude.
- *Fees:* Be sure your divorce professionals' fees are in line with the fees normally charged in your area for the experience and qualifications that he or she has. Keep your own record of dealings with them, and question any billings that don't match your record.

  Make sure your attorney is open and informative about how he or she bills—including phone calls, responding to e-mails, and work delegated to various assistants or junior attorneys. Also find out whether he or she sends fully itemized bills on a frequent basis. Ask about ways that you can save money by preparing things in certain ways, doing certain things yourself (filling out forms, doing research, mailing notices), or having a paralegal do them for far less cost.

  If you're short on funds, be open with your attorney about that fact. Will he or she cut you off in midstream if a bill isn't paid—even if he or she is filing a temporary order to have your fees paid by your spouse?

Will he or she hold your files hostage if you don't pay in full when you see that you'll be unable to keep up the payments and need to preserve funds to use a different approach? If there's a retainer involved, is it reasonable for the kind of case being conducted? Is the unused portion of your retainer refundable should you terminate the attorney's services?

- *Cooperative efforts:* Prefer an attorney who's receptive to preliminary efforts you have made (possibly with your spouse) to develop a settlement proposal using financial and legal software such as *Split-Up* and *Family Lawyer*. Good attorneys should be able to use what you've done as a starting point for the documents that they prepare.

- *Cost-effective communication:* Prepare for each meeting or phone call with your attorney by writing a list of questions and information you need to provide. Better yet, if your attorney makes regular, timely use of e-mail, send questions and information that way.

  Use your attorney's time strictly for legal business. Talk about your marriage and spouse only to the extent that it is pertinent to how you're conducting the divorce. Therapists and friends are far more economical and effective sounding boards for dealing with your emotions.

- *Discover the savings:* Do your own discovery by providing copies of all the financial and legal documents your attorney would normally formally request through your spouse's attorney. Your attorney might still have to bill you for some discovery and forensic accounting if it's clear that things are missing, have been prepared incompletely or fraudulently, or need elaboration—but you'll still have saved hundreds or thousands of dollars.

- *Documentation:* Provide a complete marital history and accounting of relevant events and expenditures during the divorce, instead of paying your attorney for the time it takes him or her to ask you questions about your marriage.

Gather Family and Financial Information and Records

Regardless of whether you own little more than the threadbare clothes on your back or you own single clothing items worth more than most people's net worth, divorce requires you to divvy up what you own and owe between the two of you and transfer title or refinance accordingly. In addition, you must take steps to update, convert, or cancel registrations, insurance policies, contracts, wills, trusts, and other records and documents. Furthermore, any professionals advising or representing you in your divorce action will need copies or online access to all these materials, documents, and sources of information.

You could gather up all your paperwork, stuff it in a gigantic plastic yard-waste bag, and drop it off at the offices of your attorney and financial advisor. Or you could have your attorney get everything from your spouse's attorney via the discovery process. Better yet, you could save several hundreds or thousands of dollars by organizing it all and making the copies yourself.

We highly recommend the "self" option, first to protect the environment but more importantly to protect you. By becoming as familiar as possible with what's at stake, you will fare better through the divorce process than you would without that knowledge. No matter what, don't rely on your spouse to do the bagging (or filing or copying)—and not just because he or she never takes out the trash anyway. For two reasons, you want to be sure that before your first "work meetings" with any of your divorce professionals, you have your own complete set of copies of everything and that you are familiar with all that information. First, you want to review everything and prepare a list of questions that occur to you, and second, you want to be able to answer your attorney's or financial advisor's questions promptly, without having to pay for "reading time" during your consultations. Also, you will pay for less of your hired professionals' reading time by packaging the material with a cover document that itemizes everything and is annotated with any comments or questions about the items. Finally, be sure to keep a full set of copies and make additional copies from them of any documents needed by your divorce professionals.

In addition to specific documents and records, many attorneys and financial planners will ask you to fill out questionnaires, information forms, and financial inventories to help them make an initial assessment of your situation before they dig into the details. Because you've completed your "divorce scavenger hunt," you won't find this task as overwhelming as it might have been. In fact, you should welcome the required effort because an attorney who doesn't have such forms has to get the information somehow, which means much more expensive consultation time with you. Or it means a really expensive unfavorable settlement because he or she never got the information!

Most attorneys use similar forms—differing mainly to accommodate differences in state law. To give you a specific idea of what to expect, the list in Figure 5-1 covers virtually everything you, your attorney, or your financial advisor(s) might need during the divorce process. (Also look at some of the copies of actual attorney information forms contained in or referred to in the Resource Appendix.)

FIGURE 5-1

The Paper Chase: Documents for Divorce Proceedings It Will be Useful for You to Have

1. *Financial affidavit:* A completed affidavit or declaration covering assets, income, and liabilities.
2. *Tax records:* Income tax records, including estimated tax returns, W-2, 1099, and K-1 forms, payroll stubs, and all other evidence of income since the filing of your last return.
3. *Income tax returns:* Personal, corporate, partnerships, joint ventures, or other income tax returns, state and federal, including W-2, 1099, and K-1 forms, in your possession or control from the inception of the marriage.
4. *Banking information:* Monthly bank statements, passbooks, check stubs, registers, deposit slips, canceled checks, certificates of deposit, money management and retirement accounts in your possession or control from banks, savings and loan institutions, brokerages, and/or federal credit unions, which have been maintained at any time for or by you, individually or in joint name or as a trustee or guardian, and in which you sign or have any legal or equitable interest.
5. *Financial statements:* Submitted to banks, lending institutions, or any persons or entities prepared by or on your behalf at any time during the last five years.
6. *Loan applications:* Applications and statements of loan accounts for all loans applied for, whether approved or not, for the last five years.
7. *Broker's statements:* All statements of account from securities and commodities dealers and mutual funds you maintained and received during the marriage and held individually, jointly, or as a trustee or guardian.
8. *Stocks, bonds, and mutual funds:* Certificates held individually, jointly, or as a trustee or guardian, including any stock brokerage accounts and statements owned during the marriage.
9. *Stock options:* All records pertaining to stock options held in any corporation or other entity, exercised or not.

FIGURE 5-1   *Continued*

10. *Pension, profit sharing, deferred compensation agreements, and retirement plans:* Or any other kind of plan owned by you or by any corporation in which you are or have been a participant during the marriage.

11. *Wills and trust agreements:* Executed by you or in which you have a present or contingent interest or in which you are named a beneficiary, trustee, executor, or guardian, and from which benefits have been received, are being received, or will be received and which are or were in existence during the past five years, including inter vivos trusts (those made while the parties are living). All records of declaration of trust and minute books for all trusts to which you are a party, including the certificates, if any, indicating such interest and copies of all statements, receipts, disbursements, investments, and other transactions.

12. *Life insurance:* Certificates of life insurance currently in existence, insuring your life or the life of any other person, in which you are named as either primary or contingent beneficiary, including any disability insurance currently in existence.

13. *General insurance:* Insurance policies, including, but not limited to, annuities, health, accident, casualty, motor vehicles of any kind, property liability, including contents insurance in which you are or have been named insured for the last three years.

14. *Outstanding debts:* Documents reflecting all debts owed to you or by you, secured or unsecured, including personal loans and lawsuits now pending or previously filed in any court, showing the name of the debtor and/or creditors, the date each debt was incurred, the total amount, and the unpaid balance.

15. *Accounts payable and receivable:* Ledgers in your possession and control that are personal or business related, together with all accounts and journals.

16. *Cash receipt books:* Evidence of budgets, cash projections, and other financial documents in your possession. This applies to all items that existed at any time throughout your marriage.

17. *Real property:* All deeds, closing statements, tax bills, appraisals, mortgages, leases, and other evidence (including monthly payments and present principal and interest balances) of any type of

interest or ownership, whether as owner, coowner, fiduciary, trust beneficiary, partner, limited partner, shareholder, joint venture, mortgagee, or otherwise, during the term of the marriage; together with evidence of all contributions in cash or otherwise, made by you or on your behalf, toward the acquisition of such real estate.

18. *Sale and option agreements:* On any real estate owned by either you either individually, through another person or entity, jointly or as trustee or guardian.

19. *Personal property:* Documents, invoices, contracts and appraisals on all personal property, including furniture, fixtures, furnishings, equipment, antiques, and any type of collections, owned by you individually, jointly, as trustee or guardian, or through any other person or entity during the term of the marriage, together with the amount of the respective liens.

20. *Motor vehicles:* Purchase orders, financing agreements, appraisals, lease agreements, registrations, and payment books to all motor vehicles owned by you, including airplanes, boats, or any other type of vehicle or craft.

21. *Corporate interests:* All records indicating any kind of personal interest in any corporation (foreign or domestic) or any other entities not evidenced by certificates or other instruments.

22. *Employment records:* During the term of the marriage, showing evidence of wages, salaries, bonuses, commissions, expense accounts, and other benefits or deductions of any kind that were, are, or may be paid, available, credited, or withheld for any purpose.

23. *Fringe benefits:* All records serving as evidence of any benefits available to you from any business entity in which you have legal or equitable ownership interest, including, without limitation, auto, travel, entertainment, education, and personal and living expenses.

24. *Employment contracts:* Under which you are performing services or for which someone is indebted to you for services and/or merchandise and materials already furnished.

FIGURE 5-1   *Continued*

---

25. *Business records:* If you are self-employed, a partner, or own more than 10 percent of the outstanding capital stock of any corporation, produce the documents requested above with respect to that business.

26. *Charge accounts:* For your personal or business use, including all statements and receipts, together with a list of those businesses for which you are or have been authorized to charge items to another person's or entity's account.

27. *Membership cards:* Documents identifying rights in any country club, key club, private clubs, associations, or fraternal organizations, together with all monthly statements.

28. *Judgments:* Any pleadings to which you have been a party, either as plaintiff or defendant, during the marriage.

29. *Gifts:* All records pertaining to gifts of any kind made to you or by you to any person or entity.

30. *Charitable contributions:* Receipts, canceled checks, or other tangible evidence of charitable donations you have made.

31. *Medical bills:* Prescriptions, evaluation reports, or diagnosis for psychiatric treatment or medical disability received during the last five years.

32. *Inventory of safe deposit boxes:* Of husband, wife, or business.

Comprehensive List of (Primarily) Financial Information You Might Need. Copyright, Moriarty and Dee, Attorneys at Law, 1109 Delaware Avenue, Buffalo, New York, 14209-1699, Phone: 716-881-6400, www.moriartydee.com/divorce/paper.html.

File or Respond (Including Court Orders)

You know you're ready for the divorce to proceed when your spouse won't be able to catch you with your pants down if he or she decides to file. And you should be ready, now that you've paid the bills and made strategic (necessary) major expenditures, planned how you're going to financially cope, lined up the professionals you (might) need, copied or printed out every relevant record you could get your hands on, and documented your divorce strategy and all pertinent marital history details. Furthermore, your preparation should allow you to broach the subject with less tension, with the goal of making it a mutual decision to proceed.

Mutual agreement to file is the most desirable way to go at this point, it lessens the possibility that either of you will sabotage negotiations because you were humiliated, enraged, or flooded with other negative emotions when you were served divorce papers by surprise. Furthermore, pursuing a mutual agreement will allow you to discuss the fact that no matter who files, the financial arrangements sought will probably seem excessive. At this point and in this context, you can also discuss the fact that the financial arrangements being suggested are only preliminary and should not arouse panic. To make this point, you can compare your negotiations to those used when buying a house. Just as you "low-ball" a bit so that you don't mistakenly offer too much when trying to buy a house, you should "high-ball" (within reason) in your divorce petition to make sure you've asked for enough.

If your spouse doesn't react well to your overtures, and you are prepared and know that the divorce is necessary, go ahead and file now so that you can commence with the separation, and the financial and other actions that go with it. Depending on just how hostile your spouse is, though, you might want to send a "no-hard-feelings" type of note to indicate your desire to move forward in the best interests of both of you and your children.

In addition to the divorce petition, in which you specify the financial and custody terms you seek upon divorce, your filing could include the following temporary (*pendente lite*) orders, which we recommend you have an attorney prepare, depending on your circumstances:

- *Taking care of business:* Orders concerning who stays in the house, who pays which bills, who is responsible for the children, and who provides the other temporary support.
- *Accounts and titling:* Restraining orders that temporarily freeze joint and credit accounts and limit either spouse's right to change title to property or beneficiaries of insurance and death benefits.
- *Legal costs:* Temporary order requiring one spouse to pay the legal and associated costs (such as costs for needed experts on the divorce team) of the other spouse. Typically, this is requested by a spouse who has low income and limited access to assets from a spouse who has higher income or access to substantial assets—particularly when the moneyed spouse is aggressively litigating to minimize what the other spouse gets.
- *Bankruptcy:* Temporary order preventing a spouse from filing bankruptcy until after the divorce is final, thus ensuring that the property is awarded equitably in the settlement.

- *Inappropriate conduct:* Restraining orders to inhibit inappropriate conduct—such as calling all his or her friends and ranting about what an "expletive-deleted" he or she is. Think carefully about such orders because they will embarrass your spouse and make negotiation more difficult. However, if after considering the repercussions, you still believe such orders are necessary—particularly if your spouse's behavior threatens your ability to properly function in your job—then you should file them.
- *Physical proximity or harassment:* Don't think twice about these. Do what you must, immediately—and arrange the appropriate (additional) physical security that might be necessary from the filing's repercussions.

Protect Yourself Financially and Secure a Source of Funds

You don't necessarily need certain restraining orders, though, to protect yourself financially—if you and your spouse can formally agree to certain arrangements that will protect you both.

Joint Accounts for Shared Expenses

Produce a document that you both sign, stating how this account will be managed: what each of you will contribute to it from your paychecks and what expenses it will cover—such as home mortgage and maintenance, child care, and other child expenses. You might want to cancel any ATM access to it and arrange for it to require both signatures on any check written on it or any withdrawal from it.

If you're fortunate enough to have more money to start with in this or other accounts than you'll need to cover these expenses, then it might seem wise to split it up and allocate it to your separate accounts. However, depending on your state's laws, this might complicate the property-distribution determination, so it's probably best to shift just enough money to each of your separate accounts to keep you both going until the next paycheck(s); then shift the rest to another joint account that you'll freeze after consolidating all other joint liquid assets into it.

Separate Accounts for Separate Expenses

Once you're living apart, you'll each be paying for your own food, clothing, toiletries, and related expenses, so these accounts will be meant to cover those, as well as become the repository for any portion of your paychecks that you're not putting in the joint account. However, having separate accounts doesn't preclude your agreeing to or securing a court order for temporary spousal support that one of you pays to the other to deposit in the dependent's separate account.

Personal Property Protection

If you have jewelry or other expensive small items that you fear your spouse might try to sell out from under you, open up your own safe deposit box and store them there. You might want to store medium-sized items, such as small pieces of furniture, that can still easily be removed with a third party or sign an agreement with your spouse that those are effectively frozen and cannot be sold or taken until the divorce judgment. Finally, you might think that bigger items are safe, but nothing stops your spouse from contracting a sale of a premium grand piano to someone for later delivery, so you might want to also include those items in a signed agreement.

Joint-Title Assets
If you and your spouse both own stocks, mutual funds, or other investments, depending on how you set up the account, it might now be possible for either of you to sell them without the other's concurrence. So contact your investment company or bank to request a document that puts in place a procedure to establish formally that both of you must sign for any transaction regarding such assets.

Separate versus Marital Property
Avoid transactions that would reclassify your separate property as marital property. Through a process called *transmutation,* described in Chapter 8, the court can convert separate property back into marital property. One way to avoid that is to agree with your spouse in writing about any separate property that was really meant to be separate and not just kept in a separate account. That would distinguish such accounts from other accounts that might have been kept in one spouse's name for marital purposes, perhaps because the account was at one spouse's employer's credit union.

Prevent the Use of Credit by One Spouse in the Name of the Other Spouse
With a few modifications, Figure 5-2 contains verbatim advice from the Federal Trade Commission regarding the handling of credit accounts in anticipation of divorce.

FIGURE 5-2 Federal Trade Commission Information on Credit Accounts and Divorce

There are two types of credit accounts: individual and joint. You can permit authorized persons to use the account with either. When you apply for credit—whether a charge card or a mortgage loan—you'll be asked to select one type. (Authors' Note: Be aware that responsibility for paying a debt is an individual credit-record and legal issue. It does not determine if the debt is considered separate or marital for purposes of equitable distribution.)

- *Individual account:* Your income, assets, and credit history are considered by the creditor. Whether you are married or single, you alone are responsible for paying off the debt. The account will appear on your credit report, and it may appear on the credit report of any "authorized" user. However, if you live in a community property state (Arizona, California, Idaho, Louisiana, Nevada, New Mexico, Texas, Washington, or Wisconsin), you and your spouse may be responsible for debts incurred during the marriage, and the individual debts of one spouse may appear on the credit report of the other.

  Advantages and disadvantages: If you're not employed outside the home, work part-time, or have a low-paying job, it may be difficult to demonstrate a strong financial picture without your spouse's income. But if you open an account in your name and you alone are responsible for it, no one can negatively affect your credit record.

- *Joint account:* Your income, financial assets, and credit history—and your spouse's—are considerations for a joint account. No matter who handles the household bills, you and your spouse are responsible for seeing that debts are paid. A creditor who reports the credit history of a joint account to credit bureaus must report it in both names (if the account was opened after June 1, 1977).

  Advantages and disadvantages: An application combining the financial resources of two people may present a stronger case to a creditor who is granting a loan or credit card. But because two people applied together for the credit, each is responsible for the debt. This is true even if a divorce decree assigns separate debt obligations to each spouse. Former spouses who run up bills and don't pay them can hurt their ex-partner's credit histories on jointly held accounts.

- *Individual accounts with additional account "users"*: If you open an individual account, you may authorize another person to use it. If you name your spouse as the authorized user, a creditor who reports the credit history to a credit bureau must report it in your spouse's name as well as in yours (if the account was opened after June 1, 1977). A creditor also may report the credit history in the name of any other authorized user.

  Advantages and disadvantages: User accounts often are opened for convenience. They benefit people who might not qualify for credit on their own, such as students or homemakers. While these people may use the account, you—not they—are contractually liable for paying the debt.

- Regarding all credit accounts: If you're considering divorce or separation, pay special attention to the status of your credit accounts. If you maintain joint accounts during this time, it's important to make regular payments so that your credit record won't suffer. As long as there's an outstanding balance on a joint account, you and your spouse are responsible for it.

  If you divorce, you may want to close joint accounts or accounts in which your former spouse was an authorized user. Or ask the creditor to convert these accounts to individual accounts. By law, a creditor cannot close a joint account because of a change in marital status, but it can do so at the request of either spouse. A creditor, however, does not have to change joint accounts to individual accounts. The creditor can require you to reapply for credit on an individual basis and then, based on your new application, extend or deny you credit. In the case of a mortgage or home equity loan, a lender is likely to require refinancing to remove a spouse from the obligation.

Separate from Your Spouse

Even if you give your spouse credit for being fully trustworthy, like the credit commercial suggests, some things are priceless. So whether your separation is warmly informal or icy formal, in addition to originals or copies (as appropriate) of vital financial and medical records, make sure you either take irreplaceable items if you move out or arrange for a third party to securely hold them, because you might not be able to get back in. These include family pictures, videos, and keepsakes; items from family celebrations; special baby books and toys; children's academic and sports awards; and academic, art, and craft projects.

Informal Spousal Separation

Most couples set up informal separations, which do not involve legal documents filed with the court. Nevertheless, couples with informal arrangements should agree on the following items—from a list provided by veteran divorce attorney Lee Borden (from his Web site, www.divorceinfo.com) before physically separating:

1. Who is moving out? Where? When?
2. What access will the spouse who is moving out have to the marital home? If you're trying to avoid changing the locks, you might try this simple understanding: The spouse who is moving out may retain a key or have access to a key if needed. He or she will agree that he or she will never enter the marital home without knocking first. If no one is home, he or she will enter only in an emergency and will leave a message on the answering machine or on a bulletin board explaining that he or she was there and describing exactly what he or she did. Several of my clients have used this understanding successfully.
3. Where will the children spend what time? How will they get from one place to another? Who will take them to school and pick them up? Under what circumstances may the children leave town?
4. When and in what way will you tell the children?
5. When and in what way will you tell parents? Family members? Friends? Other adults?
6. Who gets access to which bank accounts? For what purpose can he or she use the money? (*Note:* You don't need to make the legal division now if you trust each other. Just make sure you have a good, clear understanding about who will use what money and for what purpose.)

7. Who gets to use which credit cards? For what purpose can each of you use which card(s)? What limits do you agree to place on the use of each card?
8. What consequences will flow if one of you violates the agreement?
9. Who will pay what bills?
10. Will one of you pay support to the other? If so, should you agree in writing to the support so that you can treat it as alimony for tax purposes? See Chapter 7 for the rules on what constitutes spousal support for tax purposes.
11. Will you both agree not to sell any major assets, make any extraordinary purchases, or make any major withdrawals from family accounts without consulting with the other?
12. How will you communicate with each other? Will you meet in person? How often? Will you talk by phone at work? Or at home? By fax? By e-mail? Will you communicate only through an intermediary? Who is the intermediary, and how will each of you communicate with him or her?

Putting these things in writing assures the spouse moving out that the home-based spouse can't later charge desertion and obtain an overly favorable divorce judgment. Furthermore, you might include a clause that says the separation is not due to marital-breakup fault by either party, thus assuring both of you that the other won't later charge fault in order to obtain economic advantage. (It's harder to prove that fault broke up a marriage if both parties remain living together.) While some items on Borden's list aren't financial, they all have a financial impact in that making your separation as nonvolatile as possible will probably save you money in legal fees.

Formal Separation

However, you might need a formal separation that involves preparing a legal document that might have to be filed with the court because your spouse simply won't come to agreement on these issues, or for the following additional reasons cited by Borden:

- *Time period requirement:* Some states require that a couple seeking a divorce has been separated for some period of time, so maybe it's needed to start the clock running.

- *Separate but delaying divorce:* Some couples need to be separated, but they need to remain legally married, perhaps so one can continue to be insured for medical or other purposes by the other's company. Formal legal separation makes this possible.
- *Buying time:* Sometimes there's no question that the couple is moving toward divorce, but they know it will take some time to work everything out. If their incomes are substantially different, it may be worth it to develop a written separation agreement so the person paying alimony can deduct the alimony on his or her tax return. A paying spouse in a higher tax bracket might be able to pay the receiving spouse the agreed-upon spousal support, plus an amount to cover the taxes the receiving spouse will owe, and be better off than making nondeductible/nontaxable support payments. If you agree to this, make sure you meet all the qualifications for the payments to be classified as spousal support—including living in separate residences and not filing a joint tax return.
- *Religion:* Sometimes one of the spouses has a religious objection to divorce. A formal separation may allow the spouses to remain married even as they live apart.

If you formally separate, you should certainly try to include all the items on Borden's informal separation list that your spouse agrees to on an addendum to your legal separation filing. But you might also have to include temporary orders that address some of them—especially spousal and child support.

Separation Date

Regardless of which form of separation you use, make sure you do what your state requires to "start the separation clock" and time your various actions by the significance of that date according to these guidelines:

- *Date determination:* Determine whether your state bases the separation date on one spouse's physically separating from the marital residence, the date divorce papers are filed with the court, or the date one spouse officially informs the other by serving notice of intention to file.
- *Financial consequences:* Determine how your state treats the separation date with regard to expenditures made and debts incurred by either spouse, and funds received by either spouse. In some states, the separation date is tantamount to the divorce date in that most or all financial

inflows and outflows from separation onward "belong" to the spouse who made or received them; in others, only the inflows and outflows that are for the benefit of an individual spouse belong to that person, and in still others, all inflows and outflows are marital until the actual divorce date.

Because of the potentially huge difference the definition of separation date can make, it's imperative you know how your state treats it and act accordingly.

The separation date can affect specific types of financial transactions differently:

- *Mortgage, other loans and credit:* While the separation date in your state might mean that all loan obligations and use of credit belong to a specific spouse according to your mutual agreement or a court order, creditors will still hold both of you responsible for all debt carried or incurred before this date and until the divorce is final—so the protective measures mentioned earlier are critical.
- *Retirement funds:* For purposes of division, all pensions, 401(k),403(b), various types of IRA, and other retirement accounts are valued as of the date of divorce, so gains and losses in them between the separation date and the divorce date remain marital property. However, additional contributions to them after the separation date are usually separate property.
- *Tax returns:* In many states, income earned by each party after the separation date is treated as that party's separate income, which can affect your decision or obligation to file either jointly or separately for the years during which the separation was in effect.
- *Businesses and investments:* In many states, the division of investments and businesses is based on the value as of the separation date, so capital gains and losses taking place between then and the divorce date belong to the owner spouse (or are prorated accordingly if the business has been divided in the settlement). In other states, everything is divided as of the divorce date, so that all gains and losses during the separation period are marital property. Because such assets are often a major part of a divorce settlement, it's critical to know how your state treats them.
- *Spousal support or alimony:* Few states remain that follow an absolute letter of law about a defined marriage length (typically 10 years) being the Maginot Line for purposes of deeming a marriage long term and awarding long-term spousal support. But even they differ in whether

the divorce date or separation date is considered the "end" of the marriage. Thus, if a marriage has lasted 9 years and 7 months until the date of separation, and the divorce occurs 6 months later, certain states will treat that as an under-10-years short-term marriage (usually meaning there is no long-term spousal support awarded), and others will treat it as an over-10-years long-term marriage (usually meaning there is long-term spousal support awarded). So be wary, as this could be the most crucial issue in your divorce.

Negotiate an Agreement

Regardless of which is the most crucial issue, the most crucial activity in the divorce process is usually the negotiation. It's important now to remember our theme, financial self-defense.

But let's be clear: Your financial "defense" doesn't mean being like Mike (Michael Douglas), the gone-ballistic bazooka-blasting laid-off defense worker in *Falling Down* who found he was no longer "economically viable." Instead, keep your sanity and negotiate for your fair share. In Chapters 7 and 8, you'll learn just what that is, and you're more likely to get it if you use the following negotiation principles suggested by Lee Borden. You can find the detailed version on his Web site (www.divorceinfo.com/negotiating.htm), but here's a brief summary:

- *Keep your eyes on the prize.* Instead of handing your "rotten" spouse a laundry list of concessions that you demand because he or she deserves deprivation, make a private list of priorities to remind yourself what's truly essential and important in a fair settlement. Think *strategically:* Ask yourself these questions as you negotiate and work through divorce settlement issues: How much is this issue worth to me in today's dollars? How likely am I to win? What will it cost financially and personally to fight about it? The answers tell you whether and how hard to fight about each issue and about your willingness to compromise.
- *Ask for help.* In addition to the various professionals, support groups, and related resources we've mentioned and list in the Resource Appendix, consider a "divorce coach" who's versed in the issues you face and who can act as a sounding board and offer advice as appropriate to help you think through your options. He or she could either be one of the new professional personal coaches or a friend who shared a "good" divorce with an ex-spouse.

- *Set the stage.* Avoid a toxic negotiating climate by moving past what was wrong or bad, or right or good, about your marriage and spouse. Keep your finger off "hot buttons," and focus on a positive coparenting transition with your ex-spouse. Offer positive reinforcement relative to resolving issues regarding that and the divorce overall. Before starting negotiations, plan your first three moves—what you will say and do, the most likely ways in which your spouse will respond, and how you will respond to (not necessarily reject) them.
- *Listen.* Neither go on the offensive or be defensive, but instead hear what your spouse is actually saying. Begin your response by summarizing your understanding of what was said, and you'll likely gain your spouse's confidence in having a constructive dialogue.
- *Hit 'em straight.* It's best that you talk to your spouse directly, not through someone else. This isn't a real estate transaction conducted through agents but a real state of crisis requiring direct communication to make sure no signals get crossed. It can be helpful to have a mediator or collaborative attorney there for support and two-way facilitation. It is seldom truly helpful to talk through adversarial attorneys.
- *Don't be afraid to moosh.* Negotiation is all about "mooshing"— trading one thing for another. Usually it's about tangible things such as money and property, but sometimes it's about something tangible in exchange for an intangible concession, such as resolving a coparenting conflict.
- *Expect it to feel weird.* Perhaps you wouldn't now be negotiating divorce if you'd applied these principles in your marriage, so you're likely to feel uncomfortable using them, and your spouse might be suspicious. But you're aiming for divorce success, despite marriage failure, so proceed confidently, and you'll overcome your discomfort and your spouse's reaction.
- *Clarify.* Typical divorce settlements clearly spell out financial issues agreements, but they often don't cover many specifics affecting finances—such as timing various account terminations or transfers, and coparenting details that could affect how much driving each party must do or who should be providing what meals before and/or after the changeovers. It's better to spell things out in tedious detail now, even if you and your spouse later decide to relax enforcement of the technicalities. However, don't specify all the details until after you've made agreement on the big issues or you could get bogged down arguing over little things.

- *Keep your promises.* Divorces are all about broken promises, and success-ful postdivorce relationships are about rebuilding trust between you regarding coparenting and support obligations. If you might be late meeting a financial or coparenting commitment, say so. If you've made a promise, let your ex-spouse know ASAP if you have to change your plans.

Cashing Out of Your Marriage

As the bell rings ending Round 3, we've followed the money from the divorce initiation to agreement on financial matters, so that you'll understand what's involved and what the financial issues are. Our intent has been to enable you to take ownership of your divorce. But we've stopped short of an in-depth look at those financial issues because including them here would be like providing a detailed explanation of how your car works in its owner's manual. After all, you're unlikely to do much sophisticated work on today's complex cars if you're not a mechanic or on today's financially complex divorces if you're not a divorce attorney or financial advisor.

Yet you might want to combine do-it-yourself with knowing enough to take an active role with your divorce professionals, just as you might want to do minor car repairs and know enough to make sure you're getting top-notch mechanical work when you do pay for repairs. So taking a page from the mechanics' manuals that auto manufacturers make available for your purchase, we've included a "divorce financial mechanics manual" in the form provided in Part III (Chapters 7 and 8)—hopefully one that is far more readable though! But before you dive into that, the concluding Round 4 (Chapter 6) completes our round-by-round description of the divorce financial fight, where you'll learn how to finalize your divorce and follow it up with a number of necessary steps to keep you financially afloat when you begin postdivorce life.

Chapter 6

(Round 4): Prepare for Postdivorce Financial Life

I n Chapters 3 through 5, we've covered the basics of the divorce process, with particular emphasis on finances, from the time you first start thinking about it until you've negotiated a settlement. Through all that, we've always kept an eye to the future—how you'll end up after the divorce is granted, immediately and in the long term. In this final chapter of Part II, we look at what you'll have to do in immediate anticipation of and following the divorce decree.

Unless you're leaving an abusive relationship, your reentry to single life should be far less treacherous than when astronauts reenter the atmosphere. However, it can still be as scary as driving through a dangerous neighborhood without knowing exactly where you're going, "Unfortunately, most attorneys provide little help navigating you through the scary final stretch of your divorce journey," says Craig Ross. That's why we've provided you this detailed map of what to do to get to your postdivorce destination.

Establishing Your New Financial Identity

Divorcing women burdened by the typical unfair share of household chores will quickly discover that postdivorce "housekeeping" requires doing even more—paperwork, that is. Many women who adopted their husband's name upon marriage will want to legally change it for life after the divorce, and that can be accomplished fairly easily. However, women who change their names need to make sure that they record that change with the Social Security Administration, their employers, and financial institutions.

However, both men and women must retitle property, revise insurance coverage, notify employers regarding family changes, and make many other changes. And, although this onerous chore is more often the province of the men, if either or both spouses move from the marital home, it goes without saying that they must give their new address to anyone they do business with. Here's a closer look at what either or both spouses must do to establish individual postdivorce financial identities.

Name, Marital Status, and Address Changes

What's in a name? Aside from your sanity as a new single, your name could hold the key to your financial future, so here's information on making name and related changes.

Names

In many states, women who wish to change their names upon divorce can do it as part of the divorce decree. This Web site provides complete details for name changes in every state: www.namechangelaw.com/states.htm.

Social Security

If you change your name, you must also notify the Social Security Administration to ensure that your earnings are properly credited to your record. This is a good time too for both men and women to check their earnings records and make any allowable, necessary corrections.

To change the name shown on your card, complete Form SS-5 (download at www.ssa.gov/online/ss-5.html, or call 1-800-772-1213) and submit evidence of your identity regarding both your old and new names. Your new card will retain the same number but have your new name. Request an earnings statement on the Web (www.ssa.gov/pebes/) or by phone.

Employer Notification

Immediately notify your employer upon divorce concerning name change and change of address—as well as to make coverage, dependent, and beneficiary changes for your 401(k), medical insurance, and other employee benefits. You should also notify former employers regarding your name and status change to protect any vested benefits you've earned from them.

Financial Accounts and Credit

First, refer to Chapter 8 (and its reference to the Resource Appendix) for detailed explanation of how to assign debt responsibility per your settlement so that neither party will be affected after divorce by the other's failure to pay debt. Then notify all financial institutions with which you hold loans, or savings, checking, brokerage, credit, and line-of-credit accounts. Change title, transfer and/or refinance debt as appropriate on these accounts and on any securities or other property held or collateralized by them. You won't be able to change title on a joint credit account, though, but either spouse can close it and transfer the balance into a new account.

Unfortunately, if you've been primarily a homemaker or part-time employed spouse, then you're likely to have difficulty getting your own credit account. But even women with good jobs sometimes have difficulty getting credit after divorce, and either ex-spouse could have difficulty due to the other ex-spouse's poor credit history. But don't despair, "Women and Divorce" (www.in.gov/dfi/consumer/MiniLessons/Women_&_Divorce_Mini.doc), a comprehensive state of Indiana publication, has information useful to any U.S. resident of either gender—such as how the Fair Credit Reporting Act can help you counter credit discrimination.

Home, Automobiles, and Other Titled Personal Property
Depending on whether you have a mortgage or how you handle it upon divorce, you might not be required to change title through your town or county and get new title insurance on the home, so make sure you do if its ownership has been affected by the divorce. That change should also change the billing for your property tax, but check to make sure that it does. Similarly, you must change automobile, boat, motorcycle, and other titles through your state department of motor vehicles or related local government organizations.

Tax Filing

After you've separated but before the divorce is final, it's usually to your advantage to file jointly. However, although you might get protection from the "innocent spouse relief" rules (covered later) if your joint return is filed inaccurately, if you have strong reason to doubt your spouse's financial integrity, you might want to choose to file "married filing separately." Or, if you were separated at least 6 months of the year and provided primary support to one or more children during that period, you may file as head of household (HOH). Once the divorce occurs, you must file as either HOH or single starting with the tax year that you divorce. However, because you might have shared various tax-deductible expenses or income with your spouse while still married during that year, you'll each need to make all relevant records available to the other.

Even then, though, you'll probably still remain tax connected to your spouse for years to come. For example, when it comes time to sell investments or other property on which there are capital gains and losses, its taxation depends on its cost basis (purchase price, transaction costs, and improvements). You should try to get all this information, preferably with actual documentation, before divorce, but you might still find yourself having to ask your spouse to look up records or details that you overlooked. Read on for the major immediate and continuing tax issues you must deal with connected with your divorce.

New Filing Status and Withholding

Once you no longer file jointly, your new status and sole income will undoubtedly change your tax liability. So file a new form W-4 with your employer to adjust your tax-withholding allowances so that they'll approximately equal your estimated liability. Regardless of your custody or visitation arrangement, only one spouse is allowed to file as HOH if you have only one child: the spouse who houses the child for more than half the year (188 days qualifies—except in leap year!). So if you have total joint custody, work out who gets the extra day.) With at least two children, this "half-year-plus rule" enables you both to file as HOH by each keeping one child more than half the year.

HOH filers' advantages over single filers include a higher standard deduction. That puts less pressure on them to take on all the financial responsibilities of home ownership, because their standard deduction might even exceed what they would get if they owned a home and itemized mortgage and other deductions. Furthermore, it takes more income to reach higher tax brackets, so HOH filers typically pay less total tax than singles. And HOH filers don't start losing the child and dependent-care credits until they reach higher (adjusted gross) income "phase-out amounts" (when you start losing an increasing portion of the credit) than those for single filers.

Claiming Exemptions, Deductions, and Credits

Normally, if you have one child, the parent filing as HOH will also claim an exemption for the child. However, the non-HOH parent can claim the exemption if the HOH parent has signed an agreement to that effect (IRS Form 8332). Normally, if one parent is making much more than the other and is paying child support, it makes sense for the higher-earning parent to get the exemption because that parent's higher bracket allows more to be saved in taxes, thus preserving more of the split family's collective fund. If necessary, this swap can be compensated by raising the child support payment by the amount of tax savings lost by the HOH parent. With two or more children, it's possible to allocate the exemptions between the parents.

Sometimes, though, the higher-earning spouse makes too much. When adjusted gross income exceeds $174,400 for HOH filers or $139,500 for single filers, the exemptions start phasing out, so the lower-earning spouse may actually benefit more from them. Compare multiple tax projection scenarios to determine who will benefit the most from the exemption(s). The figures we used are for the 2003 tax year and are scheduled to be adjusted annually.

It's even trickier to determine what child-related education deductions or credits either parent can take. For example, only one parent can claim the Hope Credit (college tuition) for a given child, even if both pay at least the full credit amount toward the child's college education—and the parent claiming the credit must also be the parent claiming that child's exemption. You also have choices regarding the Child Tax Credit, which is worth $1000 per child up to age 16 in 2003. It can be claimed by the parent who claims the dependency exemption but it is also subject to (adjusted gross) income phaseouts starting at $110,000 for married couples filing jointly, $75,000 for unmarried persons, and $55,000 for married persons filing separate tax returns.

Generally, though, the parent who directly pays a deductible or credit-eligible expense claims the associated deduction or credit. That's why, for example, an HOH parent paying child care expenses directly gets the child care deduction, even if the funds were actually provided by the other parent—for example, through child support payments. The child and dependent care credit can only be claimed by the custodial parent, as opposed to the child tax credit, which can only be claimed by the parent claiming that child's tax exemption.

Claiming the Earned Income Credit
During separation or after divorce, if your income is low (including spousal support, but not child support—which isn't income), you might be eligible for a several-thousand-dollar Earned Income Tax Credit (EITC) when filing federal taxes (plus a smaller state EITC in 17 states). You can find full information on the federal EITC at www.irs.gov/eitc. But here's how to tell whether you'll be eligible, what you might expect, and how you should factor the possibility into the settlement you negotiate:

- *Children's living arrangement:* To qualify, you must either be the custodial parent or be sharing custody and housing the child more than half the year. Thus, parents of three or more children who share custody can both qualify for the EITC if they each earn less than the income limits and arrange custody so that each spouse's household has at least one child living slightly more than half the year in it. [*Note:* The EITC is also available to certain unmarried low-income individuals with no children who earn(ed) up to $11,230 (in 2003).]

- *EITC eligibility and credit amounts (2003 Tax Year):* To qualify for the credit, you must have earned income—money earned from work. Although you can file for the EITC while still married, you must file jointly, so unless you and your spouse both have low incomes, you probably won't qualify. However if the spouses lived separately for at least 6 months, then the custodial spouse can file as Head of Household (HOH). For detailed information about filing as HOH, see IRS Publication 501, Exemptions, Standard Deduction, and Filing Information.

  The higher your income up to the following threshold amounts that vary by the number of children, the closer you get to the maximum credits associated with those threshold amounts. The particulars for single or HOH filers are:
  - No children, $6250 for maximum $382 credit.
  - One child, $13,750 for maximum $2547 credit.
  - Two or more children, $13,750 for maximum $4207 credit.

  As you exceed these threshold earning amounts, your credit starts phasing out at about the same rate at which it accrued until you get no EITC if you earn more than $11,250 with no children, $29,666 with one child or $33,692 with two or more children. Maximum incomes and corresponding credits are scheduled to increase in 2004.

  It's fairly easy for some taxpayers to compute the EITC using the IRS worksheet. However, the calculation can become complicated if you receive spousal support, which you must add to your earned income to see if it reduces or eliminates the amount of EITC you'd receive without spousal support.

- *Angling to qualify:* Normally, the EITC will help only a lower-earning spouse whose income after divorce will be low (we hope only temporarily) and who'll be getting little or no spousal support. That can happen for bad reasons when that spouse has been a homemaker or has worked only limited hours, and the other spouse has a low income or has lost a job. In that case, the EITC could make the difference between eating peanut butter for every meal or actually having a healthy varied diet.

But there's another case in which you'll benefit by structuring your settlement to become EITC-eligible. If the value of property you and your spouse are dividing is high but your current earning capacity is very small, while your spouse's earnings are modest, consider a larger property settlement instead of spousal support. Then go back to school while working limited part-time hours in which you try to earn about $15,000 annually until you've graduated, using that income plus some of the "excess" property settlement to pay living expenses during your schooling. In that way, you'll get the maximum EIC during the few years it takes to substantially increase your earning power, and that will be far more than your spouse will lose by not getting a tax deduction for paying spousal support instead of giving you extra property. However, you must not have "disqualified income" of $2600 or more (2003 limit). Disqualified income includes investment income, capital gains and rental income.

Home Sale Taxation

If you and your spouse plan to sell the marital home either together or after it's given to one spouse, timing is critical to avoid or minimize capital-gains taxes. Fortunately, tax law regarding houses sold in conjunction with divorce is liberal in allowing most divorces to go ahead as quickly as possible, but allowing ample time after the divorce to sell the home without incurring more tax than would have applied during the marriage. Trying to cover all possible scenarios would require a separate book, and even summarizing it goes beyond the scope of this chapter, so we've included that information in the more "financially heavy" Chapter 7.

Deducting Divorce Professional Fees

Yet another reason for trying to resolve your divorce without undue attorney involvement is that, contrary to popular belief, most of what you would pay a divorce attorney isn't tax deductible. You would think that legal advice, mediation, and other professional assistance intended to help you get your fair share of the pie would qualify. But numerous tax court rulings have established that the only qualifying professional advice is that related to the "production or collection of income or for the management, conservation, or maintenance of property held for the production of income." Regarding divorce, this mainly means advice related to spousal support—and taxes in general.

Fortunately, though, there's enough latitude in tax planning and "production of income" to make the following types of advice potentially tax deductible: selling the family home; determining tax basis of property; drafting a QDRO for division of a pension; estate planning that minimizes tax consequences of changing estate plan for divorce; determining the best balance between property and support payments in a settlement; determining how to time the divorce and what filing status each spouse should use to gain maximum tax advantage; determining who should pay what to take maximum advantage of exemptions, tax credits, and deductions; cost of career counseling to assess earning power for purposes of determining spousal support; and forensic accounting or financial discovery for purposes of determining spousal support or correctly filing taxes. Here are specifics on various types of advice that might include a deductible portion of fees:

- *Attorney tax advice:* Have the attorneys itemize their bills to split out the fees for advice related to spousal support and taxes.
- *Financial planning fees:* You should have wider latitude in deducting the fees charged by financial advisors. That's because they are helping you determine what combination of property and support income or obligations will help both parties grow or preserve their net worth in the future. However, you might want to consult with a CPA who has been involved in the case for specific recommendations on what portion of the fees is deductible. And just as with attorney fees, these are also miscellaneous expenses, so you should consider having the party who derives the most tax benefit pay both fees in return for property compensation.
- *Other professionals:* If you've used a property appraiser to establish value or an actuary to give advice on pension plans, their fees are probably deductible because their determinations are crucial in considering tax effects and might be related to income generation as well.

Unfortunately, even if you have a number of qualified expenses, they can only be taken as miscellaneous deductions, of which you can deduct only the portion that exceeds 2 percent of your adjusted gross income (AGI). And you might not get even all of the limited deduction if you and your spouse will do your taxes as separate filers because your divorce will occur before year-end. One way to partially offset this is to arrange your settlement so that the spouse who will get the biggest tax bang for the buck is responsible for both spouses' divorce-professional fees. You'll have to do the math to determine which spouse will get the higher tax benefit by paying both fees. The settlement should then be adjusted to give that spouse the amount of extra property in the settlement, less the tax benefit received, that compensates for paying the other spouse's fees. Sometimes, though, your financial advisors might determine that it's better to pay the fees separately and have the spouse who will be paying support get more property in exchange for paying the other spouse extra (tax-deductible) spousal support, which can then be used to pay attorney fees. Warning: Don't try to arrange this without top-flight tax advice.

Legal Tax Matters
If you've been a financially uninvolved partner who unknowingly let your spouse orchestrate tax fraud by fiddling with the books or failing to pay what was owed, you might discover it during the divorce or when you start taking

charge of your own finances afterward. Or worse, the IRS might come knocking on your door to give you the news.

Talk about the final measure in a crescendo of marital nightmares! Fortunately, you can land on your feet instead of in a jail cot (a stiff fine and probation is more likely if no fraud was committed), or seat in bankruptcy court. Just qualify for relief as an "innocent spouse" in one of the following three ways:

1. *Fudged filing discovered predivorce:* On a joint return your spouse prepared and you signed, numbers were fudged in order to lower tax liability, and you didn't know about it and had no reason to know about it, the IRS deems it unfair to hold you liable. This applies in cases in which you're not yet divorced or legally separated and have lived apart less than 12 months—which usually means you've discovered it during negotiations because the IRS doesn't audit that quickly.
2. *Other fudged filing:* The same offenses have occurred, but you've discovered them after legal separation, living apart more than 12 months, or divorce. In this case you can't completely escape financial liability, but if the IRS deems you eligible, you'll be responsible only for what you would have owed, plus interest and penalties, had you and your spouse filed as "married, filing separately."
3. *Honest return, larcenous spouse:* This applies if you and your spouse filed a correct joint return, but unbeknownst to you, the amount owed wasn't fully paid and your spouse pocketed the difference. You'll get "equitable relief" if you're divorced or separated and the IRS decides that spousal abuse or economic hardship justifies absolving you of liability.

The Innocent Spouse Relief Rules might provide you a miraculous deliverance from a tax quagmire, but it could take some serious digging to prove your case. Check out IRS Publication 971 (www.irs.gov/pub/irs-pdf/p971.pdf) for what forms to file and how to file them.

Insurance Changes and Estate Planning

In Chapter 4, we covered insurance changes needed upon separation, which in some cases are the same as what you'll need after divorce. However, you should review each existing policy and area of potential insurance need to ensure that you haven't missed anything so you won't get tripped up on a technicality when filing a claim. Note that instead of including it here, we've bundled life insurance with estate planning in the next section.

Health Insurance

Good health insurance, vital for financial protection, is recognized as a necessary child support expense in every state. It's often best to have kids covered under an employee group policy with whichever of you has that coverage—and if both spouses have policies providing good coverage, evaluate which provides the best benefit for the best benefit-to-cost ratio (taking into account deductibles, coinsurance, preventive care, and so on). If only one spouse has employer coverage and he or she is not the custodial parent, make sure that policy allows kids to be covered as dependents—often a problem if the kids live in a different state than the covered employee.

A spouse without employer coverage who had been covered under the ex-spouse's plan can continue that coverage with the COBRA provision that allows coverage at 102 percent of the combined employer-employee premium that the insurer charges. If your spouse's employer required only minimal cost sharing, you're likely to be shocked at how high that premium is, and you should shop for a better individual insurance deal. Usually, though, you'll want to start out with the COBRA coverage if you've been recently treated for a potentially ongoing and expensive condition. Although the Health Insurance Portability and Accountability Act (HIPAA) guarantees your ability to find coverage when you lose your health insurance, it doesn't prevent insurers from charging you a lot more if you have a preexisting condition or from putting restrictions on your coverage of such conditions.

Get help finding affordable coverage from your state department of insurance (www.naic.org/1regulator/usamap.htm), and the U.S. Department of Labor's excellent compilation of information (www.dol.gov/ebsa/consumer_info_health.html) on COBRA, shopping for insurance, and other issues involved in obtaining health insurance privately or through an employer. Or, if you are starting a new business, you may be able to get coverage through a small-business organization in your state or through a professional organization. But even if you don't need to change coverage upon divorce, make sure you both notify your insurers of your change in family status.

Automobile Insurance

First, plan on increasing your budget to allow for the extra caffeine you'll need now that your spouse will no longer be directing your driving. More importantly, you must update your titles and coverage to accurately reflect who owns which cars as a consequence of the settlement, and who is listed as named insured and drivers for those cars.

Failing to update automobile insurance and titling could be catastrophic. For example, suppose the settlement gave the car to one spouse, so the other spouse dropped the coverage on it before the title was changed. The still-owning spouse remains liable but isn't covered should the spouse have an accident.

Homeowner's Insurance

If you both continue living where you've each been living between the separation and divorce, you've probably already made the most important changes, but now you should notify the insurer(s) about the divorce, title changes, and custody arrangement. If both of you or the nonresiding spouse will continue owning the marital home, then make sure this is clear to the agent so that the coverage properly protects the nonresiding spouse.

Also, even if no further moves occurred upon divorce, you'll both probably add or remove some property to or from your respective premises. So make sure your coverage reflects what property each of you will have "permanently" in your respective domiciles. This involves both the overall property limits of your coverage and any riders you might newly or no longer need for valuables.

Umbrella Insurance

It would be nice if this umbrella coverage kept you from getting soaked in the settlement, but hopefully this book will do that. Instead, it's another example of living apart costing more than living together; you both now need the "umbrella" of extra liability coverage over the limits of your automobile and homeowner's policies—particularly with kids and their friends now having a choice of places at which to wreak their havoc. And if you're continuing full or shared ownership of your ex-spouse's residence, be sure (as with homeowner's) that the agent knows it and that you remain as a named insured to protect you from liability on that residence as well as the one where you now will live.

Life Insurance and Estate Planning

Life insurance is the swiss army knife of divorce finances, with so many choices and decisions depending on whether and how it should be used to guarantee parts of the settlement, meet normal estate planning needs, and address needs related to previous or planned future marriages.

Life and Disability Insurance to Back the Settlement

When your divorce settlement includes child support and possibly spousal support, the receiving spouse relies on those payments. So your settlement should require life insurance to guarantee payments in the likely event that the payer isn't wealthy enough to prefund a trust from available assets. To ensure that the insurance remains in place, the payer should not also be the owner, thus preventing the payer from canceling the policy.

Instead, the receiving spouse should be named as both the beneficiary and owner coincident with the divorce, so that he or she can make the payments if the ex-spouse doesn't. Better yet, if the premiums are substantial, the settlement should include an additional periodic separate payment to cover the premium amounts. This amount can be structured as additional spousal support, with tax consequences, or a nonsupport payment without tax consequences. Or the payer could prefund an irrevocable life insurance trust that automatically makes the premium payments to continue the policy, with a provision to make payments from the policy's death.

Unfortunately, the support payer's death isn't the only or least financial risk to the child(ren)'s welfare. Before age 65, about a third of the adult population becomes disabled to the extent of not being able to continue work, the average disability lasting more than three years. Although many employers still offer long-term disability insurance to replace from 60 to 80 percent of income during disability, it's a costly benefit that employers are increasingly eliminating. A spouse who will pay support and doesn't have the coverage should consider getting it—perhaps sharing the cost with the support-receiving spouse, based on the proportion of the benefit that would go toward support.

Disability insurance is a complex product because there are so many different options concerning the types of disabilities it covers, the minimum disability duration before coverage begins, and the percentage of income it pays. A term-life insurance policy is often the most cost-effective solution to replace spousal and child support, and college funding, should the payer die. If the insurance is meant to cover long-term spousal-support payments, the otherwise large continuing premiums can be kept manageable by reducing the amount of the coverage over time, as the number of years that support is needed decreases. An unbiased financial advisor can help you determine appropriate cost-effective life and disability insurance from financially solid companies.

Estate Planning

Many books and articles about divorce will caution you about the dangers of trusting your spouse to manage an inheritance for your children while they're still minors—when they certainly shouldn't be managing it themselves. And caution is called for if you have an antagonistic divorce. When you and your spouse coop-erate in crafting your divorce to the extent that you're acting in the best interests of all parties involved, particularly your children, then who better to manage the money for them then the person left who loves them the most?

That said, consider naming someone else as cotrustee, along with your ex-spouse. For one thing, should your spouse remarry, then other parties have entered the picture whose goals might conflict with what's in your children's best interests. Your ex-spouse might actually be relieved that the new spouse's knowledge of a cotrustee's veto power would counteract such pressure.

In addition to decisions about providing for your children, there are several other reasons to revisit your estate plan upon divorce:

- *No estate plan:* If you're one of more than 50 million adult Americans who don't have one, it's especially crucial that you get one now that your children's fate would be less certain upon your death. Those com-mercials don't lie: if you die without a will your assets will pass accord-ing to the laws of intestacy in your state, so your assets are unlikely to be distributed in the manner needed or that you'd prefer. Your estate plan should also provide for the guardianship of your children.
- *Invalidated upon divorce:* In some states, your will is automatically invalid upon your divorce, so it's tantamount to not having one
- *Outdated provisions:* Even if your will isn't automatically invalidated, it might contain no-longer-appropriate standard features included in most married couples' wills—such as everything going to your spouse, or spe-cial trusts set up to benefit your spouse and avoid estate taxes. Such pro-visions must be replaced or you may inadvertently leave your ex-spouse the bulk of your estate.
- *Spouse as executor or trustee:* While you might want your ex-spouse to administer money intended for the children, you don't want your spouse to have total power over all the provisions in your will, so ex-spouses should be replaced if they were designated as executors or trustees.
- *Lifetime gifting:* Perhaps you and your spouse have customarily made certain annual gifts to family members or to charities, or have created some charitable trusts. Those should all be revisited in light of your new financial circumstances because both your estate tax and income tax sit-uations have changed dramatically due to the divorce, so those plans must be modified accordingly.
- *Beneficiary designations:* In many cases the largest part of some estates are life insurance policies and financial accounts that pass outside the

will by virtue of their own beneficiary designations. So you must also change the beneficiary designations on life insurance policies, pension plans, IRAs, 401(k)'s, and other accounts, because just changing your will won't affect how these big-ticket items pass upon your death.

Tying Up Loose Ends

When followed through completely and conscientiously, the divorce process is not only emotionally exhausting but also just plain hard work. So there's a natural tendency to relax once you've reached a final settlement that just awaits court approval and the issuance of the divorce decree. However, in addition to all the financial bookkeeping and general housekeeping matters already discussed, it's critical that you deal with the following issues before allowing the divorce judgment to be entered.

Finalizing the Divorce

Determine exactly how your state handles the official granting of the divorce so that you'll know exactly when it takes place and what paperwork and fees you must pay to have it recorded.

Benefit Plan Paperwork

Your agreement might have involved qualified domestic relations orders (QDROs) related to benefit plans, or a cash and/or property settlement in lieu of rights to such plans. Where the nonowning spouse has given up rights such as being named beneficiary of an IRA or 401(k) or survivor's rights to a pension, the other spouse must make sure to file the necessary paperwork with the spouse's waiver signatures notarized or witnessed as appropriate. In turn, where QDROs are part of the settlement, the spouse that benefits must make sure the paperwork is properly completed and signed before the divorce and then filed with the employer after the divorce.

Divorce Fees

When a case gets settled in court, the judge determines how responsibility for the collective fees spent to obtain the divorce should be split between the spouses. But when you craft a settlement with your spouse, it should include how that split should be made, regardless of who actually paid what so far. For example, the lower-income spouse might have gotten a temporary order to make the higher-income spouse pay fees during the divorce, but the settlement might call for a "refund" of some of those fees. Or, the lower-income spouse might have shelled out considerable funds to ensure getting a fair settlement, and the settlement might call for some "reimbursement" by the higher-income spouse. These fees include not only attorney fees but also the cost of financial advisors, CPAs, counseling and other professionals, court fees, and other costs associated with obtaining the divorce. The final settlement should be "reconciled" by adding or subtracting property from one spouse in accordance with how these fees are split.

Filing Bankruptcy

If you are both filing for bankruptcy, it's "cleanest" to have the bankruptcies completed before the divorce. That way you'll have most of both spouse's debts discharged and your settlement can then deal with whatever property and nondischargeable debt remains—without your having to worry that a creditor is going to later come after you for additional marital debt. Equally important, though, if one spouse is likely to have substantial property-transfer obligations to the other and is planning to divorce, the other spouse must promptly file for a stay against having those obligations discharged by the bankruptcy, or face losing property to which he or she is entitled. The matter should then still be resolved before the divorce so that the nonbankrupt spouse isn't chased by the bankrupt spouse's creditors.

Single-Life Financial Planning

Hopefully, you won't be bankrupt when you begin single life, but you'll probably feel economically chastened, whether you're the higher-earning or lower-earning spouse. To counter that and think positively, make financial planning a constant companion that you vow not to divorce. In Chapters 7 and 8 we'll cover the financial planning considerations that should factor into negotiating a settlement, but here's the financial planning you should begin to do once you commence single life.

Budgeting

The preseparation and postseparation budgets you prepared earlier are an important source of information in establishing your settlement objectives, but they're far more than negotiating tools. When you do reach a settlement, it probably won't allow you the total amount you'd budgeted postseparation, so now's the time to use that budget as a starting point for budgeting based on the actual property, earnings, and expenses you know you'll have when starting single life. To make sure you budget better now than you may have done during your marriage, take a close look at your preseparation budget to brainstorm about your budgeting weaknesses so you don't allow them to undermine you now.

If you've been primarily a homemaker, won't get long-term spousal support, and won't soon get Social Security and a sizeable portion of your spouse's pension, you must take immediate steps to upgrade your earning power, regardless of how generous your property settlement seems. Most people in your position end up eating into their cushion by having to sell off property or regularly supplementing their income with withdrawals from savings. If you'll eventually do that anyway, better you tap some of those funds now to invest in your financial future. By getting the needed additional training or schooling and starting to put it to use you will increase your earning power enough so you'll begin reversing the trend and building up your savings.

The higher-earning spouse faces a different problem, possibly having to dip into savings to pay rent or mortgage (or both!), other normal expenses, and child support and spousal support. In addition, taxes will take a far bigger chunk of income because the "family" income remains almost the same but he or she is no longer in the lower bracket created by having been married. He or she must slam on the spending brakes in a big way, although slower cash outflow shouldn't be necessary forever. Doing this means counteracting the tendency to spend big with newfound freedom or to jump into another marriage if a serious new relationship accompanied the split.

These financial limitations might seem overwhelming if the higher-earning spouse faces paying long-term or lifetime spousal support. Despite bar talk about its unfairness, though, most long-term payers have a high enough income to manage the payments without undue discomfort after a few years—partly due to the tax deductions they provide. But more important, statistics suggest that those who've been primary breadwinners in a long-term marriage have been on continually upward career path, with correspondingly increasing salaries that eventually grow enough to swallow the support payments.

Gearing Savings and Investments to Yourself (New Risk Tolerance)

One key component of your new budget should be the amount you save and invest. Tight financial circumstances might severely limit how much you can put aside initially, but it's important to view some amount of savings as mandatory and then increase it as your earnings increase. At first, your savings should be aimed at accumulating an emergency fund to cover specifically unexpected but generally inevitable expenses such as major home and car repairs, emergency trips for a family illness, or overall expenses should you lose your job. Put those savings in a money-market account because they must be immediately accessible.

Once you've accumulated an adequate emergency reserve of at least three months' worth of take-home pay, or you have set it aside from the proceeds of the property division, then start investing your savings in a company 401(k) or similar plan—at least to the maximum amount that your employer (partially) matches. Next, set aside the maximum annual amount you can put in an IRA annually—preferably a Roth IRA (no tax deduction but totally tax free earnings) if you meet the eligibility requirements. It's not enough though to simply save. You must direct the investment of these savings in an appropriate manner considering your gender and age: the younger you are, the more of the investment should be in moderate-risk diversified equities (stocks) such as mutual funds so that you can achieve long-term growth that exceeds inflation.

Similarly, examine the investments you've brought from your marriage in either separate accounts or from the property division, and consider reinvesting them in light of your new single circumstances and goals. For example, as a woman investing only for yourself, you're working on a longer timeframe because you'll live on average of five years longer than a man. And as a single man, if you don't plan to remarry, you'll want your investments to be a bit more conservative because you can expect to live a few years less than the average man. (Hmm, maybe we should have mentioned that earlier in case you're the one who first decided to get divorced.)

We don't have room here for a full-blown investment guide. But you can easily find numerous books about basic investing principles and financial institution Web sites that contain "investing primers" or otherwise-named sections on investing. You should also consider consulting a certified financial planner (CFP) or CPA who is a personal financial specialist (PFS)—whose recommendations won't be influenced by the scent of commissions that he or she might earn from your investment—to help you determine your investment goals, investment time horizon, and risk tolerance. Finally, we specifically recommend the following nonprofit organizations and government sources of personal finance and investment information:

- American Savings Education Council (www.asec.org)
- Jumpstart Coalition for Personal Financial Literacy (www.jumpstart-coalition.org)

- Credit Union National Association (www.cuna.org)
- Cooperative State Research, Education and Extension Service (www.reeusda.gov/ecs/map.htm)
- Get the Facts: The SEC's Roadmap to Saving and Investing (www.sec.gov/investor/pubs/roadmap.htm)

Funding Your Child(ren)'s College Education and Wedding

In planning your budgeting and investing, don't forget two important items that are easier to overlook in your new single status and that require cooperation with your spouse: your child(ren)'s college educations and weddings. Although many states now consider it your obligation to help your child pay for college, most don't make it a specific part of required child support payments. So unless you were planning to borrow all the money anyway, don't be caught short by failing to include it in your budget. Furthermore, strive for three-way communication between the child and parents so that you can determine what your child's college goals are and what's feasible for each party to contribute.

However, don't sacrifice other true needs in favor of saving for college or your retirement. For one thing, college loans are currently available at very attractive rates. Also, money invested in specific retirement savings plans is generally not counted by colleges in determining your ability to pay when determining your child's financial need when offering financial aid, so it's actually counterproductive to shortchange your retirement savings just to save for college. Here are some good sources on planning to fund your child(ren)'s college education(s):

- FinAid (www.finaid.org/)
- National Institute of Certified College Planners (www.niccp.com)
- Federal Student Aid Homepage (www.ed.gov/offices/OSFAP/Students/)
- College Board: Paying for College (www.collegeboard.com/paying/0,3309,6-0-0-0,00.html?orig=art)
- Raymond D. Loewe with KC Dempster, *J.K. Lasser Pro: New Strategies for College Funding: An Advisor's Guide*, John Wiley & Sons, New York, 2002

Of course, there's no requirement that you help your child pay for a wedding, but given the higher rate of divorce among those whose parents divorced, it's probably best not to send the message that they're totally on their own. Restraint, though, certainly is understandable and appropriate given that today's average wedding costs more than $20,000. It's probably best that you follow the college three-way-communication example and agree to a total amount you'll provide and how you'll split it between you.

The financial and emotional pressures of divorce make this kind of planning the last thing you'd prefer to do any time soon. But starting now will go a long way toward setting a constructive tone for the continued relationship you must have with your ex-spouse as good, cooperating parents, and facilitate communication about other financial matters such as support adjustments, in either direction, that you'll want to make as needed without going to court.

Considering Remarriage

The good news is that remarrying after divorce gives you a chance to do things better financially than you did the first time, particularly now that you're familiar with the financial ramifications of divorce. The bad news is multifold. First, debt, support obligations, and other financial encumbrances from your first marriage will make it more difficult to make the best financial moves. Second, financial habits are more ingrained from age and (bad) experience, so "cash compatibility" is more difficult. Finally, your first marriage at least gave you an even break—a 50-50 chance of success—while only about one of three divorced individuals who remarry make it to "death do us part." So if you do jump the broom again, it's that much more crucial to protect yourself from being financially swept away.

Our advice probably won't pertain to or influence you much if you're already making wedding plans while still going through your divorce. And it only scratches the surface, given the need for a full book to adequately cover marital finances. Nevertheless, we offer some remarriage financial planning guidelines.

Getting on Your Financial Feet
If financial issues significantly contributed to this marriage's failure, or if you didn't have a sufficient financial role, take time now to become financially autonomous and competent in single life. Resolve to be a full financial decision-making partner in a new marriage, regardless of how your income compares to a new spouse's. Don't even think of remarrying for financial security, regardless of how dire your circumstances, because from what we've seen, it's bound to come out badly.

Full Exploration and Disclosure
Second marriage should have romance but favor reality. If extensive discussions about finances disturb your prospective new mate, it's good to find out now and bail out, pronto! Fully discuss your situations, expectations, and definite ideas about how finances should be handled.

Prenuptial Agreements

Prospective partners with kids or substantial assets have a right and responsibility to protect them. If you or your prospective spouse want a prenup, and you probably should, it's smart—not unreasonable—provided that it isn't proffered in a coercive take-it-or-leave-it manner. Even if the proposal is generous, if there's no give and take, it's an ominous sign that you'll have marital communication problems. Furthermore, for any prenup to work, it's essential to document considerable discussion about it, have mutual full disclosure of financial history and condition, and allow sufficient elapsed time from when it was proposed until when it is finalized. Don't assume, though, that even the most carefully prepared prenup will be iron-clad upon divorce. "For example, in Michigan a prenup must be considered both fair at the time of creation and fair at the time of divorce," says Craig Ross.

Separate and Joint Property and Accounts

Take great pains to keep premaritally separate property separate and not comingled with marital property. When dipping into separate property to enrich the marital property pool, document each "dip" as its own one-time event with no intention that the source becomes marital property. Furthermore, unless you're in a community property state that requires equal splitting of all marital property, you might want a prenup to address the extent to which salary or other separate earnings are to be put in separate accounts and considered separate should a divorce occur.

Supporting Your Own and Partner's Kids

Be crystal clear, in writing, on whether and how much either of you will support the other's kids. Be particularly wary if your new spouse's kids have very different financial circumstances than your own, because that can undermine the marriage. Make sure that you can count on each other to stay out of the other's business regarding communication with ex-spouses about financial matters such as timely payment or adjustment of support. Depending on their age, suitably communicate with the children about these understandings so that they know what to expect, and the possibly different financial ground rules governing each "side" of your new blended family.

Support Modifications and Enforcement

Yogi Berra, the Hall of Fame Yankee happily married forever to Carmen, might not seem to be the ideal source of divorce advice, but if he were asked, he'd probably say, "It ain't even over when it's over." Being smarter than the average bear, he'd know that any court decision in a divorce case is subject to appeal and that even negotiated agreements aren't necessarily final if circumstances warrant . However, he might not be helpful regarding the enforcement of support agreements, likely favoring a 34-ounce Louisville slugger for deadbeat dads. Most important, though, Yogi's quick-answer philosophy suggests that there's always a solution, so here are some guidelines when you must play extra innings with your divorce agreement.

Overall Modification

When the court has rendered the decision incorporated in the divorce decree, it is subject to appeal, with states differing on the conditions under which appeals will be considered. As in criminal law, a decision that can be shown to conflict with existing law or public policy is the best candidate for appeal. Another reason, though, is when full financial disclosure was not made or disclosure was either intentionally or inadvertently in error.

Divorce decrees based on settlements can also be overturned, although that's very difficult if they contain language stating they're not subject to modification. Even then, though, they're not inviolate if they can be shown to be based on incomplete, false, or erroneous disclosure—or seriously conflict with existing law or be against the public's interest. However, the most common reason they are overturned is that the agreed settlement or settlement based on a prenuptial agreement can be shown to have been made under undue duress.

Specific Modifications

A divorce decree can also be modified just on specifics—particularly regarding child custody, and child and spousal support. Because custody is so complex and not financial, we won't cover it here, but the Resource Appendix points to some information about it. Generally, child support is expected to be modified when there's been a significant change of circumstances involving either spouse's income or the expenses needed to raise the child(ren). Spousal support, however, is not generally subject to modification in most states. However, the court can consider modification under certain circumstances such as the payer's hardship due to involuntary unemployment or other changed circumstances. Of course, both spouses can agree to modifications without a court decision.

Child Support Modification

Because child support determination is based on parents' relative abilities to provide support, when a receiving spouse providing the bulk of care for young children is able to earn more money, child support should be revisited—as it should also be if the paying spouse receives a big raise. You need only recalculate what your state's guideline would award based on your state's calculator to see the income-change impact on the guideline calculation. Preferably, though, you and your spouse originally agreed to the support amount rather than having it imposed, and you should be able to reach an agreement on the changes without a judge's intervention.

Changes in circumstances that affect expenses are also potential grounds for changing support—but remarriage is usually not one of them. Despite the additional financial obligations, your original obligation to your children remains unchanged. However, your new obligations might limit or rule out raising your obligation if your child support is revisited because your spouse's financial circumstances have worsened. Furthermore, there's "good news" should you divorce again and also take on a support commitment from the second marriage; in some states that warrants redetermination of support for your child(ren). Ain't life grand!?

Divorce Decree Enforcement

Nonpayment or late payment of child support and spousal support are the most commonly recognized divorce financial compliance problems. However, nonpayment of assigned debt—resulting in creditors' going after the other spouse—also occurs frequently, along with failure to transfer certain proscribed property at a specified date after divorce. The party seeking enforcement has various remedies, depending on the type of noncompliance.

Failure to Pay Child Support

First try dealing directly with a spouse who is in arrears on child support because the repercussions for enforcement actions could be embarrassment that will lead to recriminations. After all, it could be just a matter of a temporary cash flow problem, even when it occurs multiple times. However, you can't afford to get too far behind before it becomes a serious or chronic problem, so you can make use of free government assistance to achieve enforcement.

The Uniform Interstate Family Support Act (UIFSA) is the federal law that governs child support enforcement within and between states via a national database that facilitates tracking nonpayers, under the auspices of the federal

Office of Child Support Enforcement (OSCE) (www.acf.dhhs.gov /programs/cse/). The following summarizes your enforcement alternatives:

Child Support Enforcement
(Extract from OSCE Web Site)

The Child Support Enforcement (CSE) office can help with collecting the money due no matter where the noncustodial parent lives. The CSE office may need to know where the noncustodial parent is living or where he or she is working. When a parent has disappeared, it is usually possible for the CSE office to find him or her with the help of state agencies, such as the department of motor vehicles, or the federal Parent Locator Service. Your caseworker can tell you what information is needed to find an absent parent or his or her employer.

The most successful way to collect child support is by direct withholding from the obligated parent's paycheck. Most child support orders require the employer to withhold the money that is ordered for child support and send it to the CSE office. Your Child Support Enforcement office can tell you about this procedure.

Federal and state income tax refunds may be withheld to collect unpaid child support. States also have laws that allow them to use liens on real and personal property; orders to withhold and deliver property; or seizure and sale of property with the proceeds applied to the support debt. Many states routinely report child support debts to credit bureaus, and smart parents are bringing their payments current so that their credit won't be affected.

The OCSE services are free to people on public assistance and otherwise for a nominal fee. See this Web page www.acf.dhhs.gov/programs/cse/pubs/2002 /reports/essentials/c10.html for detailed information on OCSE methods of collecting child support, and this page www.acf.dhhs.gov/programs/cse/extinf.htm for information on your state's CSE office.

Enforcing Spousal Support and Other Divorce Decree Provisions
In some states, the OCSE will also enforce spousal support orders using the same remedy alternatives, and other states have agencies separate from the OCSE for that purpose.

However, you might have to go to court to enforce spousal support or other provisions. Usually, you start by getting the court to issue an ex-parte (doesn't require notice) "order to show cause" to the noncomplying spouse to appear at a contempt hearing, which can lead to a court-issued contempt citation. If the noncomplying spouse is found in contempt, the court can assess fines, court costs, and interest to compensate the spouse forced to seek legal remedy. The court can also use the same methods or others (for example, publishing non-complying spouses' names in the paper or issuing "wanted posters") to achieve compliance, or even order that spouse's jailing. This complex enforcement mechanism suggests how much easier life will be for both of you by coming to an equitable agreement that doesn't unduly stress either of you.

From Planning the Fight to Fighting It

Most sports allow timeouts or other action breaks—such as baseball's pitcher-mound visits or side changes in tennis. They provide time to possibly reverse your opponent's momentum by catching your breath, clearing your head, and regaining focus on a winning strategy. But boxing offers no respite from the three-minute-round eternity that spells doom you if you allow the crushing blow to land. So it is crucial to be fully prepared before the bell rings to start the fight. That means being prepared to carry out your strategy and protect yourself at all times.

The divorce process is similarly unforgiving of critical mistakes. So we designed this four-round Part II as a strategic guide for you to thoroughly internalize so you'll be able to call upon it to keep you steady no matter how desperate circumstances seem during your divorce. Now let's move on to Part III, where we'll learn the divorce financial-fight equivalent of the punching, fancy footwork, and clinching techniques that help boxers get the referees' decision and the winning share.

Part III

Dealing with Divorce Financial Issues

Sixties' pop icon Neil Sedaka never did identify the "they" who said that breaking up is hard to do, and he was talking about puppy love, not dog-eat-dog divorce. What makes breaking up a marriage so hard—even if you don't have a family dog to "divide"—is that it involves far more than divvying up the loot and what's left of the good china after each of you has taken turns throwing it at each other. At a minimum, you must deal with the unique laws of your state regarding how property should or can be divided and divide up both unsheltered and tax-sheltered accounts such as IRAs and 401(k)s—without running afoul of employer regulations and tax laws. You must also deal with the marital residence, determine child and possibly spousal support, and incorporate the value of health insurance and other basic benefits that will no longer be available to the other spouse from each spouse's benefit plan.

But don't worry, we'll break down all the financial details of breaking up in this section, starting with Chapter 7. Chapter 8 then moves into more complex issues that the majority of couples don't face, such as vacation homes or investment real estate, coordination of child support from multiple marriages, bells and whistles in more complex spousal support situations, traditional (defined-benefit) pension plans, stock options and other complex employee benefits, and spouse-owned businesses.

It's bad enough that Neil Sedaka was so right—even worse that his cloying song might now be relentlessly racing through your head, leaving you at the breaking (up) point. By understanding these aspects of a divorce settlement, though, you'll be in a far better position to defend your financial interests. Perhaps it's no coincidence that "Kung Fu Fighting" ranked just below the 1975 remade release of "Breaking Up Is Hard to Do."

Chapter 7

Basic Divorce Financial Issues

Think of divorce complexity the way an auto-repair business thinks of cars scheduled for service. Every car needs an oil change and lube, tire-pressure check, and other basics—but only some need a tune-up, new brake linings, and other additional services. This chapter covers the basic service items for every divorce, while Chapter 8 covers the more extensive service items.

Don't make the mistake of regarding your basic (divorce) service as routine. It might be more complex because you have a more sophisticated car (marriage). Furthermore, if you have a more basic mass-produced car (typical middle-class marriage), it's still *yours*, so you want to give it your full attention. So either way, keep your eye on the mechanic (your divorce attorney) or the repair manual (mostly do-it-yourself divorce) to ensure that these aspects of your finances leave your marriage in the best possible condition.

Property

No matter what the final outcome of your property division, if it's done well, chances are that both you and your spouse will think the other one got the better deal. It stinks, but not in comparison to Anatevka's residents in *Fiddler on the Roof*, who had three days to sell their homes and move out with whatever property they could shlep with them. Even if your home has a second mortgage, chances are that you'll walk away with at least some equity, and it's likely you'll be able to squeeze out enough cash to hire a moving van to take as much property as you're awarded. So go ahead and play the world's smallest fiddle to accompany your tale of (a) woe(fully inadequate share). But end it with the crescendo of Tevye's unfailing optimism—which learning these family law and financial principles of property division should give you.

A Primer on Property Division Principles

We could give you detailed technical explanations of yours, mine, and ours in relation to who owns property in a marriage and who should receive what in divorce. But then, in addition to the sign-offs from our editor and publisher, we'd have to get this book approved by the FDA as a sleep-inducing drug. So instead, let's consider the TV commercials every major holiday season that are meant to make you feel like the most inferior human in history if you don't surprise your spouse by gift packaging a set of keys to an obscenely expensive new car.

In most states, such a key giver will have made a flashy gesture that means nothing. If the couple divorces, the gift recipient isn't automatically entitled to the car—but very well might be entitled to responsibility for a good chunk of the huge loan or lease agreement used to acquire it. On the other hand (as Tevye often said), you might even be entitled to a luxury car that your spouse bought solely for himself or herself, with a hands-off warning to you. Put another way, in divorce, possession is nine tenths of the "flaw." So buckle up for a quick joy-riding spin through the head-spinning back roads of property division.

Who Owns What before Divorce

Your first step in splitting property is to inventory all financial and physical assets titled in either or both spouses' name. Your natural tendency might be to let each item's titling dictate its placement in one of three columns: his, hers, or ours. But in establishing actual ownership under family law, either how it was acquired or where you lived when you acquired it often overrides how it was subsequently titled. So instead of relying only on title, use the partial sample in Figure 7-1 as a model for setting up an inventory sheet.

The only entry that isn't self-explanatory is the Property Type column, separate (husband or wife), marital, community, or not sure, which are defined as follows:

- *"Separate-husband" or "separate-wife"*: This is the husband or wife's actual "separate property"—defined as *not* acquired together or from either spouse's earnings *during* the marriage. In most states, separate property is instead acquired before the marriage or during the marriage from (nonspousal) gifts, inheritances, designation in writing by one

Property (Describe)	Property Type (Community, Marital, Separate-Wife, Separate-Husband, or Not Sure)	When/Where Acquired (Any Special Circumstances?)	Purchase Price and (Down) Payment Source	Loan Amount, Balance, and Payment Source	Current FMV (Fair Market Value)
Motorcycle	Separate (H)	1995, New Jersey, Before Marriage	$8250, $4250 down payment (H) pre-marriage	$4000, Paid Off by Husband Before Marriage	$5500
Piano	Community	1998, California	$20,000, from joint account	None	$17,000
XYZ Stock	Not sure	Employee Stock Purchase Plan shares continuously acquired in several states before and during marriage	Account statements contain purchase dates, amounts, prices. Husband's payroll deduction.	None	$78,400
Boat	Marital/Separate (W)	1999, Connecticut	$80,000, $35,000 down Payment from Wife's Trust	$45,000, $20,000 Joint Account	$70,000

FIGURE 7-1   Partial (Sample) Property Inventory Sheet

spouse for assignment to the other, or earnings or price appreciation associated with separate property. Although the property itself might have "begun life" as separate, sometimes the appreciation on it since it was acquired is considered marital property.

- *"Marital" or "community property"*: The 41 equitable-distribution states as opposed to the nine community property states (and D.C.) recognize "marital property"—as opposed to the nine community property states. (See next page.) Theoretically, marital property is all property, regardless of how it's titled, that isn't the separate property of either spouse. Thus, if both spouses have their own separate accounts in their own names, in which they electronically deposit their own paychecks, the funds in those accounts are still marital property—because the income of either spouse during the marriage isn't separate property. Furthermore, determining marital property is trickier when one spouse owns a business, but we'll try to cover the basics—although the laws and how the courts interpret them differ significantly between states.

First, even if a business is incorporated in only the owning spouse's name, if it was started during the marriage, the value of that business is marital property—but if it was started before the marriage, and uses only business assets to keep it going or grow it, then it's normally that spouse's alone. However, if nonbusiness (marital) assets were used also, then the business becomes partially marital property. In addition, if the owner's spouse makes nonmonetary contributions to the business that help it increase its value, some portion of that increased value could be marital property. Finally, even if the owner's spouse had no involvement, and no marital assets were used, the spouse still might be entitled to some portion of the "passive" increase in business value that occurs for various reasons, such as a town adopting more restrictive zoning which would make it difficult for new competitive businesses to be established.

Returning to general property principles, if either spouse allows separate property to be commingled with marital property (for example, by putting it in a joint account), then it becomes marital property, with two exceptions: first, if what amounts to a written IOU from the other spouse documents that it remains the original owner's separate property; or second, if a paper trail "follows the money" back to the original spouse, so that everyone, including the court (if involved), agrees that it is separate property—but don't count on either of these exceptions.

So what about that luxury-car surprise gift from one spouse to the other? If the recipient didn't include a signed note saying "I've given this car to my spouse on XYZ date," the car is marital property even if the title is in the recipient spouse's name. However, we shall see soon that even though a piece of property is technically classified as marital, the circumstances behind how that property was brought into the marriage and subsequently handled can play a big part in how marital property is divided—except in the few states whose laws mandate that marital property is divided 50-50. The B movie line "what's yours is mine and what's mine is yours" almost perfectly describes such "C" (community) property.

Community property combines the concept of marital property with *equal* (not equitable) distribution. In other words, in the nine community property states, all property that would be considered marital property in the other 41 states (plus the District of Columbia) is considered to be half-owned by each spouse, regardless of how it's titled—while the spouses each own the property defined as their separate property before the marriage or received as an inheritance or a (nonspousal or documented-spousal) gift during the marriage.

- *Not sure:* You might not be sure who owns something if you disagree or can't remember whether it was purchased with separate or marital funds. Or you might not be sure if it's marital or community property if you acquired it in a different state and you've lived in both equitable distribution (marital property) and community property states. To help with that, we'll now offer some guidelines on how to tell.

Splitting When All Things Are Equal

Although community property is half-owned by each spouse, its treatment upon divorce differs among the nine community property states:

- California, Louisiana, and New Mexico are "pure" in absolutely requiring community property to be divided equally upon divorce.
- Idaho, Nevada, and Wisconsin allow a judge to split community property unequally for a "compelling reason."
- Arizona, Washington, and Texas treat community property almost like equitable distribution states treat marital property. The judge should start with the presumption of an equal split, but he or she is allowed full discretion in how to divide it.

To complicate matters further, community property states differ in how they treat property acquired in an equitable distribution state a couple lived in earlier. Such "quasi community property" is generally treated the way it would be treated if it had been acquired in the current (community) state of residence. That usually translates into such property being considered community property, but some community property states treat specific situations differently.

Community property laws can make it either easier or harder to reach a fair agreement. If you've been a homemaker whose spouse has had considerable financial success during your marriage, you'll usually be entitled to half of the property that success acquired, and you won't have to fight the vicious battles that often take place in those circumstances in equitable distribution states. But pity the successful executive whose career is hanging in the balance because of a spouse inattentive to family needs—perhaps even multiply unfaithful. In a no-fault (only) community property state, he or she can file and the executive must fight tooth and nail to keep the spouse from getting the "presumptive half" to which he or she is entitled—and that's only in the five states that allow discretion. If these possibilities shock you, welcome to the community!

Splitting When All Things Are Equitable

Just as all community property is subject to division—but usually 50-50—in community property states, all marital property is subject to division—very often not 50-50—in equitable distribution states. Furthermore, unlike community property states where a homemaker or low-earning spouse of a wealthy spouse is protected by the 50-50 division, determination of equitable division is often considered in combination with spousal support. For example, depending on the specific wording of an equitable state's laws, the judge might award a much higher earning spouse in a long-term marriage a much higher percentage of the property if spousal support is going to be substantial and permanent. Conversely, if the marriage is not long enough to make permanent spousal support justifiable, the judge might award the economically weaker spouse a much higher than equal property share.

So it's important that you try to get you and your spouse on the same page in understanding that an unequal split is not an inequitable split, per se. If that bothers you, then it might help to think of the period until your divorce as the time you spend trapped in a dark, narrow cave; in both situations, flexibility (physical and fiscal, respectively) might be the key to getting out safely with minimal injury. In exercising that flexibility with regards to splitting marital property, here are the factors that judges might consider:

- *Marital vital statistics:* The current age and health of each spouse and the marriage's length.

- *Before and after financial status:* Each spouse's marriage-starting education, income, and net worth, current separate assets, current and future earnings prospects, and "live" (properly executed) binding agreements between spouses regarding disposition of some or all assets.
- *Marital roles and (positive or negative) contributions:* Each spouse's role in the marriage (primary breadwinner, shared breadwinners, homemaker, and so on). How much each spouse contributed from earnings, other assets contributed to the marriage, nonmonetary asset-preserving or asset-building contributions—such as obsessively clipping and redeeming coupons, doing all home repairs, or telemarketing for a spouse's new business—and economically detrimental actions that consumed assets—such as gambling or carrying on an expensive affair.
- *Nature of assets:* Which assets have embedded tax liabilities or deductible losses, carry liquidation penalties, are expensive to liquidate (such as estate sale or auctioneer commissions), or are particularly easy or difficult to liquidate quickly for full value? Which assets serve continuing needs that mitigate against liquidation and favor sole ownership by one party (such as the marital home, a cash-value life insurance policy, or a business)?
- *Asset protection expenses:* By divorcing, the (joint) custodial spouse(s) must protect assets via new health, life, disability, auto, and homeowner insurance, as well as possibly other forms of insurance that weren't previously needed.
- *Current separate and combined debts:* Examine these closely because of continuing liability of both spouses for debts incurred during marriage by either. The possibility of predivorce joint bankruptcy or postdivorce separate bankruptcies must be weighed.
- *Coordination with spousal maintenance:* If a spousal maintenance agreement has been reached, the judge might take that amount into account in determining how to divide property to achieve an overall equitable marital settlement. Or, for tax efficiency, the judge might decide to award high "front-loaded" (see below) spousal support so that a wealthier spouse can gain more tax advantage from delayed transfer of some property or otherwise benefit by delaying liquidation of some assets. At the opposite extreme, the judge might determine that spousal maintenance that might otherwise be called for should be totally front-loaded in the form of a higher share of property—perhaps because of the risk of bankruptcy or to give a large immediate cash infusion to a new business that offers high income potential.

Whether and to what extent each of the equitable distribution states use these factors in splitting property varies widely. For example, some states start with a presumption that equitable means equal, while others don't—an unequal split is more likely to be initially awarded and upheld in appellate court where equal isn't presumed. A recent survey of all equitable distribution states revealed that disparity in amounts of property each spouse brought into the marriage and disparities in future earning capacity were two of the top three reasons that judges awarded unequal marital-property splits—the other being when an unequal split wouldn't be equitable relative to the length of the marriage.

You can get an idea of the factors your state uses in property division by looking at Figure 7-2.

Splitting Hairs in Difficult Divisions

Even if they could, legal Las Vegas sporting books aren't ever likely to establish odds on the outcome of litigated divorce cases. Cases documented by the National Legal Research Group family law newsletters reveal the incredible range of discretion and number of novel arguments that judges exercise and accept. Although appellate courts often strike down some of these overly creative lower-court interpretations, the expense of litigation precludes many similar decisions from ever being appealed.

So instead of betting on the courts, you're better off coming to an imperfect agreement with your spouse—definitely based on full disclosure and preferably including documentation of the reasoning behind the way things have been divided. And that's where it might well be worth involving attorneys after you've come to an agreement to make sure the division will be acceptable to the court and that it be as appeal proof as possible. (While there's far less chance of successfully appealing a divorce decree based on an agreement reached between you, and not by a judge's decision, it can happen) These are the kinds of cases that seem to cause the most problems regarding court decisions or appeals on property division:

- *Timing of property valuation:* If considerable time elapses between the agreement and the final divorce decree, courts often reconsider awards. For example, if one spouse gets the house but Hannibal Lecter has moved in next door in the interim two years between agreement and decree, presumably driving the market value down in inverse proportion to rising appetite, judges will be inclined to let that party feast on more of the spouse('s assets).

FIGURE 7-2   Property Distribution Methods by State

STATE	PROPERTY DISTRIBUTION	PROPERTY MODEL*	INCREASE IN VALUE OF SEPARATE PROPERTY
ALABAMA:	Equitable Distribution	No Property Model	Separate Property
ALASKA:	Equitable Distribution	All Property Model	Marital Property
ARIZONA:	Community Property	Dual Property Model	Separate Property
ARKANSAS:	Equitable Distribution	Dual Property Model	Separate Property
CALIFORNIA:	Community Property	Dual Property Model	Separate Property
COLORADO:	Equitable Distribution	Dual Property Model	Marital Property
CONNECTICUT:	Equitable Distribution	All Property Model	Marital Property
DELAWARE:	Equitable Distribution	Dual Property Model	Separate Property
DIST OF COLUMBIA:	Equitable Distribution	Dual Property Model	Separate Property
FLORIDA:	Equitable Distribution	Dual Property Model	Separate Property
GEORGIA:	Equitable Distribution	Dual Property Model	Separate Property
HAWAII:	Equitable Distribution	All Property Model	Marital Property
IDAHO:	Community Property	Dual Property Model	Separate Property
ILLINOIS:	Equitable Distribution	Dual Property Model	Separate Property
INDIANA:	Equitable Distribution	All Property Model	Marital Property
IOWA:	Equitable Distribution	All Property Model	Marital Property
KANSAS:	Equitable Distribution	All Property Model	Marital Property
KENTUCKY:	Equitable Distribution	Dual Property Model	Separate Property
LOUISIANA:	Community Property	Dual Property Model	Separate Property
MAINE:	Equitable Distribution	Dual Property Model	Separate Property
MARYLAND:	Equitable Distribution	Dual Property Model	Separate Property
MASSACHUSETTS:	Equitable Distribution	All Property Model	Marital Property
MICHIGAN:	Equitable Distribution	All Property Model	Marital Property
MINNESOTA:	Equitable Distribution	Dual Property Model	Separate Property
MISSISSIPPI:	Title	Dual Property Model	Separate Property
MISSOURI:	Equitable Distribution	Dual Property Model	Separate Property
MONTANA:	Equitable Distribution	All Property Model	Marital Property
NEBRASKA:	Equitable Distribution	Dual Property Model	Separate Property
NEVADA:	Community Property	Dual Property Model	Marital Property
NEW HAMPSHIRE:	Equitable Distribution	All Property Model	Marital Property
NEW JERSEY:	Equitable Distribution	Dual Property Model	Separate Property
NEW MEXICO:	Community Property	Dual Property Model	Marital Property
NEW YORK:	Equitable Distribution	Dual Property Model	Separate Property
NORTH CAROLINA:	Equitable Distribution	Dual Property Model	Separate Property
NORTH DAKOTA:	Equitable Distribution	All Property Model	Marital Property
OHIO:	Equitable Distribution	Dual Property Model	Separate Property
OKLAHOMA:	Equitable Distribution	Dual Property Model	Separate Property
OREGON:	Equitable Distribution	All Property Model	Marital Property
PENNSYLVANIA:	Equitable Distribution	Dual Property Model	Marital Property
RHODE ISLAND:	Equitable Distribution	Dual Property Model	Separate Property
SOUTH CAROLINA:	Equitable Distribution	Dual Property Model	Separate Property
SOUTH DAKOTA:	Equitable Distribution	All Property Model	Marital Property
TENNESSEE:	Equitable Distribution	Dual Property Model	Separate Property
TEXAS:	Community Property	Dual Property Model	Separate Property
UTAH:	Equitable Distribution	All Property Model	Marital Property

FIGURE 7-2   *Continued*

STATE	PROPERTY DISTRIBUTION	PROPERTY MODEL	INCREASE IN VALUE OF SEPARATE PROPERTY
VERMONT:	Equitable Distribution	All Property Model	Marital Property
VIRGINIA:	Equitable Distribution	Dual Property Model	Separate Property
WASHINGTON:	Community Property	Dual Property Model	Separate Property
WEST VIRGINIA:	Equitable Distribution	Dual Property Model	Separate Property
WISCONSIN:	Community Property	Dual Property Model	Separate Property
WYOMING:	Equitable Distribution	All Property Model	Marital Property

*"All Property Model" means that in appropriate circumstances the court may include separate property with the property to be divided. "Dual Property Model" means that the court may only divide marital property or community property–but not separate property.
Used with permission of Pension Appraisers Inc. ©Copyright 2001-2003, All Rights Reserved, Pension Appraisers, Inc.
http://www.pensionappraisers.com/popup/propertymodeltable.shtml

- *Separation agreements:* Couples often divide some or all property coincident to separation, sometimes with a formal separation agreement. But when that agreement is made anticipating an extended separation before divorce, a new look at how equitable that division remains a few years later could result in a court mandating a revised property division.
- *Separate accounts used as continued source of marital funds:* It's not unusual for a judge to decide that separate accounts brought into a marriage can be "invaded" to effect an overall equitable settlement, even if they've never held marital assets. But much more frequently, judges have granted the nonowning spouse's request to reclassify such separate accounts as marital property if they've served as a continuing source of funds used in the marriage. Returning to the earlier car gift example, if a separate account is not regularly used for marital funds but the owning spouse taps it for occasional interspousal gifts, such as the luxury car mentioned earlier, the account will probably remain separate, but the gifts are more likely to be seen as the separate property of the receiving spouse.
- *Attorney fees:* Checks cut to attorneys by both parties clearly consume part of the marital estate, and settlements usually apportion them as debits against the respective divided assets. When they're substantial, though, they're frequently the source of contention and their allocation becomes subject to a judge's interpretation.
- *Homemaker services:* Your likely strong (pro or con) opinion of the National Organization for Women notwithstanding, NOW's visible imprint on family law is unmistakable when the recognition of homemaker services is considered as a contributing factor in property divi-

sion. Although judges might not accept NOW's calculated value of homemaker services, they're increasingly considering their value, and homemakers have had success getting more of their value recognized in trial or on appeal. But establishing their value is a point of contention that you and your spouse are better off resolving yourselves rather than leaving it to judges whose participation in domestic chores at their homes is a closely guarded secret.

Specific Property Division Issues

In addition to understanding the general law governing all property, you must also understand how specific types of property are treated. While this section won't offer specific advice about a husband's power tools or a wife's power hair-styling equipment (or vice versa), it will address personal property as a whole, as well as all your various financial assets.

Marital Residence

When ditching a spouse, who should keep the house(?)—or so the question was once worded. Today, though, should anybody keep the house? In the past, far too many wives discovered, too late, that a house became an albatross of strangling maintenance obligations; the cash embedded in home equity could-n't be tapped because they couldn't afford the interest on a home-equity line of credit, assuming the bank would grant one. Worse, they were trapped by the tax liability they would incur under previous tax law if they sold a house before age 55, and then bought a less expensive home or rented.

With careful planning and sound strategy, though, you might be able to turn the trap into a triumph—starting with using the house as a powerful bargaining chip to break a stalemate. Suppose you and your spouse are far apart in negotiations because the domestic spouse wants to keep the house but is holding out for enough other assets and spousal support to ensure being able to afford it. If the domestic spouse then indicates willingness to sell it, he or she might elicit concessions on the other property because the other spouse will no longer view him or her as being unrealistic and unreasonable.

Fortunately, unless you've made an enormous profit on your house, you can now decide to keep or sell it on a purely economic basis, independent of taxes, due to recent tax-law changes. Chances are that you don't have more than $250,000 appreciation on the house, and it will probably be a good while until you do. Unless your gain upon sale exceeds that amount, whoever ends up with the house has from now until eternity to sell it tax free and only has to pay tax on the amount over $250,000 if it should appreciate that much. Furthermore, if the house already has more than a $250,000 built-in gain now, you can still sell it tax free in the following circumstances as long as you each have lived in it as a primary residence at least two (not necessarily at the same time) of the last five years. (Note: In some of these scenarios, under certain "hardship" circumstances, a spouse who lived in the home less than 2 of the last 5 years at the time of sale can claim a partial exclusion.)

- Sell the jointly owned house before the divorce and file jointly for the $500,000 exclusion.
- Sell the jointly owned home before or within one year after the divorce and file individually (married file separate, head of household, or single—depending on when sold) to collectively exclude up to $500,000 of the gain by each excluding up to $250,000. If the divorcing couple continues joint ownership despite only one spouse's living in the house, and it is not sold within a year of divorce, then each ex-spouse will owe taxes on his or her separate return on half of the portion of the gain exceeding $250,000.
- The divorce settlement stipulates that one spouse will own the house while the other spouse occupies it, either indefinitely or for a specific designated period. Upon ultimate sale, the nonoccupant owner spouse qualifies for the $250,000 exclusion without having had to live in it for at least 2 of the past 5 years.
- The spouse who gets the house later remarries and upon eventual sale is able to take the whole $500,000 exclusion with the new spouse, even though that spouse would have had to pay tax on the gain above $250,000 without the remarriage.
- Under certain conditions, such as a slumping housing market, it might be desirable for both parties to continue owning the house and for one to continue living in it, or for both to move out and rent it for an indeterminate period after the divorce. Or if one spouse gets the house, that spouse might move out and rent it out. To still qualify for the exclusion(s)—the amount(s) depending on the circumstances—however, the owner(s) must have lived in the house for at least two of the five years immediately prior to the sale—which might require one spouse to move back in for two years before selling. Of course, the rental income will cause other tax complications, so the spouses should get a financial advisor's help before pursuing that strategy.
- The divorce decree gives the house to one spouse but that spouse lacks sufficient property from the settlement to pay for it. If the other spouse

doesn't need the money immediately, a *divorce lien* can be arranged to enable the owning spouse to pay off the other spouse over a period of time while the lien serves as collateral.

Two cautions regarding all this however. First, gain will be computed as sales price minus the sum of transaction costs, improvements, and the original purchase price. If you also had gains on homes you owned before the 1997 law was enacted, you were required to roll over those gains to reduce the basis in your current home in determining total gain. For example, suppose you bought a house in 1975 for $110,000 and sold it in 1988 for $310,000—for a gain of $200,000. You then bought a new home the same year for $330,000, which you're now selling for $680,000, for an apparent gain of $350,000. But because your basis in the new house is reduced to $130,000 because of the rolled-over $200,000 gain, your total gain on your current home's sale is $550,000, the difference between $130,000 and $680,000. Thus, you will owe capital-gains tax on $50,000, the excess gain over the $500,000 married-owner (tax-free gain) limit.

Second, we've covered these possibilities here in order to give you an idea of the various possibilities and tax consequences regarding the largest asset which you'll likely be dealing with in your divorce. So, you should definitely check with your divorce professional regarding any of these possibilities, particularly the divorce and postdivorce nonresident ownership, to ensure compliance with the requirements you must meet to get the tax exclusion you expect.

Of course, whoever ends up with the house might plan to remain in it for as long as possible, so be sure you understand the long-term ramifications:

- *Mortgage:* It's not just that one spouse has to be able to keep paying it. The other spouse has worries if the house title is transferred but the mortgage remains in both names, which puts the nonowning spouse on the hook with the bank. It's much better to get it refinanced in solely the owning spouse's name, but that depends on whether he or she will qualify for the loan.
- *Property tax:* When houses appreciate significantly after divorce, that's good, right? Well, eventually, but meanwhile you're caught in a rising property-tax spiral. And you might face repeatedly rising homeowner's association dues. Oh, you don't know if you're in a homeowner's association? There's at least a 50-50 chance that you are if your house is less than 10 years old.
- *Upkeep:* As each year goes by, the closer the house comes to needing a new roof and another paint job, a new furnace and major appliances, redecorating and remodeling. Don't forget the yard, particularly if you're

in a homeowner's association that can sue you if you don't keep the house up to sometimes arbitrary standards not fully spelled out in the covenants. You might think that those expenses would later help you in terms of reducing the gain on the home when you sell it, but they don't; only actual improvements increase the cost basis of your home, thus reducing the potentially taxable gain.

- *Income tax:* OK, so single home ownership is expensive, but you'll benefit from a huge break on your taxes, right? Think again if you don't have a good income. Your low tax bracket will not enable you to capitalize much on the deductions you can take for those property taxes and mortgage interest. Therefore, if your combined job income and any spousal support is a modest total, and you can find a place with much lower rent than your current combined mortgage and property tax payment (if your property tax isn't already built in as escrow on your mortgage payment), put down a deposit! Even considering the continued appreciation on the house, you're probably better off renting or buying a more modest home to make sure you don't end up in foreclosure or bankrupt.

Employer and Other Retirement Plans

Next to home equity, your biggest asset is probably the total of the amounts you and your spouse have in retirement plans. If either of you are in the minority of employees who have traditional pension plans, you should understand that the portion of such plans that is considered "earned" during the marriage is marital property subject to equitable division. But the formulas and legalities for doing that are quite complicated, so we've included a lengthy section on them in Chapter 8.

Pensions

Ideally, if the pension either spouse is earning is expected to be modest, you and your spouse should just agree to split future payments of it either equally or based on the ratio between the number of years of marriage in which the employee has been accruing years of service, versus the number of years in total it will take to earn it. For example, if 18 years of it have been earned during the marriage and it will take 30 to earn it fully, then it is common to conclude that the spouse gets 60 percent (18/30) of half of it, or 30 percent of each payment. More on this in Chapter 8.

However, many spouses who expect a pension resist to splitting it at all, feeling that the pension should belong to them alone. Consequently it is often helpful to explore settlement options that use additional property or higher spousal support to replace the portion of the pension to which the other spouse would be entitled. To determine the value of replacing the pension share, you must estimate what the payments will be at the time of retirement, and then do a *present-value analysis* of them to determine the current *lump-sum value* of the future pension. Most large government and some private employers have password-protected Web sites or other information or tools that enable you to make that estimate on your own. Or they might provide sketchier information that's still enough to make a reasonable estimate. Either way, these estimates depend on predictions concerning your future salary growth and years of service—so you have to do some "what-if" analysis to try out different scenarios (which you can easily do with the in *Split-Up Pension Evaluator* www.splitup.com/products/product_pension_calculator.htm.

However, don't rely on such estimates if you find pensions, or math in general, confusing, or if the pension is expected to be a significant amount of the total assets. You can use them as a starting point to help you formulate a negotiating position but should obtain a formal valuation by an actuary (in complex cases) or otherwise qualified financial professional before coming to any final settlement agreement. Here's a valuation example and some ways to get formal pension valuations:

Sample Pension Valuation Report
www.divorcesource.com/webcarte/samplereport.shtml
Pension Appraisers Online Valuation
www.divorcesource.com/webcarte/pensionvaluations.shtml
Legal Economic Evaluations, Inc.
www.legaleconomic.com/family_law_pension_valuations.html

Defined-Contribution Plans and IRA Plans

Meanwhile, you may be among the individuals who have some form of non-employer IRA plan, as well as among the majority of employees who have 401(k), 403(b), SEP IRA or SIMPLE IRA, or other defined-contribution (DC) plans. All DC plans are subject to equitable division, along with traditional or Roth IRAs in which you've deposited earnings for tax-deferred or tax-free growth. On the surface, it would seem quite easy to split such plans because their value can be determined as of the close of the markets on any given day, but little is truly easy in divorce:

- *Plans begun before marriage:* You must determine the final balance that's marital versus separate property. This calculation includes subtracting the starting balance from the end balance. You then determine what part of the difference represents growth of the original starting balance during the marriage because that should be added to the starting balance to determine the total amount of separate property, the remainder being marital property.

How? Well in financial-planner geek-speak, it requires setting up a cash flow analysis of when all funds went into the plan and then calculating an overall uniform rate of return that would make those inflows grow to the ending balance. You'd then apply that rate to the marriage-starting balance. You can do it on a good financial calculator, but who wants a reputation as a geek when you're about to become single? Furthermore, your state might have some mandated methods or methods derived from case precedents, so this one is worth a brief consultation with a professional if a lot of money is at stake. But if you and your spouse are both reasonably knowledgeable about things financial, you can probably come to some reasonable agreement that will make the calculations simpler.

- *Valuation timing.* Undue delays between separation dates and divorce decrees often raise problems as to the proper "fair" valuation date. If a plan is split based on the value at the date of separation, you generally add or subtract the pro rata appreciation or depletion until the plan assets are actually transferred. In addition, you usually will subtract any postseparation contributions.
- *DC-Plan Vesting.* Unlike IRA plans, which individuals control themselves, DC plans are controlled by employers and usually have vesting periods for the employer's matching contributions. When that vesting is gradual, there's no problem because the current-balance summary shows the part that remains unvested. But when the vesting is "cliff vesting," it means that it takes place all at once at the end of the vesting period. Thus, the portion of unvested contributions subject to division must be calculated with a formula that prorates them by the percentage of the vesting period that has been completed.
- *Employee Retirement Income Security Act (ERISA) Plan (partial) distributions upon divorce:* If your divorce gives you a share of a 401(k) or other ERISA plan, regardless of age, you can take a distribution at the time of the divorce without paying an early withdrawal penalty, but you will owe taxes on that distribution. Thus, if you're less than age 59.5, determine how much you're likely to need from such plans in the next few years and take that amount as a distribution at the time of divorce, and roll the rest directly over into your own IRA. Otherwise, you'll pay taxes and an early withdrawal penalty on any after-divorce distribution you take before age 59.5. For example, if you're getting half of a $200,000 401(k), and require $55,000 now, you'll probably need $70,000 to $80,000 of it (before taxes), and roll the remaining $20,000 to $30,000 over into a new IRA.

- *Qualified domestic relations orders (QDRO):* DC plans are governed under ERISA—a federal law directing employers to release the spousal share of the employee's account only upon receipt of a properly executed qualified domestic relations order (QDRO). QDROs can be complex, so make sure that yours is drafted by an attorney, with expertise in employee benefit plans, possibly in conjunction with a benefits professional. Finally, because IRAs aren't ERISA plans, they're not "qualified" plans, so they do not require a QDRO. (Note, however, that tax-court rulings have created slight ambiguity concerning IRA plans set up by employers for their employees. If an employer has set up a SEP-IRA or SIMPLE-IRA plan for you or your spouse, double check with your attorney on the need for a QDRO.)

Nonemployer IRAs

Roth, traditional, tax-deferred-only IRAs, self-employed SEP-IRAs and SIMPLE-IRAs, and self-employed defined-contribution Keogh plans are not "qualified" ERISA plans. So they are not handled with a QDRO. Instead, specifications for how they are divided are detailed in the marital settlement agreement itself rather than in a QDRO. Here's how distributions are treated:

- *Roth IRAs:* If you're getting a distribution and are at least age 59.5, and if the account is at least five years old, then you can cash in all or part of it and owe no taxes and no withdrawal penalty. You can also choose to have any part you don't cash in transferred as a rollover directly into your own Roth IRA, where it will continue to accumulate tax free and you won't owe taxes or penalties if and when you later withdraw it. If you're under age 59.5, in a few limited circumstances you can also take a distribution without any taxes or penalties.
- *Other IRAs:* Because other IRAs only defer tax on net investment gains, then you'll pay current taxes on any distribution you take. Because they're not ERISA plans, if you're under age 59.5, in most circumstances you'll also pay the 10 percent penalty on such distributions. However, you can avoid current tax and penalties by having the share you get upon divorce directly rolled over into a new IRA that you establish.

Other Savings and Investments

Whew, we've now covered the hard part of financial accounts, so the rest is a piece of cake. Uh . . . wrong! There's nothing cakelike about dividing divorce pie—and worse, with no-fault divorce you can't even ensure that your spouse gets his or her just desserts. The best we can do is give you instructions for picking through the leftover "cash-e-rolls":

- *Liquid assets:* No real tricks here, unless there's a question of commingled assets that both of you know include some truly separate property. If your spouse was the commingling klutz who made the mistake, you can probably rely on the court to be a stickler and rule the whole account as marital. But you can go a long way toward a spirit of true cooperation by agreeing with your spouse on any parts that really are separate and subtracting those parts away to determine the total marital liquid assets to divide.
- *Market investments:* Remember the good early days when you and your spouse were getting to first base, then second and third bases? Well, it's time for basis again, the financial kind. In dividing capital assets, it's imperative that you know their *basis*, which, if you bought it yourself, is defined as the market purchase price, plus the transaction costs. (For mutual funds, you must also add any capital gains distributions and reinvested dividends since they were purchased.) The difference between the basis and the price when the investment is sold is the realized gain or loss. All these gains and losses are combined with some complex rules to determine how much tax you owe due to net gains or how much you can deduct from taxable income due to net losses. Because there's no way of knowing what the market price will be when the investments are eventually sold, you should base your negotiations on the current unrealized gains and losses, which are calculated by determining the difference between basis and current market price for each investment. Your basis is defined differently, though, if you inherited the investment or received it as a gift. If you inherited it, then the basis is what it was worth on the date of death of the person who willed it to you. But if it was a gift, then the basis is the giver's original basis when he or she acquired it.

Your objective should be to determine the net value (taking into account tax impacts) of the investments to ensure you're getting a fair deal when splitting them. We don't intend to teach you tax preparation, but you should know the basics of what's involved in the calculation. To determine the proper tax rates, you must know when assets were purchased to determine which transactions are long-term or short-term gains or losses. Because you probably bought at a number of different times, you must calculate each gain or loss separately. Furthermore, the tax is not truly independent for each gain or loss, because what matters is what the total tax bill or savings will be when you combine everything into four categories: short-term gain, short-term loss, long-term gain, and long-term loss.

Based on tax rules, you determine aggregate tax by further combining those categories in a specified way. If you have numerous investments, you can literally have thousands of permutations and combinations for dividing them into his and her baskets, determining what each of you would net in each scenario, and choosing the scenario with the largest combined net value.

Let's just say, as Clint Eastwood fans, that if you have a lot of investments that total a high-dollar value to divide up, and we saw you reaching for the calculator to try doing it yourself, we'd say, "Go ahead and make our day!" Professionals use sophisticated software to input all the basis and selling price information and quickly run through the permutations and combinations to optimize the result, for fees that are usually much less than what you stand to gain by determining the minimal tax scenario. Furthermore, a professional can also tell you whether it's better, from a combined tax standpoint, to sell some of the investments while you're married.

Finally, as with retirement accounts, problems crop up with investments that were brought into the marriage. These might include employer stock plans in which either of you regularly invested a monthly amount toward continued purchase of employer stock. Clearly, all stock purchased after marriage is marital property, and the current value of stock held before the marriage (not including reinvested dividends) should remain separate property. But if any stock was sold and commingled with marital funds, that amount becomes marital property.

Also, either of you might have separate brokerage accounts in which you've been trading throughout the marriage. While it's clear that any investments that remained intact during the marriage remain separate property, what about investments that you sold within the brokerage account, leaving them there in cash form or using the proceeds to make other investments? And what if you used marital funds, such as part of your salary, to make further investments in that account? There are no obvious answers to these situations, but you and your spouse can work together to fairly determine what part should be separate and what part is marital—if you have the will and sense of fairness to do so. Otherwise, a judge will rely, in a sometimes unpredictable way, on existing statutes and precedent cases to make the determination.

- *Cash value insurance:* Where was that divorce-insurance salesperson when he or she was really needed? Never mind. If the support-paying spouse ever purchased permanent life insurance, that policy might be golden now if its cash value is considerably less than its face value. Then it can be used to guarantee the continuation of payments should the paying spouse die prematurely (but don't get any ideas), which we cover in Chapter 8.

Otherwise, the cash value of life insurance purchased after the marriage is part of the marital property to be divided. But it should be evaluated carefully for both its tax consequences, upon sale, to either spouse, and as an investment that might not be ripe for liquidation. If its value is greater than the amount of premiums paid on it, then cashing it in would generate a taxable capital gain.

However, if the policy is relatively new, there not only won't be a capital gain but there might even be early-surrender penalties, which might not be tax deductible, that further reduce the puny cash value it has attained. So if its face value isn't enough to be used to guarantee payments, or it's not needed for that purpose, then it should be regarded as an investment that's guaranteed to produce a fairly good return as payments continue and its cash value races to catch up with the premiums paid into it. It's best not to cash it now and to make sure that the spouse who ends up owning it can keep up the premium payments. Again, if a considerable amount of money is involved, seek a financial advisor's opinion.

- *Annuities:* These present a similar, yet sometimes nightmarishly complex problems. In simplest terms, an *annuity* is an investment vehicle— usually purchased with a series of payments over many years preceding retirement, or a one-time payment at or near retirement—that provides an income stream during retirement. Some annuities also have death benefits, but they're usually not structured to serve the purpose of guaranteeing future payments to meet support obligations.

    Transferring annuity ownership in a settlement might be desirable to a recipient spouse only if the annuity has nearly matured. Otherwise, an annuity is often a risky (variable annuity bought partly for tax-deferred growth) or inferior-return (fixed annuity bought for guaranteed income) investment. Worse, they come with a decreasing scale (by each additional year owned) of large early-surrender (cash-in) charges due to the sizeable sales commissions that are built into the payments.

Personal Property

In *Minority Report*, people are arrested for their murderous intentions based on the psychic powers of three isolated, unusual beings. It didn't break any box-office records, but perhaps Tom Cruise won't continue suffering in poverty after getting the cold (mountain) shoulder from Nicole if it's licensed as a divorce-training film offering these lessons:

- Spouses needn't have psychic abilities to know what each other is thinking while dividing emotion-laden personal property—and it's a good thing they can't be arrested for it.
- Isolation is definitely an advantage; it's far better that only one spouse be there at a time when sizing up what he or she wants.
- Three people with or without psychic powers working together is often a good way to solve emotional issues; it's called "mediation."
- Don't spend a majority of divorce-decision time dividing what is usually only a small minority percentage of your assets.

Putting these lessons in concrete terms is an article by Anne Lober, an attorney with Divorce Helpline (www.divorcehelp.com), a California firm specializing in nonadversarial approaches to divorce resolution. Here's a condensed, adapted version of some of her suggestions:

1. Using two colors of Post-its, survey the house together, alternately marking desired items. Then make a his-and-hers two-column list from the result, and horse-trade if necessary from the lists you generate to come up with a financially and emotionally fair solution.
2. Skip the Post-its and just inventory all the items, listing them on one big sheet. Alternately initial things you want and continue as in suggestion 1.
3. With whatever division technique you end up using to come up with a split of roughly equal value, entertain cash offers for particular items to come up with a fair but unequal split. Of course, if one of you is staying in the marital home, an equal split probably doesn't make sense, so modify this approach by allowing for a tradeoff of less cash and more personal property, based on market (not replacement) value for the person remaining.

If you can't agree on any of these, Craig Ross has found that this often works: Have one person place personal items such as photos and videos in two "equal" piles. The other spouse gets to choose which pile he or she wants. From there, you can do further horse-trading with cash or items, and where possible, each party can reproduce items in the other pile at his or her own expense.

Dividing Debt

It's too late to do anything about your dead marriage, but now is definitely the time to do something about your debt (from) marriage. We could inundate you with a "debtly dull" list of everything you couldn't possibly want to know about family law in regards to debt and bankruptcy, but instead we'll offer you the following guidelines and refer you to a detailed example you'll find on the Split-Up Web site:

1. Identify all of your debts, including normal bills, taxes, mortgages and home-equity line-of-credit balances, loan and credit card balances, and legal judgments.
2. Classify each debt as to title (whose name it's in or if it's joint), who's responsible (100 percent, 50-50, 75-25, or other), whom the law will hold responsible (which spouse the creditor can come after), and whether any property is tied to the debt with a lien (such as a car to a car loan), or other unusual debts.
3. Identify all your property as to title, who you've agreed actually owns it (or what proportion of it), and whether it's tied to a loan.
4. For each item of property or debt, assign it a positive value for its market value, a negative value for what's owed, or either a positive or negative net value for any combination of debt and property tied to the debt.
5. Use this information to assign property and debt so that you end up with your agreed overall division of property—such as 50-50 or 60-40. Furthermore, nobody should be assigned a debt for which the other party can be legally pursued, so certain debts will normally have to be paid off or refinanced so that each ends up in the name of the party to whom it's assigned.

"Refinancing your marital consumer debt so that the parties leave the marriage with only debt in their own names is a great idea," says Craig Ross, "but it must not be easy because I rarely see it." That's why we've supplemented this procedure, which could be more complicated, in your case, than it appears with material on the Split-Up Web site (www.divorcesoftware.com/divorce_finance _book/debt_division procedure) There you'll find a more detailed comprehensive procedure, supplemented by the aforementioned full-fledged example.

Perhaps you'll still decide that you're unable to agree or don't want to try this yourselves. You should still at least organize the information as we have specified, so that you can negotiate or go to court having decided on these classifications, which will save a lot of time and money. You'll also be more aware of your vulnerabilities regarding debt that you could be responsible for based on the marriage, even if it hasn't been assigned to you.

Putting Property and Debt in Proper Perspective

It's only recently that historians have discovered the true antecedents of modern family and financial law, Patrick O' Henry's fiery fighting words "Give me liberty or give me debt." After all, in those days, liberty translated into property—because only property owners had full democratic privileges—and how could the common man afford it without borrowing?

Forgive us if that bit of blarney got your Irish up, but we did it to make a point: Because of the undue reverence we attach to property, it's easy to become irrationally consumed by the need to fight for the last dollar or piece of silverware. Instead, remember that property is just stuff, and even it's worth a million dollars, it's not as valuable as the $5 worth of chemicals that have been molded into your children. So do fight for what you need, but don't feel the need to fight.

Spousal Support

Do you owe your spouse a living, or vice versa? No, but most states recognize that everybody coming out of a marriage is owed a lifestyle that is as close as possible to the lifestyle they have a right to expect based on their lives before the marriage, the circumstances of the marriage and their independent prospects for the future. Yet on Internet "sound-off-type" bulletin boards, it's common to find divorce-related posts about how "she needs to get on with her life and not just think she can sponge off me for the rest of it," or "he can't just throw me out like a rancid piece of meat and think he can get away without paying for it." In some ways, both of those viewpoints totally miss the point of prevailing family law, and in others they're right on.

No matter how much you want to, you can neither erase the past created by you, your spouse, your children, and your marriage nor can you automatically perpetuate it. To view the issue of spousal support fairly, then, you need to acknowledge that marriage put each of you in a role that has become increasingly entrenched, the way clay hardens with age. But just as you can soften and remold high-quality clay no matter how old it is, people of character and integrity can remold themselves almost no matter how entrenched they've become in their marital roles. It just takes more time—the older the clay or the longer the marriage—to do the necessary bending while avoiding breaking.

Hence the dual concepts of rehabilitative support and long-term support. The more moldable the clay, the easier the transformation. In childless, relatively short marriages of a young spouse of modest means to a wealthier spouse, the laws don't provide much time for remolding. The economically lesser spouse enjoyed a period of elevated lifestyle while losing some opportunity to build self and a different family life. So that spouse might be entitled to some property consideration to make the transition from affluence to where he or she might have been otherwise had the marriage not occurred. But when children are involved, it's often an economically lesser spouse who takes on a role as homemaker. So even in a short-term marriage, that role has begun to harden and can't be remolded for some time. Thus, the courts often recognize both a property compensation and short-term support—in addition to child support—to help that homemaker spouse make up for and catch up to the lost earning power due to that marital role.

Of course, in many marriages where spouses have children and similar earning capacities, neither becomes a long-term homemaker, so perhaps the standard solution should be totally equal division of marital property, no spousal support, and joint custody that obviates the need for child support. Many judges would make that decision without blinking, but that doesn't mean you and your spouse should necessarily make that decision if you want to truly be fair.

For one thing, women still often take up to six months of unpaid leave with each child's birth. Many also get on the "mommy career track" that recognizes their family obligations in subtle ways—such as part-time hours for a year or so, flexible hours afterward, and no significant business travel or high-profile projects demanding 80-hour weeks. After several years of that, many mothers' careers lag, and they suffer diminished earning power and retirement-savings buildup. But increasingly it's the man who falls behind. Many couples end up putting whoever is less driven or more parentally inclined on the "parent track"—so "daddy trackers" who similarly sacrifice career are no longer a rarity. Thus, a truly fair settlement of most marriages involving one "parent track" spouse should tilt somewhat toward that spouse—with an uneven property split, spousal support, or a combination of both depending on such factors as available cash-equivalent assets and the tax situation. To determine how best to do this so that the parent-track spouse can comfortably and expeditiously upgrade earning power and become self-sufficient, cash flow projections for alternative scenarios involving property division and rehabilitative spousal support of various amounts and durations are crucial tools.

Most ranters on both sides have started to accept that philosophy. We're a long way, though, from the recognition of just how much roles have hardened in a longer-term marriage or in a marriage that began at the now commonly more advanced age than it might have 40 years ago.

Consider someone in his or her early 30s who has enjoyed a successful career, marries, and then becomes the homemaker when children enter the picture. A significant percentage of nonhomemaker spouses don't recognize just how molded or hardened he or she has become if the marriage ends less than 10 years later. Yet family law treats 10 years as the Maginot line between short-term and long-term marriage, so in a marriage falling short of the line, what becomes of the 40 year old with two young children who has been mostly out of the workforce during the prime career-ascendancy years? Law aside, ethics, fair play, humanity, and common sense all point to that spouse's being definitely entitled to extended help; without it, he or she has no chance of living even close to the marital lifestyle. So, getting back to the earlier rants, can you see a midway point that recognizes the validity of both arguments? Women, particularly, once argued in a fault-based divorce system that they were entitled to permanent alimony because they "gave him the best years of my life." Now, the no-fault reality is that a homemaker who has given the best economic-ascendancy years of life is entitled to some combination of generous property division and spousal support to compensate for earnings that will be considerably lower from here on than he or she would have had otherwise, not to mention lost pension and less Social Security buildup. And a spouse who has been in a truly long term marriage and has been devoted more to home, children, and spouse than to career might very well be entitled to lifetime support. Otherwise, he or she will have no chance to even come close to perpetuating the marital lifestyle, after really having given the best years of life in every way.

That said, it's been a long time since only one spouse wore the pants in the family. So in determining a fair settlement, we must also determine to what extent the homemaker spouse, within the bounds of possibility and plausibility, endeavored to have contributed to current or future family wealth by maintaining or increasing earning power through continued education, establishing a home business, working part-time, or productively managing the family finances. Furthermore, whatever help that lesser spouse is entitled to must be calculated within the bounds of the higher-earning spouse's capabilities to maintain at least some semblance of a reasonable lifestyle while supporting the ex-spouse and kids.

Forgive us for making a short socioeconomic story long, but we felt it necessary to avoid its losing something in the translation. Now that you unmistakably understand our philosophy in the context of current family law, let's put it into practice in determining spousal support.

Conditions for Spousal Support Award and Termination

Unlike child support, for which every state has exact formulas that are at least used as a starting point, most states don't yet (see sidebar) have spousal support formulas—and for seemingly good reason. Variables such as length of marriage, ages and health of the spouses, salaries and salary inhibition from homemaking, tax brackets and property division, and financial fault in the marriage make such formulas quite complex. If these variables sound familiar, it's because they are from the set of factors used to determine division of property in equitable distribution states (see earlier section). That's not surprising because property and spousal support are inextricably linked to the point that one man or woman's spousal support is another's majority property division.

Support for More Use of Mathematical Spousal-Support Formulas

While formula-based alimony guidelines are a major challenge, Craig Ross, the divorce expert we've frequently quoted, knows that Washtenaw and several other major Michigan counties use them. After all, he was their original chief author, and his Support 2004 software (www.marginsoft.com) embodies that methodology. It's been endorsed by the Family Law Section of the State Bar of Michigan—and he's also developed state-specific versions for mathematical guidelines used in parts of Kentucky and Washington. In addition, select counties in California, Pennsylvania, Kansas, and New Mexico now use mathematical alimony guidelines for at least some components of spousal-support determination.

Nevertheless, in a pure sense, family law philosophy generally starts by presuming a divorce should end a long-term marriage by equalizing property and income between the spouses—after subtracting the amount each spent on the children from his or her respective income. Few model marriages merit that exact treatment, but assuming we're dealing with one and have divided the property equally, here's the mathematical approach you'd use to create equal incomes:

1. Determine the net incomes of the higher-income and lower-income spouse.
2. Subtract child support paid from the higher net income to get net adjusted higher income.
3. Add the child support received to the lower net income and then subtract child-related expenses from the net lower income to get net adjusted lower income.
4. Subtract net adjusted lower income from net adjusted higher income and divide by 2.

By having the higher-income spouse then pay the result of step 4 to the lower-income spouse, the two spouses would have theoretically equal incomes after child support and additional child expenses. Mathematically inclined readers will immediately see flaws in this, such as the definition of net income, whether net income is the appropriate number, and tax effects related to the children—such as who gets favored filing status, various exemptions, deductions, and credits. Notwithstanding these technicalities, our purpose is to demonstrate a theoretically simple way of thinking about the objective of spousal support in a long-term marriage and how you might start from that point and take into account all the other factors to make adjustments.

In Chapter 9, though, we'll reveal a holistic approach to equitable property division and spousal support that overcomes many of these flaws and is easy to understand visually by use of graphs. Don't worry, though, we won't require that you listen to new-age music or wear 3-D goggles while you're reading it. Meanwhile, let's move on to the details of spousal support before you have to listen to old-age music and read with inch-thick glasses.

Rehabilitative Spousal Support

The largest percentage of cases that account for the increased divorce rate are shorter-term marriages. Where these involve no children, or haven't lasted long enough to firmly establish a "marital financial lifestyle," spousal support is rarely awarded because the spouses easily revert to their own premarital lifestyles. But when marriages are lengthier or involve children, that transition isn't simple, so if it's difficult for one spouse to become self-supporting after divorce, even taking into account child support, then either a favorable property settlement or short-term spousal support is often awarded to help "rehabilitate" that spouse back to a self-supporting state. The longer the marriage, however, the more awards go beyond the spouse simply becoming self-supporting towards being able to continue the marital financial lifestyle.

When significant marital property isn't involved, it's generally not practical or feasible to accomplish that rehabilitation by dividing property in favor of the economically lesser spouse, so spousal support is used. That's often an advantage to the paying spouse, anyway, because the payments are tax deductible to the higher-bracket payer and taxable to the lower-bracket recipient. In contrast, property transfer at divorce is a nontaxable event—although it can have tax consequences later when capital-gain property is sold.

The amount of support might cover getting further education to increase earning power, hiring child care help over an extended period for the long hours required to get that education or to put in long work hours, the down payment on a small condo, and similar items. So, theoretically, we'd calculate rehabilitative support along similar lines to our earlier income equalization calculation:

1. Determine the self-supporting, marital financial lifestyle, or in-between level of income to be achieved as appropriate to the marital circumstances.
2. Subtract the actual postdivorce income from the goal income to determine the income deficit.
3. Determine the time it will take to reach the goal income via rehabilitation.
4. Add the rehabilitative items that otherwise might have been paid for in the form of a favorable property division.
5. Divide the result of step 4 by the length of time in step 3 to get the "annual rehabilitative adjustment amount" (in other words, spreading the adjustment over the rehabilitation period).
6. Add the income deficit in step 2 to the annual rehabilitative adjustment amount step 5 to determine the annual amount of rehabilitative spousal support.

Ideally this method provides the recipient a self-supporting income until he or she is able to earn one, and the extra needed for rehabilitation. However, because expenses might occur unevenly or it might be tax advantageous, payments are sometimes structured unevenly by front-loading some of the rehabilitation amount. Or the recipient or payer might be uncomfortable with the period of time and want to shorten it or stretch it out to reduce financial pressure. It's far better to work it out between you to factor in these preferences and needs than to rely on the courts. Finally, you must factor in your mutual economic reality, which probably won't match this ideal.

Long-Term Spousal Support

What could be better than receiving a long-term spousal support award that will ensure the recipient's ability to maintain the marital lifestyle? Well, plenty—although that doesn't mean it isn't necessary and appropriate in many cases. If you've been in a long-term marriage in which one of you will fall far short of being able to continue the marital lifestyle after the divorce if you simply divide marital property 50-50 (again, see Chapter 9), read on for what to consider.

Lifetime Support Not Ideal for Either Spouse

Lifetime support obligations rub rough both ways. The paying spouse hates being tied to the receiving ex-spouse long after children are grown and after remarriage. The receiving spouse must be concerned about the continued payment. While life insurance might be acquired to guarantee payment upon the payer's death, and long-term disability insurance upon the payer's premature (before retirement) incapacity for work, what about job loss, early retirement, lower-paying, higher-satisfaction career changes, and simple loss of drive? While the recipient can go to court if payments become erratic or stop, we no longer have debtor prisons, and there's only so much the court system can do. Furthermore, although states such as Michigan commit the payer to full payments over the entire period designated in the spousal-support ruling or agreement, that's not the general rule. In many states, a payer whose circumstances have changed can conceivably get payments reduced or their term shortened—putting the kabosh on the recipient's plans if expected support were to suddenly decline or end.

Support and Court

Getting and keeping substantial permanent support almost always means court appearances, now and possibly later. Before demanding it, the potential recipient must step into the payer's shoes, and vice versa. Any reasonable person will resist substantial continued payments to anyone for the rest of their lives. If that weren't true, then half the B crime movies in existence never would have been made. So as undesirable as court seems, it's likely the case will end up there. From the opposite perspective when potential recipients weigh being shorted out of lifetime support that they feel is clearly indicated, court will be seem mandatory if a suitable support offer is otherwise not forthcoming.

Finite Support Creates a Future

By going on a program of lifetime support, in some ways both parties are also on a form of life support—living in the past, or not living with a zest toward the future. Life spans continue to increase, so even if divorce occurs well past 50, there's plenty to look forward to if you're not constantly reminded of the life that was and no longer is.

Don't misunderstand, we're not suggesting that lifetime support isn't often deserved. But practical considerations call for creative solutions out of court, such as finite periods with larger payments, highly tilted property settlements with front-loaded alimony (see next subsection), or permanent payments that start considerably higher and continually decrease. Some of these solutions might not result in the recipient's getting as much as was possible from fighting tooth and nail, but they should be considered if they're at least close to fair. The less the fighting, the less the professional fees and bitterness, the better for the kids and effective co-parenting, and the more emotionally equipped the supported spouse will be to move on constructively with the next phase of life.

Spousal Support Rules

Whether you or a judge determines spousal support, most state laws allow wide discretion, but you want to be sure that any agreement you make is accepted by the court. Thus, be aware of the following conditions that usually apply.

Spousal Support versus Child Support

Tax consequences are the biggest difference between spousal support and child support. The payer can deduct spousal support and the payee reports it as taxable income. Child support is neither deductible nor taxable. Except in a few states, you can't disguise child support as spousal support—to the dismay of high-bracket payers who want to be able to deduct higher amounts. Couples often err in tying reductions or termination of spousal support to the cessation of child support, which causes the spousal support to be reclassified as child support, thus no longer deductible to the payer.

You also can't tie the cessation of spousal support to any particular event in the children's lives such as entering high school or college. If the IRS determines that spousal support is improperly tied to child-related events, it might reclassify some or all of the payments as child support, which requires recalculation of both the payer's taxes based on the lost deductions and the recipient's taxes based on less income. The payer will owe the additional taxes plus interest and possibly penalties. Notwithstanding these IRS parameters, you still have a lot of leeway in structuring spousal support and child support to take advantage of the tax benefits of payments between parties who may be in different marginal tax rate brackets.

Spousal Support versus Property Division

Except in community property states, you have almost total flexibility to fashion an equitable settlement from whatever mix of property division and spousal support works best for the two of you. However, if you want the spousal support payments to be totally deductible to the payer, then you must take care when front-loading them with large payments in the first few years that decline from year to year. Otherwise, you're subject to *alimony recapture*—which would make the payer reclaim as income some of nonconforming excess payments that were originally used as tax deductions against income. To avoid recapture, the second year payment must not drop by more than $15,000 from the first year, and the third year must not drop by more than $15,000 from the second. Figure 7-3 contains two examples.

There's nothing illegal about structuring your payments in a way that will require recapture, but you don't want to be caught by surprise, because just as with spousal support reclassified as child support, the payer will be liable for additional taxes and interest, plus possible penalties. IRS Publication 504 contains a worksheet that shows how recapture is calculated.

Formalized Payments

Payments must be made under an agreement that's part of the divorce decree or a later modification, and must be in cash (preferably a check so as to prove payment). When filing federal taxes and claiming the deduction, the payer must include the payee's Social Security number. Payments can also be made to third parties on behalf of the payee (for example, mortgage payments) if this is part of the written agreement.

Payment Period

Payments can be over almost any period but must end with the payee's death—another consideration favoring front-loading them or arranging life insurance that would replace them if the payer dies before the payment term

FIGURE 7-3 SPOUSAL SUPPORT RECAPTURE EXAMPLES

	Year 1	Year 2	Year 3	Recapture Calculation?
Example 1	$60,000	$45,000	$30,000	No
Example 2	$65,000	$40,000	$30,000	Yes

ends. Also, in most states, payments normally end if the payee remarries (perhaps another form of death after a divorce?!), but the parties can agree to different terms that don't necessarily preclude continued payment—such as renegotiating payments—upon the payee's remarriage. As mentioned earlier, payments shouldn't terminate within six months on either side of a "child-related contingency," such as turning 18, graduating from high school, or getting married; otherwise, they could be deemed child support. These rules become even more complex when you have more than one child.

Revising the Support Agreement or Ruling

Depending on your state's laws, both the payer and receiver have the option of going back to court to attempt a reduction or increase in payments and a shortening or lengthening of the term of spousal support. However, it's not something you should count on, and you and your spouse will usually be mutually best served by coming to a "nonmodifiable" support agreement, if that's possible in your state, to avoid any future surprises.

Child Support

If your family is neither in severe economic distress nor quite wealthy, you should find child support one of the easier issues to resolve in your divorce—as long as you're willing to ignore the "unfairness hype" (too little, too much) by "divorcing" it from the yours-or-mine issues of property, spousal support, and child custody. After all, state formulas are based on well-defined elements that are consistent with the reality that the split-up family unit cannot live at the same standard that the intact family did. Consequently, they tend to err on the side of not making the payer feel too squeezed—thus usually awarding not quite enough to enable kids to continue living in the way to which they were accustomed. If you can't put your children's interests first, then perhaps you deserve the outcome that renowned financial planner and author Adrienne Berg reported about a New York couple: They haggled so much over who should get the house that the judge awarded it to their 8-year-old child.

Of course, the house isn't really a child support issue, but the story's message is clear: Don't be children about child support or which of you gets the best and most toys. Lopsided settlements intensify anxiety and instability inherent in divorce, and children often blame themselves for the "losing" parent's predicament. Here's how mature adults should deal with it.

Definition of Child Support

Child support laws have become increasingly controversial with intensified scrutiny of just what constitutes child support and how long it should last. The specific expenses that child support is intended to cover vary from state to state, but this statement from the Kansas guidelines is typical: "The purpose of child support is to provide for the needs of the child. The needs of the child are not limited to direct needs for food, clothing, school, and entertainment. Child support is also to be used to provide for housing, utilities, transportation, and other indirect expenses related to the day-to-day care and well-being of the child."

Normally, child support ends at the age of majority—18 in most states but 21 in some. However, when children require continued support as adults due to disabilities or other circumstances, most states allow courts to order support indefinitely.

Formula-Based Child Support Determination

State formulas for child support are somewhat of a "black box"—in that you enter a few key items of salary and other financial information and out pops the award determination. Inside the box, though, the gears are crunching through a series of basic steps depending on which of three models that state uses to build its formula: Percentage of Income, Income Shares, or Melson.

Percentage of Income Model

The Percentage of Income Model is used in only 13 states and is keyed to the higher-income spouse's income, not even taking into account the lower-income spouse's income.

Income Shares and Melson Models

Thirty-five states use the predominant Income Shares Model, which in qualitative terms goes something like this:

1. Determine each spouse's income before any adjustments. Although this seems straightforward, it is complicated in cases when income isn't just salary from an employer—such as income derived from the earner's owned business, or compensation that includes substantial stock options. Furthermore, courts will sometimes use *imputed income* (what the parent could or should be earning) in cases in which it's established that the parent is underemployed by choice.

2. Determine the support needed based on the combined incomes, children's ages, and other factors that vary significantly between different states.

3. Adjust the incomes by subtracting any spousal support paid from the higher (payer) income and adding it to the lower (receiver). Many states have additional adjustments based on each spouse's tax liability, tax credits the custodial spouse receives for child care payments, support payments for children from a previous marriage, and amounts specifically agreed to by the spouses for medical insurance.

4. Apportion the child support responsibility in proportion to each spouse's adjusted incomes. For example, suppose the support needed based on step 2 is $1000 per month, one spouse's adjusted income is $60,000, and the other's is $40,000. Then the higher-earning spouse is responsible for 60 percent of the needed support, or $600 monthly.

5. Adjust the final total downward in relation to the amount of time the paying spouse has custody in a joint (physical) custody situation. Many states also make downward adjustments when the paying spouse exceeds a certain threshold of visitation (percentage of nights a year the child spends there). This adjustment is not necessarily strictly proportional because the receiving spouse still has to pay for the "support infrastructure" whether the child is there or not, and states make it in a variety of different ways.

In addition, the Melson Model—developed by a Delaware family court judge, and also used in Hawaii and Montana—is an "advanced" version of the Income Shares Model. You can find out more about these models and which one your state uses at the National Conference of State Legislatures Web site (www.ncsl.org/programs/cyf/models.htm).

Regardless of model or state, for many middle-class couples, the formulaic result often ends up being used as the actual amount of child support agreed to or awarded. But circumstances often warrant adjustment. For example, suppose the property settlement was tilted significantly toward the lower-earning spouse and included substantial assets that could be liquidated and reinvested in bonds or other income-producing securities. Then the court might consider the recipient's income to be understated in the formula and impute a higher income to recalculate based on the potential additional income.

Child Support Formula Limitations

The formulas serve as little more than a starting point in the case of children with special needs or other unusual circumstances. For example, if the custodial spouse moves to another state, then the paying spouse's cost of visitation will increase substantially, quite possibly warranting a downward adjustment in support to partially make up for the travel costs.

The bigger problem, though, comes in the way that formulas impute the total cost of supporting a child. Men's groups have been extremely vocal in claims that most formulas actually build in a margin for additional child support, while some advocacy groups for children and families have argued that the formulas are skimpy based on the spending of typical families for their children.

One of your authors, Alan Feigenbaum, weighs in on this subject in both directions as the author of the book *A Parent's Guide to Money, Raising Financially Savvy Children* (Parent's Guide Press, October 2002). On the one hand, statistics definitely support the finding that child support formulas generally fall well short of what we do spend on our children. On the other, there's no question that we excessively spend on our children because as parents we've abdicated to their clamoring for wants rather than focusing on their needs. While the result of child support formulas might well be close to meeting true needs, how can we, with a straight face, pull the rug out from under the spending patterns to which children have become accustomed? Shared sacrifice is necessary in divorce, and that would indicate finding some middle ground between the higher levels of spending on children that existed before the divorce and the sparse levels produced by many of the formulas.

That overspending is probably one reason why most state formulas apply to only those incomes below a certain level. They're not flexible enough to work for more affluent families, making child support determination a more treacherous battleground. If you fall into this category, or otherwise intend to deviate from the amount specified by the child support formulas, be aware that you're walking a tightrope between falling into too much of a squeeze on the paying partner on one side, and giving your child a message that he or she is worth only that much on the other. And make no mistake, if financial pressures are greatly exacerbated in either household due to the stinginess or excess of the child support award, your child(ren) will know about it due to spoken or subtle recriminations for which he, she, or they might end up even serving as the conduit.

Paying for College

To address these limitations, support rules are changing to a degree—particularly a college degree. State legislatures and courts are increasingly recognizing that support should include expenses for college or other postsecondary education. Most states with a majority age of 21 now include college expenses, but many other states have specifically ruled or legislated the college education obligation.

Based on the accelerated trend, it's only a matter of time until many states that don't currently require it will—and might even apply it retroactively to previously divorced parents with children who still have college ahead of them. In planning your divorce, then, you'd be wise to include a provision that apportions responsibility for providing the children funds for college. Failing that, you should at least plan to save toward that objective, because a later order could compel you to provide that support. And definitely plan on the need to coordinate with your ex-spouse; if your child applies to colleges that require the College Board's PROFILE form for financial aid, then both the custodial and noncustodial spouses have to provide detailed financial information. In addition, many other colleges have their own financial aid forms that require information from both parents.

The thought of how you'll ever pay for college might well have you rattled. Do keep in mind, though, that if required, most states won't make you pay for any college your child might want, regardless of how high the price. However, you might be expected to meet an amount somewhat in proportion to your income. Furthermore, financial aid based on your ability to pay from income and assets remains plentiful, although loans are becoming a greater percentage of the package. In concert, colleges are giving away more money in merit scholarships for the top tier of applicants—especially colleges trying to elevate themselves from moderately selective to highly selective. So make the divorce as smooth and amicable as possible, so that your child doesn't suffer the too-common postdivorce drop in academic achievement.

Child Support State-Specific Guidelines and Formulas

Child support is such a complex issue that someone could write a whole book about it; in fact, someone has. The most comprehensive source available on child support is a combination of Web site (www.supportguidelines.com) and related book: *Child Support Guidelines, Interpretation and Application* (Aspen Law & Business, 1996 and supplements). The Web site has comprehensive links to online child support calculators, as well as full child support guidelines that spell out what child support is meant to cover and what goes into calculating it in each of the 50 states. Don't ignore the guidelines; to make the results meaningful, issues such as complex income calculations must be resolved through use of the guidelines before numbers are put into the formulas.

Postdivorce Child Support Adjustments

Because child support is an issue unto itself financially and it is not tied to the agreements made about property and spousal support, it is subject to change at any time to reflect changed circumstances, such as the following:

- Either spouse's income changes significantly.
- Spousal support payments end.
- The cost of supporting the children changes significantly.
- One of the children reaches majority age, 18 or 21 depending on your state.
- Changes in custody arrangements or visitation.

Preferably, you and your spouse should be able to work out a new amount and simply formalize it through the court—particularly if the amount you previously agreed to was based on your state's support calculator. But even if you can't, there's no reason to make it another battle. Perhaps the circumstances are complicated enough that the two of you just can't easily figure it out. In that case, you should be able to go to court without the need for battling it out between the attorneys. Whether you work it out with your spouse or go to court, if you're the custodial spouse, you'll help your cause by having tracked the child-related expenses. While the support guidelines don't require you to prove how you've spent the money, they do require you to demonstrate why a change is necessary due to changed circumstances such as higher expenses.

Enforcing Child Support Payment

Unfortunately, even when child support is awarded or agreed to, it isn't always paid. Those who fear that they'll never see a dollar from what the court awards can take heart in a late-2002 news story about the federal court conviction (with prison time) of the author of *Dirty Divorce Tricks*. Robert H. Morrison had defied a 1990 Arizona order by failing to pay child support, cutting off contact with his son, and living in California under assumed names until authorities caught up with him.

Fortunately for custodial spouses who depend on it, child support enforcement has come a long way since 1990. The federal Office of Child Support Enforcement (OCSE) in the U.S. Department of Health and Human Services acts as an umbrella organization for the 51 state enforcement programs. Nationwide collections have increased dramatically since the 1996 welfare-reform legislation granted the OCSE increased enforcement powers and funds to facilitate interstate enforcement. Although the programs originated to help ex-spouses without financial resources to legally pursue enforcement, they now fully serve everybody—regardless of income.

If you should need the OSCE, it can help garnish a payer's wages, locate and freeze accounts, and route funds to you to cover back and current payments—as well as suspend the payer's driver's license, assess civil penalties, and prosecute. Find out about the federal and state services available on this Web site: www.acf.dhhs.gov/programs/cse/index.html.

Health Insurance

Not long ago, financial responsibility for health insurance was almost an afterthought in divorce cases, but ignoring it today is extremely hazardous to your financial health. While married, you had the tremendous advantage of group family coverage—possibly from either of your employers, or as a member of various professional or other organizations. But even individual policy family coverage, which is quite expensive, is often cheaper overall than what you might collectively pay once you've divorced. It's imperative that you investigate the alternatives available so that the cost will be considered when you are arriving at a settlement.

Here are your options in descending order of preference:

- *Two employer policies:* Cover one spouse and the kids under one employer policy and the other spouse under the other employer's policy. You can choose either employer, regardless of who is the custodial spouse and whether or not a noncustodial spouse claims the children as dependents. Don't necessarily include them under the cheapest, though, if one policy offers much better coverage for kids, such as well-child visits, than the other.
- *One employer policy:* If everybody is now covered under one employer's policy, you can continue that coverage in New Hampshire and a few other states, regardless of the divorce. However, the rate might be higher because of the new status of the employee's ex-spouse.
- *Neither of first two options available:* If the spouse who had been covered as a dependent can't get employer coverage or finds that it's significantly inferior to what he or she had during the marriage, then the kids can remain on or switch to the employer-covered spouse's policy as dependents. The spouse can also continue under the ex-spouse's plan for a

period of three years with a special divorced status under the provisions of the national COBRA law (if your spouse is a snake, that's purely coincidental). However, the total cost of coverage for the "family" will now be much higher because the COBRA-covered spouse's premium will be 102 percent of what that employer is charged by the insurer to provide that coverage. If you use this option, you'll want to begin looking for other coverage immediately, preferably by changing jobs to an employer with good coverage or finding the best possible individual coverage.

Regardless of which path you choose, be careful of any settlement that designates one spouse to keep the other spouse covered, COBRA or otherwise, under an employer or other group plan—or that depends on one spouse paying directly for the other spouse's coverage. That spouse could conceivably drop the other spouse's coverage carelessly or maliciously, so make sure you and your spouse are on good terms if you go that route. One way to set it up is to have the independent spouse pay the dependent spouse what it costs as part of the deductible spousal support. The dependent spouse can either reimburse the payer for the after-tax amount or not, depending on the overall spousal support package.

Spousal coverage might be the least of your worries though, because escalating costs cause many settlement battles over just the kids' coverage. Noncustodial spouses can't assume that they're not responsible for covering kids because child support laws recognize health insurance as a necessity that must be budgeted. If you can't resolve this issue, the custodial parent might need a court-granted *qualified medical child support order* (QMCSO) to force the noncustodial parent to provide coverage and give the custodial spouse full access to plan information.

Just arranging coverage isn't enough. Your settlement must spell out who's responsible for any deductibles, copayments, and uninsured medical expenses. And it should also deal with the possibility of either spouse's losing health coverage or significant changes in the policy's rates or services offered. For example, many plans have recently started requiring significant employee sharing of the premium with the employer where they once were either free or much less expensive. Or they now charge significantly more for more than one child, instead of a package rate for any number of children. You might want your agreement to spell out specific dollar amounts that each spouse will provide to combine for the current responsibility and how any increases will be split between you.

Social Security

Say what you want about Social Security, but for homemakers who've been divorced from long-term marriages, it's one of the best things going. The double-good news is that ex-spouses who were married at least 10 years are entitled to benefits tied to the benefits the ex-spouse will receive, and those benefits don't cost the ex-spouse a dime. Here are the details:

- *Marriage length:* You must have been married at least 10 years, been divorced from that spouse at least two years, be at least age 62 (that age is likely to increase in the future), and not be married at the time you apply for benefits. However, if you are remarried but the second marriage occurred after you reached age 60, you are still eligible.
- *Ex-spouse's benefit:* You're entitled to either half of the benefit to which your ex-spouse is entitled or to a benefit based on your own earnings; you don't get both!
- *Multiple marriages:* If you were in more than one 10-year marriage, you're entitled to either a benefit based on your own earnings or the largest of the ex-spouse benefits.
- *Survivor's benefit:* If your ex-spouse died and you're over the age of 60, and you didn't remarry before age 60, you're entitled to the full benefit for which your deceased ex-spouse was eligible, called a *survivor's benefit.* However, if you did remarry before age 60 but otherwise meet the conditions, you become eligible for the survivor's benefit upon your divorce from or the death of your new spouse. If you're already receiving the ex-spouse's benefit at the time you become eligible for survivor's benefits, your benefit will be changed from the normal ex-spouse's benefit to the survivor's benefit.
- *Disability:* More liberal conditions apply if you become disabled.

All these conditions mean that if you are over 55 when you divorce and you were not in the workforce for a good part of your marriage, you might want to defer any new marriage until you reach the age of 60. However, if your ex-spouse was not a high earner and you have good earning potential, you'll ultimately be better off with your own benefit. In that event, you should plan to work until the age of 70 and qualify for enhanced benefits based on your own earnings, but you'll still be able to collect the ex-spouse's benefit until your own benefit kicks in.

For complete details on Social Security benefits for ex-spouses, check out this section of the Social Security Web site: www.ssa.gov/women/women2. htm#divorcedspouse.

More Complex Divorce Issues

This chapter has covered most financial issues that you're likely to confront related to your divorce. However, skim Chapter 8 to see if any of the more complex issues it covers apply to you, and read it carefully if any of the following issues apply.

- *Commingled (mixed) funds:* You and your spouse have problems regarding the classification of various financial accounts because of commingling of funds that either of you believe should be considered separate property. (Don't mistake this with your divorce being caused by too much spousal fun mingling.) Or your assets include trusts or other sophisticated financial instruments.
- *Potential hidden assets:* You have reason to believe that your spouse is hiding assets, or enough assets are at stake that you should trace assets even if you have no suspicions.
- *Complex finances:* Either spouse has a defined-benefit pension, owns a business, or has a sophisticated employee benefits package that might include stock options or nonqualified deferred compensation.
- *Major spousal support anticipated:* You plan a settlement that relies on substantial spousal support paid over a period of time, so you might need to ensure its receipt through measures such as life insurance, long-term disability insurance, or some type of trust.
- *Estate planning concerns:* You have complex estate planning issues that might be due to previous marriages, overall wealth, or the potential that one of you will remarry soon.

Chapter 8 won't answer every conceivable question, but it will address most of the "common un-common" financial issues you might face in divorce.

Chapter 8

Complex Divorce Financial Issues

As Gilda Radner so aptly put it, "there's always something." Unfortunately, just as she had little control over the something that took her away from us too soon, you probably had little control over many of the somethings that might have ended your marriage too soon. However, you *do* have some control over many of the money divorce somethings that, if neglected, could permanently undo your postmarital finances.

We covered the more straightforward somethings in Chapter 7, saving for (this) Chapter 8 those for which you'll almost certainly need sophisticated divorce-professional financial consultation. So we'll provide only enough information to ensure that even Gilda Radner's inept reporter, Emily Litella, could understand it—and maybe even your spouse . . . oh, "never mind!" In any event, don't experiment with home-grown solutions to these complexities, or your divorce could become even more of a monster than the "Young Frankenstein" for which Gilda's widower, Gene Wilder, is best known.

Property

Chapter 7 dealt with the basic divorce decisions concerning what you own and what you owe. Determining what you own, however, sometimes takes a Watergate "what did he or she own and when did he or she own it?" prosecutorial mentality. Namely, regarding commingled accounts, future income attributable to marriage, hidden assets, and similar property issues, you might have to "follow the money" to answer what, when, where, who, and why.

Apportioning Separate, Marital, and/or Community Property

You'll recall that solving the "problem of property" is a two-stage process consisting first of classifying the property as separate or marital (or community in some states), and then dividing all forms of property—sometimes including separate property. We devoted most of the Chapter 7 discussion of property to the division aspect, and we covered only the basics of classification, so let's take a closer look at some of the classification complications.

Problem Property

If Lewis Carroll, the mathematician and author of *Alice in Wonderland,* had written "Alice in Divorce Court," he might have had her say, "The property owned by either or both spouses belongs to whom it can be traced as belonging to (in whole or in part), no more and no less." However, most states have "dual classification" systems where any property item can be considered part separate (husband, wife, or both) and part marital or community. Thus, in our seemingly straightforward "Alice principle" lies one of the biggest challenges in divorce—determining the percentage ownership of the following types of property:

- *Premarital and still separate:* These are financial accounts or noncash property items that were separate before marriage and remain titled that way. Interest or dividends paid on such property, even though they might be reinvested in more of the same property (such as a stock's dividend reinvestment plan) or within the same account (such as a brokerage "sweep subaccount") are usually considered marital or community property. In all states, a property's value upon marriage remains separate property, but in many states, the subsequent gain on it is either part or all marital or community property (see Figure 7-2); some states consider the capital gain to be marital, but allow the inflation component of passive appreciation to be combined with the original separate property value.

    Thus, if a husband gives a wife a valuable diamond necklace before marriage, the wife's separate property is the necklace's value at the time of marriage, and the appreciation on the necklace is usually (in other words, "in most states") either part or all marital or community property. If, before the marriage, a wife gives a husband 100 shares of a stock, then the dividends earned from then until the marriage and the value of that stock on the day of the wedding is the husband's separate property. But the subsequent dividends and capital gain on the stock are usually marital or community property. Finally, one special case involves distributions of income or corpus—that is, the principal—from a trust established for one spouse either before or during the marriage, and trust earnings during marriage. If the trust was established before the marriage, then the value of its corpus at the time of the marriage is definitely separate property. But the treatment of trust distributions and earnings during marriage, and even the value of the trust upon gifting during marriage, depends on how it was set up and the laws of your state. We cover this more below.

- *Separate property received during marriage:* Similarly, property given to or inherited by either spouse separately during marriage remains separate property unless it is commingled. However, the subsequent appreciation during the marriage on such property is treated the same as the appreciation on property that was separate coming into the marriage.
- *"Mixed" marital/community property:* This concerns "real property" (not financial securities). It is property acquired during marriage from partly separate funds, or from funds generated during marriage from selling real property that was separate before marriage—for example, the purchasing of a home after marriage with a combination of separate and joint funds. If the spouses have agreed that the ownership in the home is not strictly marital, but that pieces of it can be attributed to each one's separate contributions, then the apportionment of its value between marital/community and separate must take that into account—a nontrivial calculation, to be sure! Furthermore, regardless of the source of funds for "purchasing" the house, if there's a mortgage being paid from marital funds, then the house will definitely be at least part marital/community property.
- *Commingled accounts:* These are premarital separate accounts infused with funds derived during marriage or from the other spouse's separate funds—or accounts established during marriage that are partially composed of funds originally in separate accounts. They're often classified as marital or community unless the person who provided the separate funds can document and successfully argue his or her continued separate ownership.
- *Premarital separate active investments:* This category includes investment real estate, collections, and other types of investments that rise and fall in value partly due to the efforts of the owner. Normally, the portion of the marital appreciation of such property due to efforts by either spouse during the marriage is marital or community property, as is the net income from rents or other payouts. However, the "natural appreciation"—that attributable to purely market forces—is often at least partly separate property. Depending on your state's law, the part of that

gain that might be attributable to "inflation" could be considered separate property that "keeps whole" the property's value at the time of
marriage.

Transmutation of Property

By the time you've completed your divorce, you might consider the whole family law system and the people in it a malformed mutation of life on Earth as it
should be. So it's no surprise that the transformation of property that was separate into marital or community property is called *transmutation*. In all the situations just described, transmutation can take place, and the onus is on you in
two ways to prove that the following is or is not the case:

1. Separate property that has been commingled with marital assets or
    separate funds used during marriage still belongs to you.
2. Property titled separately in your spouse's name is all or partly marital
    or community if transmutation has taken place.

That onus, though, is subject to the trust and goodwill that you and your
spouse can bring to the settlement process. Regardless of what a court would
decide, it behooves the two of you to do the classification yourselves, but if
complex situations such as these exist, make sure you at least consult an attorney to determine the court's likely classification in your jurisdiction. And if a
lot of property is involved, and you're unable to agree, you might want to retain
the services of a forensic accountant to "map the money flow" and classify property accordingly.

Hidden, Overlooked, Protected, and Dissipated Property

It's hard enough to classify property when you know what it is and where it is.
You really have your work cut out for you, though, when you've accidentally
forgotten about it, or—more likely—your spouse has made it hard to get at,
has hidden it, or has just plain gotten rid of it. If your spouse is sitting on his
or her assets, here's how to get your assets in gear to stop it.

Protected Assets

Short of dealing with the outright fraud involved if your spouse is hiding, dis-
sipating, or disguising the true value of assets, you might have to fight against
a possibly legal financial structure specifically established to protect your spouse's
assets from a divorce settlement. There's no shortage of vendors who push com-

prehensive asset-protection schemes to physicians, other highly paid professionals, and wealthy entrepreneurs. Underlying their strategies is a complex labyrinth of pathways to the money that's intended to discourage spouses by making it expensive and time-consuming to value and reach the assets. Here are some of their techniques:

- *Corporate liens:* They create shell corporations that hold liens on marital or separate property.
- *Privacy-protected assets:* They create financial structures that own assets, with the identity of that ownership protected by privacy.
- *Layering:* They create a layer of financial structures that each own parts or all of each other
- *Friendly foreign and domestic jurisdictions:* They hold assets in offshore trusts or limited liability companies in Panama, the Cayman Islands, and other foreign jurisdictions whose laws help keep them out of reach of rulings. Protective trusts and various protective corporate structures can also be used in states such as Nevada and Delaware.
- *Family limited partnership (FLP):* The FLP is a complex asset-ownership arrangement that has several advantages in estate planning but can also potentially protect one spouse's assets in a divorce. When an FLP is created for either spouse's birth family, it can be used to shield that spouse's FLP "partnership interest" as separate property not subject to equitable or community division. If that doesn't succeed, the FLP offers a second layer of protection with "creative" use of an otherwise well-accepted accounting technique that "discounts" the spouse's assets held in it, thus reducing the total amount of that spouse's assets subject to division.
- *Asset protection trusts:* They set up a trust in a child's name that retains control over the assets—even though the assets should be considered marital property if they are not totally dedicated to a child's support.

If you're facing one or more of these situations because your spouse appears to be up to no good, then the law could well side with you, ultimately. But you must weigh the financial and personal cost of seeing the battle through to the end versus getting an approximate idea of what is at stake and compromising for somewhat less than you might otherwise get. In fact, some schemes can ultimately be unraveled because your spouse was the victim of an unscrupulous or unqualified advisor who set up something that is actually tax evasive or otherwise illegal—such as many of the offshore schemes once thought to be "bulletproof." A forensic accountant could advise you on whether that's the likely case, and you'll then know for sure whether you're much better off settling for assets that aren't tied up in such schemes because those that are might end up confiscated by the IRS—regardless of who gets them.

Hidden Assets

Because the formal discovery process requires full disclosure, with failure to comply possibly a criminal offense, the protector will often reveal such protected assets voluntarily—confident that they'll remain out of settlement reach. But the law is murkier in settlements without formal discovery, so the "asset protector" might follow a "didn't ask, so won't tell" strategy—turning some of the asset-protection strategies just discussed into asset concealment. Or the asset protector might simply fail to fully disclose protected assets during formal discovery—hoping they won't be found during formal discovery but taking an "oh yeah, those" approach if they are.

In addition, though, many spouses deliberately hide assets using these methods:

- *Purchasing bearer securities:* A *bearer security* is not registered to anyone anywhere. It belongs to whoever is holding it at a particular time. These securities include bearer bonds, savings bonds, and travelers' checks that aren't held in financial accounts.
- *Purchasing jewelry, rare stamps or coins, or other valuables:* These items can easily be liquidated for close to their purchase price. In some cases, the items aren't even concealed because the spouse doesn't even realize they have value.
- *Opening fraudulent accounts:* Fraudulent accounts are opened with a phony name with phony identification.
- *Using fraudulent business entities:* There are numerous variations of this basic technique: one spouse creates phony business entities that make phony loans that are then repaid, with cash the spouse wants to hide, through still other phony entities.
- *Fraudulently using a legitimate business:* One spouse uses a legitimate business entity in a fraudulent way to hide or launder money that is subsequently siphoned out to that spouse's hidden or phony-name accounts.
- *Maintaining rigged books:* One spouse manipulates figures in a business's books so that the business entity, although operating and existing legitimately, appears to be worth much less than it actually is.
- *Fraudulently colluding to hide income:* One spouse teams with a customer or employer to delay payment for services rendered or salary

owed so that the payment hasn't yet occurred and been "booked" when records are supplied to the other spouse.

Dissipated Assets

Unfortunately, it's hard to establish that criminal behavior has occurred if a spouse hides assets in another way—by literally making them disappear. A "get while the getting is good" spouse might live the high life in one or more extra-marital relationships; take expensive excursions in the guise of business trips; gamble money away at the track, casino, or in ill-advised business ventures; shoot up or snort money away; or otherwise spend down the marital pot. Or he or she might sink marital money into a successful business and then fraud-ulently hide the money or disguise the true increased value of the business. In most cases, the spouse will be ultimately accountable to the extent that such dissipation of assets can be traced.

It won't do the innocent spouse much good, though, if the guilty spouse doesn't have much in separate assets available to replace the dissipated assets, and has spent down most marital assets. The good news is that where there's smoke (the ashes of dissipated assets), it can help lead you, with the possible assistance of a trained professional, to the fire—before it burns up other hidden assets you might be able to recover in time to make up for the dissipated assets.

Finding Assets

When spouses must overcome their partners' attempts to cover their assets, it's no time to be passive, and, in fact, they must be ready to kick some assets in response. Their first line of financial self-defense should be the kind of personal sleuthing referred to in Chapter 2: make copies of all accessible financial records and information that might relate to finding other financial records. If they find less than seems to fit their lifestyle, or they know their spouse is secretive, the next rung of aggression is the formal discovery process, which is usually suffi-cient if the spouse is likely to fear criminal sanctions for nondisclosure. How-ever, they might need the full muscle of a "trust but verify" approach that also involves the use of a *forensic accountant*—generally a CPA trained to trace all the financial activities of a person or business entity.

Choosing an asset-finding strategy involves weighing the cost of discovery and (possibly) a forensic accountant versus the likelihood that hidden assets exist and the amounts that might be hidden. One way to initially hedge is by gathering information through personal sleuthing and engaging a forensic accountant on a limited basis to look first for surface discrepancies. That result will help you decide whether to further engage a forensic accountant to delve more deeply in a comprehensive inventory of both obvious and potentially hidden marital and spousal assets.

Complex Property Division Valuation

It can be challenging enough to find all financial and tangible property. But if your spouse is an inventor, writer, or practitioner of the fine arts—or even just a powerful thinker—you might have valuable property, and not even realize it, in the form of a written idea, sketch, or model. Perhaps your spouse has contracts relating to such intangible property for services that will be delivered in whole or in part after your divorce. Or he or she might be the current or future beneficiary of a trust. You must inventory all current and marriage-related future tangible and intangible property, because it might be subject to division or it might affect the division of divisible property. Here's why ideas are not only powerful but profitable, and why (a) trust is a valuable commodity.

Intangible, Intellectual, and Artistic Property

Suppose your spouse is a struggling writer who has made some money from having articles and stories published, and a small advance on one published book. He or she has just completed the manuscript for a second one but hasn't yet submitted it—although you've read excerpts from it and know that it's really good. What if you were to divorce and see that book on the bestseller's list two years from now? Shouldn't you be entitled to some significant share of the royalties?

In some states, the answer is clearly that you're not entitled if the book isn't under contract or hasn't been copyrighted prior to the divorce. In other states, though, the book is a work product with economic value derived in large part during the marriage—although subsequent revisions and promotion of the final product after the marriage might contribute to a lot of its ultimate value. Some states or judges recognize only its probable ultimate value, determining the portion of it that should be shared based on how much of its ultimate value the work now represents. Others grant the share of its ultimate value represented by the portion of the work completed during the marriage—much as a spouse is entitled to a share of the portion of the other spouse's pension earned during marriage.

Sorry that we can't give you more valuable advice about future value. But we can tell you not to ignore that potential value and to make sure your attorney has a good handle on your state's treatment of such property and involves or refers you to appropriate specialists to value it. To find the right specialist, you should distinguish between two types of property:

1. *Copyright or trademark:* This consists of creations that you generally would copyright or trademark to protect their originality, such as the following:
   - Computer software, video games, or an innovative Web site
   - Paintings, sculptures, photographs, or other works of fine art
   - Story, book, or play manuscripts
   - Sheet music and original-music CDs
   - TV scripts or screen plays
2. *Intellectual property:* This type of property is generally the product of new mathematical or scientific ideas, methods, or processes. It's usually characterized by warranting a patent that gives its creator ownership, or a license allowing use for a fee. Some examples:
   - Inventions or improved product designs (for example, a golf club that always strikes the ball squarely and straight)
   - New or better psychological tests (for example, to improve personnel selection)
   - New or more accurate mathematical formulas (for example, to improve weather forecasting)
   - New chemical formulations (for example, to make quantum leaps in fuel efficiency)
   - A new laboratory procedure (for example, to test DNA more quickly and cheaply)

Although we've separated the two categories, in reality the lines between them are somewhat blurred. In general, though, you'd want an attorney who specializes in artistic property for the former and one who specializes in intellectual property for the latter. In either case, the process of estimating a value for such property is definitely more art than science.

Creative Property and Future-Service Contracts

Determining your share is easier when the type of property just discussed has already been marketed so that its value is established by a contract. For example, your spouse might have a book contract that paid half the advance upon signing, the other half upon acceptance of the manuscript, and a percentage of the royalties on all copies sold after the first 10,000. Or he or she might have a contract to adapt an existing book into a screenplay, with a flat fee payable upon completion, and a percentage of the profits from the movie, video, and so on. While such contracts are straightforward, their ultimate value can only be estimated, so you must base the settlement on either a current estimate or on a certain percentage of the future earnings as they're paid out.

Next are contracts for future services that are explicit concerning income to be received. For example, suppose someone about to be divorced is either generally famous or an expert in demand based on accomplishments during marriage—such as winning an Olympic gold medal. Consequently, the celebrity spouse signs a personal-services contract for hundreds of thousands of dollars over the next five years to make appearances and give motivational speeches. Although that work will be done after the marriage, the celebrity spouse was given it because of efforts during the marriage, and it's reasonable for the other spouse to feel entitled to a significant share (although certainly less than half) of those earnings stemming from marital accomplishments.

Taking it one step further, though, suppose the celebrity spouse deliberately delays signing any such contracts until after separation or marriage in order to avoid having to share the earnings. The other spouse might reasonably assert that contract negotiations took place during the marriage, entitling that spouse to a share of the future earnings when and if the contract is signed.

That future payback for current worth doesn't have to be of Olympic proportions. Suppose that during marriage, one spouse develops a new personal-coaching technique that helps top scientists become more productive researchers. Consequently, he or she signs a lucrative five-year contract to work with the scientists in a large corporation that does extensive R&D. Clearly, this personal coaching will involve demanding hands-on work, so the spouse doing it should be entitled to a large share of the income from it. But the technique was developed and the contract signed during marriage, so it's reasonable for the other spouse to feel entitled to some of that future income. That's particularly true if the contracted spouse's work on developing the personal-coaching technique limited the other spouse's income and career growth due to having additional domestic responsibilities.

You might wonder, legitimately, how far such arguments can be taken. Like it or not, many states recognize the principle of entitlement to a portion of future earnings based on a the spouse's becoming a "valuable commodity" or producing things during a marriage that will have postmarital economic value. The entitled spouse must determine how far to carry it based on need versus greed.

Trust Assets and Income

Many marriages break down because either or both spouses fail to earn or keep the other's trust. Ironically, though, sometimes they earn at least part of it upon

divorce—(a) financial trust, that is! That could happen when a spouse is a beneficiary of a parent's or grandparent's trusts. Whether created before or during
the marriage, such trusts are generally regarded as gifts of separate property to
that spouse. Nevertheless, they often become an issue in divorce in one of the
following ways:

- *Effect on future income:* If an existing separate trust will significantly
  improve one spouse's economic circumstances after the divorce, some
  states are inclined to favor the other spouse by awarding more spousal
  support or a more favorable property split.
- *Trust appreciation:* Some states consider the trust's increase in value
  attributable to investment gain (not additional gifts into it) as marital
  property to be divided, even if the terms of the trust don't allow the
  trust to yet be invaded. (Warning: When trusts are invaded—cash is
  withdrawn—it might warrant a homeland-security code green alert.)
- *Trust income:* If the trust pays income to one of the spouses, some states
  regard that as marital property. But even in states that don't, if that
  income is used for marital purposes, or commingled with marital funds,
  it will be considered a regular addition to that spouse's income for purposes of determining child support and spousal support.
- *Trust principal invasion:* Unless a prenuptial or postnuptial agreement
  specifically protected it, all or part of a trust could be construed as marital property. That can occur if, during the marriage, the beneficiary
  spouse has repeatedly invaded its principal for marital use.
- *Spouse-established trust:* During the marriage, if either spouse has used
  employment income or other marital funds to establish a separate trust,
  that trust is usually, nonetheless, marital property. The main exception
  is when a prenuptial or postnuptial agreement addressing such trust creation specifically has preempted the other spouse's entitlement to any
  share of trust income or principal.

Spouse's or Family Business

During most of your marriage, it might have been none of your business
(although it should have been), but in planning the divorce, a business owned
by either spouse, or one in which one spouse is a significant partner with other
owners, is always the other's business. Unfortunately, though, nonowner spouses
have to make it their business to find out everything they can about such businesses because some owner-spouses are far from forthcoming.

Although that's not right, it's understandable because many owners feel they're entitled to keep all the fruits of the intensive and extensive labor that made the business successful. However, that effort is comparable in type if not degree to the efforts put into building a career, and we've already seen that the longer the marriage, the more the lower-earning spouse is entitled to continue the lifestyle funded by the career success of the higher-earning spouse. Furthermore, just as many lower-earning spouses contribute considerable intangible value to the marriage to compensate for the other spouse's single-minded career pursuits, the spouses of entrepreneurs do many things to make the owner-spouse's business success possible.

For example, the nonowner spouse might have worked substantial overtime while also holding down the home fort to compensate for the lack of the owner-spouse's income during the first few years the business was being developed and put into operation. Also, businesses almost always represent gambles that put the family's financial situation in jeopardy. When one spouse starts a business during marriage, the other has bought into the gamble—often including considerable marital debt incurred to launch the business—and deserves the payoff when the dice hit the point. Finally, nonowning spouses often make significant contributions to businesses as unofficial unpaid part-time staff.

"OK," say some business-owning spouses, "but those arguments don't apply to me because we started our businesses before our marriages." They are right, to a degree. In most states, the value of the business at the time of marriage is definitely the owner's separate property, and some of its increase during marriage might also be regarded as separate property. But the way a court would apportion that increase is largely dependent on the owner's well-documented, logical, and economic arguments for getting a larger share of the marital growth piece, and the spouse's arguments to the contrary. As we mentioned before, the best strategy is to negotiate this issue reasonably with your spouse. But to negotiate, you must know what the business is worth. To determine that, here are some of the key issues that a business valuation expert addresses:

- Is it a separate entity known as a C corp, S corp, or LLC? Or is it a partnership in the form of a Limited Liability Partnership (LLP), Limited Partnership (LP), or general partnership? All these generally use formal bookkeeping systems. Or is it an unincorporated self-employment business that might not have a formal bookkeeping system, but nonetheless might have value beyond the income it produces?
- What standard of value and method of valuation should be used? Different states use different standards of value and recognize numerous

valuation methodologies within each of the standards. These standards of value include fair market value, fair value, going concern value, and liquidation value. The professional valuation expert will choose the appropriate standard of value and valuation method valid for it based on the case law in the state where the business is located as well as the facts and circumstances related to the business itself. For example, in many states, fair market value is the general standard of value for divorce cases, while in Michigan, it is "going concern value."

- Does the business have intangible assets? Depending on the standard of value, the valuation might include recognition of business "goodwill"— which incorporates several factors: location and other convenience factors, identification with one or more brands, general reputation with the public, position in the marketplace, and relationships it has developed with customers, suppliers, and employees. Such goodwill can be a part of any type of business, ranging from a multinational megacorporation to the handyman with a listing in your local free advertising weekly.

You shouldn't have to worry about the process used to value the business in question as long as you find a well-qualified valuation professional—from among designations we described earlier. You will have to worry, though, if you and your spouse don't have enough other assets to compensate the nonowner spouse for his or her share should the owner spouse want or need to continue the business after divorce. Constructing a fair settlement in that situation usually requires creativity, cooperation, and compromise—and perhaps some fancy financial footwork by your divorce team.

Finally, if the spouse's business is really just a self-employment activity that has no value beyond the income it produces, it should be addressed in the marital settlement the same way as any regular job that has been producing income for the marriage. The lower-earning spouse is entitled to maintain some fraction of the lifestyle afforded by that source of revenue. Furthermore, such self-employment jobs often produce more income than the owner reveals to the other spouse, or provide opportunities for financial shenanigans that help hide marital assets, as we discussed earlier in this chapter (and which also apply to more formal businesses). So it usually pays to have a financial professional involved who's capable of analyzing the business or businesslike activity.

And all this just to overview one-spouse businesses. What happens if you and your spouse are dealing with a business that you own together equally, or in which one spouse owns a majority share and the other spouse owns a significant minority share? It's the exceptional divorcing couple who stays in business together or has a nonoperating spouse maintain a significant interest. Generally, then, one spouse needs to be cut out of the business—as carefully as a surgeon cuts out a brain tumor! And because your divorce already involves enough (figurative) bloodletting, we're putting some of the gorier details of splitting businesses on the Split-Up Web site (www.divorcesoftware.com/divorce_finance_book/business_splitting_ complexities.htm). In addition, check out this new book by one of your co-authors *Streetwise Business Valuation: Proven Methods to Easily Determine the True Value of Your Business* (Heather Linton, Adams Streetwise Series, February 2004).

Traditional (Defined-Benefit) Pensions

Will either you or your spouse receive a good, old-fashioned pension upon retirement—the type to which you didn't contribute a dime? If so, the portion of what the pensioner will receive that was earned during your marriage is a marital asset. That's a scary thought to pensioners—especially given increasing fears of not being able to afford retirement after the 2001–2002 stock market mini-collapse, the shaky future of Social Security and Medicare, our increasing life spans, the rising cost of living, and the uncertainty about the company's eventual ability to meet its pension commitments. People want to hold onto every last pension penny, and they will often become irrational about the pension aspect of a settlement, even if they've been genuinely constructive in every other respect.

But let's examine the future of the pensioner's spouse. Bankruptcy incidence is alarmingly high among retirement-age women, and it's no coincidence that few who've reached that age among today's population are entitled to their own pensions. And even those who aren't bankrupt often live at or not much above subsistence level—even though they never could have imagined living that way when they were younger and married, with a much more comfortable lifestyle. Although a larger percentage of future pensioners will be women, company cutbacks or discontinuations of pension plans mean that the actual numbers of women who'll get pensions will remain quite low—not to mention that far fewer men will get them either, and many more will experience the frugal retirement that's common among single women.

Therefore, when either spouse has a pension, the other must ensure that it's included in marital assets and a value for it determined so that an agreed portion can be legally paid out to the other spouse. In many cases, it makes sense to simply agree to split the pension-earner's future payments based on the part of the pension earned during the marriage and the overall split percentage to which you agree. For example, if 20 percent of the pension is earned during the marriage, and the pension-earner's spouse is getting 60 percent of other assets, then that spouse will get 12 percent of each future payment (20 percent of 60 percent). Doing this makes particular sense if the duration of the marriage is only a small part of the total years of service for which the pension will be earned.

However, in long-term marriages and many other circumstances, including the use of the forward-looking (future cash flow) approach to reaching settlement that we describe in Chapters 9 and 10, it pays to pay an expert to determine the pension's value—and here's why. First, it's hard enough to determine the current value of a pension given the uniqueness and complexity of most companies' formulas. Second how can you determine the pension's future value now, in today's dollars, when it could be 20 years or more until the pension has been fully earned—with its payments all based on unknowns: the pensioner's years of service at retirement, salary history, age at retirement, future changes to the pension formula, and other factors?

Determining the pension's value is only the beginning, though. Now, you must figure out how to split it—numerically and mechanically (is Solomon in the house?). After all, unless you live in a community property state, it's actually just one other marital asset subject to equitable division—which doesn't necessarily mean it should be split in half if you've agreed to an unequal split of assets, as in the example above. In fact, it's unlikely you'll split it in half if the spouse earning it started doing so before the marriage and will continue to do so after—making most of it that spouse's separate property. Once you've determined the split, you must still decide on how the pension-owner's spouse will get his or her share: A portion of all future payments at the time they're being disbursed? A lump sum equivalent to the current (present) value of future payments? Partial payment now in the form of a lump sum and the "balance" later in the form of a correspondingly reduced later share of actual pension payments?

Finally, once you've determined how the pension will figure into the settlement, you must make sure that the divorce documents include the necessary official paperwork that ensures delivery of the nonpensioner's share. This is done with a qualified domestic relations order (QDRO). Although the employer might provide forms for you to create such an order, you must *not* rely on them because they're often later invalidated due to numerous possible errors (the most common covered below). Instead, one or more qualified professionals, usually including a family law attorney and sometimes a benefits expert, should draw up a QDRO that specifically satisfies the conditions of both your agreed settlement and the employer's rules regarding its pensions.

Thus, just as in the case of one spouse's having a business or both spouses' sharing a business, incorporating the pension into the divorce settlement is a job that usually requires help from more than one highly trained professional. So the advice in this section comes with the caveat that you will use it strictly to better understand the options presented by any or all of the following: your attorney, CPA or financial planner, pension actuary, and/or certified employee benefits specialist (CEBS).

Pension Calculation

It's best to have an expert verify the company's pension estimate or actual calculation, and to determine each spouse's "fair" fractional pension share. Although you needn't fully understand the math, you might benefit from the "Simple Pension Calculation Mini-Lesson" on the Split-Up Web site (www.divorcesoftware.com/divorce_finance_book/pension_calculation_lesson .htm). Regardless of whether you understand the calculation, though, you should know about several factors that could significantly affect it.

Money Now, or Later?

If you and your spouse were to simply agree on a certain percentage split of all assets, including the eventual pension, complex pension-split calculations would be unnecessary. You'd simply make sure your attorney prepared an appropriate QDRO that directed the employer to split each pension payment into two checks according to the split—and whatever those amounts were at the time, so be it (although you'd want the calculation verified).

However, the rest of your settlement, including spousal support, might very well hinge on the anticipated size of the future pension, so in most cases you do want to go through this calculation. In fact, if there are sufficient assets, spouses often agree on a current lump-sum settlement of future pension benefits, and they tilt the split of all current assets accordingly. To do this, it's necessary to not only project the future benefit but to also "discount" that future stream of payments back to a current present value and then determine what part of that will have been earned during the marriage. By adding that to the total value of all other assets, you'll know the total size of the pie and can then negotiate how much of it you each should get. For example, if the marital portion of the pension is $300,000 and the rest of the assets are worth $500,000, you might decide to split the total of $800,000 evenly. The reasons you might want to do this, or not, will become clear in discussing some of the factors that follow.

Salary and Economic Assumptions

Base salary, the key to any pension calculation, is usually defined as the average of the last several years (often five) before retirement. However, as unreasonable as it sounds, in some states, courts will assume that the final five years of salary will be the same as the current most recent five years of salary because there's no reliable way of predicting future salary. In other cases, they'll use current salary but adjust it for inflation to what that salary would be in retirement-year future dollars. And in other cases, they'll allow reasonable predictions to be made based on the career path and salary history that the employee has had so far.

Dan Caine, whose Split-Up program has strong "what-if" capabilities for analyzing pension scenarios, points out several more important assumptions inherent in any pension projection: What is the assumed date until which the employee will work? Is it assumed that the employee will work until retirement, or the "cutoff" date—a date around the time of the divorce? Does your state require the use of a "coverture factor" to take into account the proportion of time the parties were married during the employment period to the total time of employment? What is the assumed date the employee will start receiving benefits? The alternatives are "regular retirement date" (usually 65) and "early retirement date" (62? 58?). Which is better? The earlier an employee retires, the more years of pension he or she collects. However, most plans reduce the monthly payout for early retirement. Consult your attorney and other divorce professionals, as well as the actual pension-plan summary document, to determine the pension-calculation assumptions made by the courts in your state and by your specific plan.

You might find that not all these or other possible assumptions are completely spelled out by your state or your plan. So there's possibly considerable room for establishing new legal precedents regarding pension division, and for arguing for sensible calculation methods if you settle out of court. Therefore, if you have a lot at stake, the pensioner's retirement isn't imminent, and you don't simply intend to divide the benefits as they're paid out, it's crucial that you don't exclusively rely on a simple calculation based only on current salary—unless proscribed by state law or the plan document. You could be totally off the mark in estimating the actual value the pension will ultimately have.

Pension Formula Differences

Many companies add complexities to the basic pension calculation, such as factoring in offsets for the Social Security benefits you're projected to receive. Others deviate from giving a constant percentage of credit for each year of service. For example, in calculating what is sometimes called the total percentage of base pension, one company might encourage long-term service by using 1.5

percent per year of service for the first 25 years, and 2 percent per year thereafter. Another might discourage service beyond normal retirement age by doing the reverse—giving less reward for each year after a certain point: for example, 2 percent each for the first 20 years and 1 percent per year thereafter. You can find out the specific formula that affects you by requesting the *summary plan description* (SPD) for your (spouse's) company's pension from the human resources department.

Pensions Grow Faster, Later

Regardless of formula specifics, you earn much more of your ultimate pension for each year of service in the latter part of a long career. That's because two important components of the calculation are, first, your average salary the last several years before you retire and, second, total years of service. Thus, the longer your work, assuming your salary keeps increasing, the higher your average salary for the last several years and the more the total years of service. Figure 8-1 illustrates an example of the dramatic growth of a typical white-collar mangerial professional's pension as years of service increase.

Company Changing Retirement Plans

You might be getting more sedentary and set in your ways as you get older, but your pension plan is doing anything but. Companies have the right to change their plans at any time, provided they preserve the benefits already earned by the employee as of the changeover day—in other words formula changes can reduce only benefits yet to be earned. With companies increasingly choosing cost cutting over loyalty to employees, your future pension will likely be less than now projected—the expected disparity larger the further you now are from retirement.

The most likely change will be a shift to a totally new type of formula called a *cash balance pension,* which has advantages for newer and younger employees because it enables them to earn more of their pensions in early years, and is "portable" if they change jobs. Unfortunately, when companies adopt cash-balance plans they "cash out" their employees from the traditional plan by starting their new plan accounts with a balance equal to what they'd have earned in the old plan had they quit or retired on the day of changeover. From that point, veteran employees find their pensions growing much more slowly than they would have under the old plan, with little or no chance that they will earn as good a final pension as they had been expecting. Perhaps this now sounds familiar because it's been a source of enormous controversy that led the IRS a few years ago to put a moratorium on companies' converting to cash

FIGURE 8-1:   Annual Pension Earned Based on Years of Service

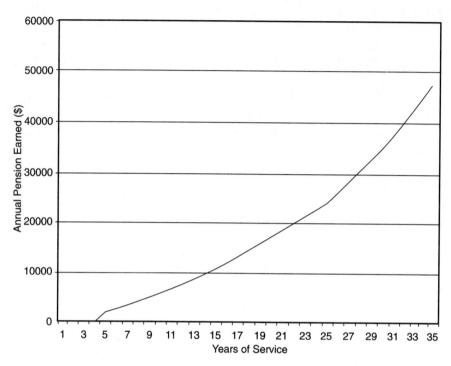

balance plans. Typical mid-career employees at IBM, for example, discovered that their future pensions would be cut by a third to a half from what they'd anticipated. Unfortunately, it appears the moratorium will soon be lifted, so future pension amounts are likely to fall short of current projections for a majority of Americans—due either to cash balance conversions or changes to stingier formulas.

Early Retirement, Job Termination, and Partial Vesting
In addition to changes that the company might make to the retirement plan, the company might also make changes to the employee's plan to retire. Despite growing protests against age discrimination, companies have too much at stake in the high salaries they pay many older workers to not aggressively pursue both incentives to retire early or disincentives to stay until retirement. Furthermore, once shed of responsibility for spousal and child support, many divorced older workers are not as driven to stay the course. So there's also a significant chance,

for these reasons, that you or your spouse won't earn the full retirement benefit you now anticipate, and you must seriously weigh the uncertain value of the future pension(s) when deciding between immediate compensation with a lump-sum settlement or regular payments starting at retirement age.

However, in evaluating various scenarios regarding retirement timing, don't just calculate early retirement at face value because companies often offer sweeteners to the formula or additional cash payments at termination. If you've agreed to a split of future retirement payments, you'll benefit from a sweetened formula automatically, but if you're negotiating for a current lump sum in lieu of future split payments, you'd miss out. Thus, you should do calculations for various scenarios involving sweeteners or additional payments because either are marital property to be divided.

Life-Expectancy Assumptions

Once they've earned it, pension recipients receive the actual pension monthly payments for as long as they live. But at retirement, many plans give them the option of taking a lump-sum payment for the future value of that stream of payments. You can think of this lump-sum payment as the amount that it would cost to buy a no-fee annuity that would provide the same monthly payments using the same interest rate and life-expectancy assumptions.

Sounds good, but there's a big difference between 10 years versus 35 years of $30,000 per year, and there's no way of knowing how long an individual employee will live. Enter the actuaries, who use life-expectancy tables to calculate pension amounts based on average life expectancy for that employer's population—but not for particular individuals, regardless of health or family health history. When the actuaries do their jobs right, the bulk of employees will live to about their life expectancies. Those employees who choose future payments and live longer than life expectancy get a "bonus" of extra years of payments while those who die prematurely get "shortchanged" by getting fewer years of payments. (Of course, its debatable whether either group really cares after the fact!)

The groups that do care, though, are those who elect a lump sum and live either less or more than life expectancy. That's because the lump-sum calculation is based on the overall life expectancy for the employee population as a whole. Thus, the ones who die prematurely will get a "bonus" and the ones who live beyond life expectancy will have been "shortchanged."

"So what," you say, "how does this apply to an employee's ex-spouse?" Consider what would happen if you weren't getting divorced and your spouse died before you, unless he or she worked for Cook County, Illinois, where dead people have historically had the same legal rights (at least in voting) as live ones. If you and your spouse didn't elect the lump sum and were receiving regular payments, then upon your spouse's death, the full pension payments would cease. Then, in most plans, provided you didn't sign something waiving the "joint and survivor" option, you'd continue getting a percentage (often 50 percent) of the full payments as a survivor's pension until you die. So you can see that the total of payments you'd eventually receive depends on how long your spouse actually lives, and lacking that prescience, a prediction of how long that *is* based on individual rather than group characteristics—namely, your spouse's health, family health history, and lifestyle (is your spouse planning to join the NASCAR circuit for a second career?).

This leads to a calculation of the estimated lump sum that your spouse would be entitled to at retirement based on a life expectancy derived from his or her individual characteristics. That could lead to a very different decision on how to split it than if it were based on general population life expectancy for your spouse's gender. After all, imagine your spouse having a heart condition and only expecting to live five years from that point. Would you consider it to be equally fair to divide the amount in that case the same way as you would divide a larger amount if your spouse were very healthy and would probably live 30 years past retirement? So if this discussion has done nothing else, we hope it has opened your mind to the equity reasons behind splitting a pension, and made you aware of some of the potential complexities involved in doing it fairly. One benefit of negotiating your property division out of court is that you can incorporate some of these individual factors into your calculation, even if the plan document or the statutory plan division rules of your state would not permit them.

Cost-of-Living Adjustments (COLAs)

Less than one quarter of employers make annual inflation adjustments to their retirees' pension payments. But if yours does, it's important to calculate some scenarios based on inflation-adjusted annually increasing pension payments.

Survivor Benefits

The survivor benefits we mentioned in discussing life expectancy are a desirable feature in most pension plans, but they do complicate matters. The "vanilla" pension formula in any particular employer's plan calculates a benefit that assumes the employee always was and will be single. However, federal laws require a married employee to elect some form of joint and survivor annuity unless their spouse waives the right to receive a survivor annuity. Consider the typical case in which the husband is earning the pension and the wife hasn't waived the right to survivor benefits because she'll need them should the husband die first. Unless the wife has died by the time the husband retires, the annual pension amount will be less than calculated by the vanilla formula. That's because it is based on the couple's having a higher "joint life expectancy" than the husband's individual life expectancy.

Whether or not you'll be splitting the pension, it's important to consider how to handle the survivor's benefit. To maximize the amount that the pension-earner alone will get, or the ex-spouses will split, the pensioner's spouse might consider waiving the right to the survivor's pension in return for some insurance. Namely, if the pensioner is currently healthy, the spouse would take out life insurance on him or her, in an amount that will make up for the lost survivor's benefit. Generally the cost of this insurance would be borne by the pensioner, either directly or in the form of additional spousal support.

In fact, the spouse should insist on such an insurance arrangement, or on reinstating the survivor benefit—which can be done if the pension is not yet being paid—if during happier times, he or she waived the survivor's benefit in favor of a larger pension amount that would help them enjoy a more prosperous retirement together. Furthermore, you'll also want to consider this method of compensating the pensioner's spouse if the pensioner wants to "get back" the survivor's benefit to hold in reserve for a new spouse in a remarriage. That's because, otherwise, the ex-spouse remains entitled to the survivor's benefit after the divorce unless he or she waives it as a condition of the settlement. Finally, any such arrangement, regardless of reason, should be in addition to any life insurance taken out in the event of premature death of a long-term spousal-support payer.

Tying the Pension Knot When Untying the Marital Knot

Next to the cash, jewelry, and other valuables you might keep in a safe-deposit box, a piece of paper indicating ownership of partial future rights to a spouse's pension deserves equally important protection. That's why it's so critical to ensure that a court or ex-spouse's employer won't find it to be as worthless as Confederate money, due to improper drafting.

That paper, the qualified domestic relations order (QDRO), is a precious end product of a divorce settlement that includes future division of an ex-spouse's pension. To get that division right, legally, you need an attorney who gives undivided attention to divorce matters—and either is quite experienced with pensions or has good referral relationships with attorneys who do. Because it's impossible to tell you how to make sure your QDRO is right in 50,000 words or less, we'll instead tell you the key things it usually covers and the most common mistakes made in preparing it.

QDRO Basics

OK, we've used a bit of literary license because a QDRO can actually be part of the divorce decree itself, or a separate document. The key thing to note, though, is that the QDRO is not enforceable by the family court but instead by federal courts under the auspices of the Department of Labor's Pension and Welfare Benefits Administration (DOL-PWBA)—which oversees employers' qualified retirement plans including profit-sharing, 401(k), and defined-benefit pension plans. That doesn't mean, though, that you have to go to federal court later to get the pension payment started. But if the employer were to refuse payment for some reason, the matter would be settled in federal court. You can help prevent that from happening by making sure that the QDRO includes at least the following:

- The names and addresses of the employee and of the "alternate payee"
- The name of the pension (or other qualified retirement) plan
- Either the dollar amount to be paid or the way the amount is to be figured
- The form of payment to be received (that is, lump sum, lifetime monthly payment, and/or widow's or widower's pension)
- When payments are to start and stop

Common QDRO Mistakes

The primary reason that spouses don't receive their share of pension (or other qualified retirement plan) benefits is that a QDRO was never prepared. Well, you now know enough to do that, but here are the five common mistakes connected with preparing and enforcing a QDRO:

1. *Neglects state's distribution laws:* The negotiation is based on incorrect or incomplete information about nuances of state rules, often those concerning equitable or community distribution and how they apply to pension plans.
2. *Neglects employer's rules:* The QDRO is drafted with incorrect or incomplete knowledge of provisions in the employer's summary plan description, such as the rules of the plan and its survivor and other benefits. The employer might then exploit a technicality to avoid paying out the benefits—a cost savings many employers would be only too happy to achieve.

3. *No employer pre-approval:* The spouse(s) fail to get the QDRO draft preapproved by the employer's plan administrator—that is, the company actually administering the plan. Just as banks preapprove mortgage loans, most administrators will review a draft QDRO for validity. Attorneys who don't take advantage of that service are foolish, irresponsible, and potentially liable. "Such pre-approval isn't a foolproof guarantee, though," cautions Craig Ross, "employers' QDRO mistakes are multiplying because widespread cost-cutting has resulted, in general, in fewer and less-qualified employees in the human-resource functions that have QDRO responsibility."

4. *Failure to file the finalized QDRO with the plan administrator:* The attorney should do this immediately upon divorce, the administrator should respond with an acceptance letter, and you should follow up to ensure that they do and that you have a copy of that letter.

5. *Doing Only One QDRO:* Some employees have more than one type of pension plan that should be addressed by a QDRO, such as an employee stock ownership plan (ESOP) or a 401(k), in addition to a defined-benefit pension. Others have vested benefits in more than one employer's plan. It's critical that for every plan in which the employee's spouse has a marital interest, a separate QDRO is prepared—whether they be multiple QDROs for one employer or separate QDROs for multiple employers.

Sometimes, though, QDRO-related mistakes are not due to QDRO errors but to arrangements made in lieu of a QDRO. For example, the pensioner's spouse might agree to make another part of the settlement richer to compensate for not taking part of the pension—thus forgoing a QDRO. But unless that agreement is drafted with appropriate contingencies, the spousal support will normally terminate if the spouse remarries—effectively (legally) cheating the spouse out of pension benefits that would have been paid under a QDRO regardless of any remarriage.

More QDRO Information

In case you're planning to sit for the Law School Aptitude Test, or get a job as a government bureaucrat, these QDRO information sources are especially (and perhaps overly!) helpful:

- *QDROs, EDROs and the Division of Employee Benefits on Divorce* (Nancy Keppelman, www.icle.org)

- *QDROs: The Division of Pensions Through Qualified Domestic Relations Orders* (Department of Welfare Pension and Welfare Benefits Administration—or DOL-PWBA)
  www.labor.gov/pwba/publications/qdros.html
- *Qualified Domestic Relations Orders* (DOL-PWBA)
  www.dol.gov/pwba/faqs/faq_qdro.html
- *Determining Qualified Status and Paying Benefits* (DOL-PWBA)
  http://www.dol.gov/pwba/faqs/faq_qdro2.html
- *Drafting Qualified Domestic Relations Orders* (DOL-PWBA)
  www.dol.gov/pwba/faqs/faq_qdro3.html
- *Falling Short, A 50-State Survey of Spousal Rights under State Pension Plans* (AARP Fulfillment, 601 East Street, NW, Washington, D.C. 20049, free)
- *Guide for Military Wives Facing Separation and Divorce* (Ex-Partners of Service Men/Women for Equality, Post Office Box 11191, Alexandria, VA 22312) www.angelfire.com/va/EXPOSE ($5)
- *New QDRO Handbook: How to Divide ERISA, Military and Civil Service Pensions and Collect Child Support from Employee Benefit Plans* (David Carrad, American Bar Association, May 2000)

Other Complex Employee Benefits

Pensions are the 800-pound gorilla of divorce-divisible benefits, but don't ignore the smaller apes and chimpanzees. In high-profile cases such as the divorce of General Electric CEO Jack Welch—whose wife made sure GE brought good things to (her) life—stock options, deferred compensation, and executive perks proved pricey primates worth millions. But even the average American's employee benefit package can be worth thousands over and above the value of its pension and tax-deferred-savings plans. In divorce negotiations, these benefits are classified as one of two species: either divisible property or salary supplements that effectively increase the salary amount used in the negotiations and calculations regarding child support and spousal support. So, don't monkey around; here's information to help you take them seriously.

Salary-Supplement Benefits

Many companies offer benefits that start fresh each year—most commonly the company contribution to various forms of insurance, or the annual amount available to buy benefits in a cafeteria plan. They might be taxable, such as the premiums the company pays for more than $50,000 of group life insurance, or nontaxable, such as family privileges at an on-site fitness facility. Regardless, many states treat them as additional income for the purposes of child support and spousal-support determination because they support a certain level of lifestyle. Although the court might not make a distinction between what is taxable and nontaxable for these calculations, we're describing them separately.

Taxable Salary-Supplement Benefits
The following benefits are taxable as either cash or their cash equivalent value:

- Personal use of a company car
- Taxable portion of company-paid parking
- Imputed interest on interest-free or below-market interest rate loans
- Average annual bonus usually earned if latest W-2 figure didn't fully reflect it

Nontaxable Salary-Supplement Benefits

- *Flexible spending accounts (medical, dependent care, commuting to work):* These benefits save employees taxes by the deposit of part of their salary in accounts used to pay for these items—with the amount deposited not being counted as income, thus not being taxed. If the employee's spouse doesn't have such a plan available from his or her employer, then the divorce will cost that spouse those tax-saving benefits. More importantly, though, that spouse might come up short on support received if the other spouse's pretax amounts deducted from salary are overlooked because they don't show up on the W-2.
- *Business use of company car*
- *Up to $190 monthly of company-paid parking*
- *Company contribution to health benefits outside of a cafeteria plan*
- *Cafeteria plan annual allotment applied to purchasing benefits* (not W-2)
- *Tuition reimbursement* (if deemed likely to have been used with no divorce)
- *Company-provided life-enhancement benefits* such as fitness facilities and healthy lifestyle programs
- *Bargain discounts for items regularly purchased through employee buying club*

Divisible Property in Other Forms of Compensation

These forms of compensation differ because they're not a regular annually renewed salary enhancement but are instead accrued to meet specific performance objectives, or triggered upon specific events. Recent tax-court decisions and IRS revenue rulings have given some of them, such as nonqualified stock options, the status of property that can be divided "incident to divorce" without tax consequences to the employee-spouse transferring them. Previously, the portion of them given to the employee's spouse at divorce was considered an "assignment of income" that was taxable to the employee-spouse giver, even though the employee's ex-spouse enjoyed the proceeds.

It's important that you're aware of both the immediate and potential deferred tax consequences of any part of a property division that involves any kind of complex property, such as stock options or deferred compensation. We recommend that you and your attorney discuss putting a clause in your settlement agreement requiring reimbursement for any taxes either party pays that the IRS or other taxing authority later determines that the other party should have paid.

Some of these complex benefits are summarized below, and you can more detail on them under this topic on the Split-Up Web site: www.divorcesoftware.com/divorce_finance_book/complex_benefits.htm

- *Golden parachutes:* Severance packages or early-retirement incentives given upon forced or solicited premature termination of employment.
- *Stock options:* Financial obligations granted by employers that enable employees to purchase designated amounts of company stock at specified prices at any time during a specified time period, regardless of the then-current stock market price. These are either qualified *incentive stock options* (ISOs) or *nonqualified stock options* (NQSOs) that have different tax treatments. You should also be aware that ISOs often trigger the alternative minimum tax (AMT) when they are exercised.
- *Employee stock ownership plans (ESOPs):* These programs award shares of company stock, based on years of service and salary, that are usually not redeemable until an employee or ex-employee retires or reaches retirement age.
- *Nonqualified deferred compensation:* This benefit is compensation promised at a future time based on work done before or at the time of granting. Because the compensation isn't guaranteed, it doesn't trigger a current tax obligation.

Divorce-Related Financial Planning Issues

You might not have to deal with those tricky stock options, but you'll probably have several personal finance options to consider in trying to develop a winning divorce plan—including budgeting, investment strategies, comparative tax impacts of alternative scenarios, and the timing of both the divorce and its associated property transfers and support payments.

Considering Your Invested Interests

When basing settlements on the current fair market value of property and assets, their investment-income potential is often overlooked. Domestic spouses receiving substantial property settlements can generate far more current income from that property than it provided during the marriage. That's because its income might be taxed (postdivorce) in a lower bracket. While current fixed-income investment yields are extremely low, they won't stay that way permanently. When evaluating a settlement proposal, consider the possibility of putting a certain portion of it into a diversified income-producing portfolio (which might include high-quality tax-free municipal bonds, for example) that can often generate more income than you can get from CDs and money market accounts.

You may wish to consult a financial advisor to help you evaluate the economic impact various settlement proposals would have on your investment strategy. Then, after the divorce, they or another advisor could help you implement a diversified investment strategy (which, for example, might emphasize mutual funds if you have a long investment horizon). Rely on such an advisor, because we're not recommending municipal bonds or mutual funds; we're just giving you examples of the types of advice you might get depending on your situation, that is appropriate for your immediate needs, future goals, and level of risk tolerance.

Finally, a warning: Many profiteers run businesses that "buy" structured settlements. They might offer you a current lump sum of cash to spend and invest, in exchange for the spousal support payments you would have received over time. If you receive a large settlement that becomes public record, you're more likely to be contacted by such businesses. Remember that they wouldn't be in business if a profit were not there to be made, and their profits come at your loss because they buy such settlements at a substantial discount to their actual current value. If you need more immediate cash than a proposed divorce settlement would provide you, consult a financial advisor to restructure your proposed settlement accordingly, without costing you part of what you deserve.

Trading Time for Money

Time is either on your side, or not. By trying out various scenarios illustrating different amounts and different payment time frames for spousal support and property settlements, you can determine what settlement best serves the needs of both sides in terms of minimizing budget strain and taxes on income.

For example, when one spouse's business is undergoing expansion, the other spouse could consider delaying part of the property settlement or that year's spousal support payments to alleviate a business cash crunch that could lead to damaging the ex-spouse financially, possibly ending the flow of any support payments. There are no definite guidelines to offer in this area, but being willing to offer and entertain a variety of possibilities is one low-cost way of demonstrating flexibility and recognition that the best settlement comes closest to meeting both parties' needs.

Budging Your Budgets

Financial planners are often amazed and appalled when clients reveal their current household budgets and identify *their* necessities and discretionary items: expensive country club memberships, new cars every three years, two months annually for each child at premium-priced summer camps, and similar expenditures labeled as "necessities" while retirement investments are labeled "discretionary." You're probably far more realistic, but even so, you and your spouse should be willing to take a hard look at the budgets you both prepare to identify true needs and differentiate the priorities of various discretionary items. If you each demonstrate flexibility to the other in doing so, you'll both be more receptive to negotiation compromises.

Some divorce attorneys would have you go to the opposite extreme and pad budgets to create bargaining room. But we suggest looking at your budget in the same way any good real estate agent would advise marketing your home: list it at a realistic price that attracts realistic offers for the most efficient route to a harmonious deal made at a fair price.

Getting the Max-Tax Benefits

Criticize our legislators and the IRS all you want, but the fact is that our tax code is really quite reasonable to divorcing families. At various times throughout the book, we've touched on tax implications of specific aspects of a settlement. Exploiting those possibilities individually can help you formulate your initial set of proposals. A good CPA, certified divorce financial analyst (CDFA), or certified financial planner with expert tax knowledge can be invaluable in plotting your taxwise strategy.

Nowhere is the tax tradeoff more evident than in balancing the property split with the amount of spousal support. Every case has an optimum amount of spousal support that will maximize the difference between the tax benefit received from the payor deducting spousal support payments, and the receiver's payment of taxes on that support. Agree beforehand on what the "real" (tax-adjusted) property split and spousal support should be. Then you can get your advisors to help determine the combination of actual spousal support payment and property settlement that, with maximum financial efficiency, will achieve the desired tax-adjusted goals you set for them. You will have to balance this taxwise planning by considering the traps for the unwary such as alimony recapture, which we discussed in Chapter 7, and the termination of spousal support that frequently occurs upon the receiving spouse's remarriage—and always upon the paying spouse's death.

Divorce-Related Estate Planning Issues

Except when mandated by the divorce settlement, or in unusual circumstances, you and your spouse should revise your estate plans so that you won't inherit from each other when one of you dies after the divorce. In addition, either of you might have reason to revise the following aspects of your estate plan in the event that one of you dies *before* the divorce is actually final—presumably not at the hands of the other!

Wills and Trusts

Are you among the 40 percent of adult Americans who don't even have a will or living trust? If so, and you're also among the 80 percent of Americans who don't get presents they actually want or that fit them, then you have a big problem: who's going to get all of that unwanted or unusable stuff someday? Now's the time to remedy that (the lack of a will, not presents you want) or your assets will be distributed in a way you probably didn't intend should you die either during or after the divorce. You'll probably want to have one will or trust in effect during divorce proceedings that doesn't totally shut out your spouse, and another one without any spousal references that you'll put in effect as a replacement immediately upon the divorce.

If you already have a will or trust, you should review and revise it now, just as you should when you anticipate any major change in your circumstances. Pay particular attention if you've been in a previous marriage—thus raising issues concerning arrangements for children, and possibly spouses. Also, if you are getting additional dollars of spousal support in exchange for giving your spouse additional dollars of property settlement, you should consider whether you want any special provisions in your will to provide more property for your children in the event that spousal support is prematurely cut short by death or remarriage. These issues are often complex, so make sure your divorce attorney brings your estate attorney into the process.

Life Insurance

If you own life insurance on yourself that names your spouse as beneficiary, consider changing the beneficiary to a life insurance trust set up for the benefit of your children. You'd hope that your spouse would use the proceeds for your children should you die, but there's no guarantee that he or she will, so this step protects the children. Another benefit of a life insurance trust is that the proceeds would not be subject to estate taxes if you are no longer the owner of the policy. However, check your state's law to determine if there are any timing issues related to your divorce that could affect whether the change is legally enforceable.

Retirement Accounts

Chances are that your spouse is named as your beneficiary on any IRA accounts you have, so you should make a change so as to designate your children—or one or more trusts established for their benefit—instead. However, you cannot automatically do the same with your 401(k) or other retirement accounts administered under federal ERISA statutes without your spouse signing a waiver allowing you to do so. These administrative details must be spelled out in your settlement agreement and in any required QDRO.

Power of Attorney

Perhaps you and your spouse have given each other power of attorney to conduct the other's financial transactions if either of you becomes incapacitated or because of frequent travel. Get these revoked pronto because such power can allow a spouse to quickly empty your accounts. Instead, you may want to create a "springing power of attorney" that would only go into effect if you were incapacitated or otherwise medically unable to carry out your own affairs either temporarily or permanently. The best person for this job may be another family member or trusted friend.

Parental Estate Planning Changes

Although gifts or bequests to one spouse during marriage are generally that spouse's separate property, receiving such payments before the divorce might negatively impact the property division share or spousal support payments that spouse receives. Similarly, such payments to children might reduce child support. So unless such payments are much larger than potential support lost, alert (grand)parents of your intent to divorce so that they can amend their estate planning documents (for example, to create a trust instead of making an outright bequest). And they might want to temporarily suspend planned annual gifting, particularly if they've been gifting maximum amounts to both you and your spouse in order to minimize ultimate taxation of their estates.

Health Care Surrogates and Living Wills

OK, this one isn't really about finances, except in having a laugh at your spouse's "expense"—but it could definitely be "costly" if you overlook it. Namely, do you want your spouse to be responsible for making healthcare decisions for you should you be in critical condition during divorce proceedings? If your spouse wants to strangle you anyway, imagine how quickly he or she might invoke a *do not resuscitate order* (DNR). Thus, just as with each financial power of attorney, you will want to modify each healthcare power of attorney to ensure that your "quality of life" wishes are carried out.

Property, Liberty, and Complexity

At the time of the French Revolution, property issues were easy: Serfs and women owned nothing. Thanks to equality, liberty, and fraternity, things are different now, but the complexity of dealing with property issues might threaten to make your divorce resemble the Reign of Terror. To deal with the often nonintuitive nature of divorce property law, consider taking seriously the optimistic Enlightenment philosophy mocked by Voltaire in *Candide*: Regardless of the settlement, (tell yourself) "it's the best of all (financial) possible worlds!" In Chapters 9 and 10 we'll show you the revolutionary way in which you can try to make this philosophy a reality in your divorce settlement.

Part IV

Reaching a Financially Fair and Feasible Divorce Settlement

*I*f we would have taken a cue from that famous George Lucas classic movie and named this book Divorce Wars, we'd now say "divorce is (almost) with you." But although they told a sort of complete story, we couldn't leave you hanging with a three-part trilogy of (Part I) philosophical, procedural, and financial fundamentals, (Part II) round-by-round fight strategies, and (Part III) in-depth understanding of financial-issues fundamentals.

We needed a Part IV to show you why war doesn't have to be the answer and why you should instead lay down your swords and (and Star Wars defense) shields and come to an equitable solution. So in Chapter 9, we show you what it means to negotiate an equitable settlement, and in Chapter 10 we present two hypothetical realistic case studies of couples reaching equitable settlements. By the time you're done, you'll be able to "quibble equitably for settlement equity"—even if you can't say it five times quickly.

Chapter 9

Negotiating Financially Sound Settlements for Postdivorce Prosperity

We don't know whether you believe that affirmative action is necessary to achieve the once-revolutionary American ideal of equal opportunity. But you'd better believe that affirmative action by the economically weaker spouse to get more than an equal share is often necessary to achieve the after-divorce equivalent of equal opportunity, an equitable settlement. In this chapter, we tell you about the equal-opportunity divorce revolution underway that takes into account a proposed settlement's financial projections over time rather than just its immediate effect at one point in time (the day of divorce).

The Divorce "Problem"

Meet one of today's typical divorced couples: two professionals, married in their mid-20s, parents by 30, another child or two before 40. Add in a substantial mortgage and other debt and subtract most of one income lost to one spouse, no longer always the wife, assuming primary homemaking responsibilities when the children arrive.

Unfortunately, they're now divorcing in their early 40s because they've grown apart, succumbed to family and/or work stress, or begun midlife angst. Fortunately, they're taking an enlightened approach to do things fairly, stay out of court, and minimize cost. So they're splitting their combined assets and debts—sharing the custody initially by having the primarily domestic spouse continue as the main custodial parent for the next few years, remaining in the house and neighborhood to which the kids are accustomed. They'll begin full joint physical custody when the youngest child is established comfortably in school by first or second grade. During that time, the custodial spouse, a hospital employee, will work flexible, part-time hours—weekends and some evenings. The other spouse becomes a weekend (and sometime weeknight) mom or dad, supplementing the custodial spouse's limited income with adequate spousal support. He or she will also provide more than the statutory amount of child support—recognizing how hard this will be on the kids and wanting them to be comfortable.

Divorce Dreams versus Reality

Sounds like a dream solution, given the nightmare of divorce, doesn't it? Unfortunately, just as Martin Luther King's "I Had a Dream" (of equality) still needs some work, our couple's divorce dream doesn't translate into equality five years later, when the spousal support has ended and both spouses are working full time. First, during the time spent primarily as a homemaker, the custodial spouse fell behind on the latest professional developments, had no salary growth, and accumulated no savings or additional credits in the hospital's retirement system. At the same salary as five years ago and without spousal support, he or she now faces the upkeep of a midlife house that needs a new roof and other repairs, and a new furnace and some appliances. He or she also needs a new car, will try to resume more of a normal social life, and also needs to return to school part-time to upgrade skills and qualify for more advanced certification.

Meanwhile, the other spouse has been promoted once or twice, with substantial accompanying salary increase. At first, the added financial obligations required maxing out a few credit cards, but the added salary has long since helped in paying those off and resuming maximum contributions to retirement savings. He or she has also pursued an active social life, is now remarried or thinking about it, and wants to "trade in" the three-bedroom condominium purchased after separation for a bigger, better house. Yet he or she recognizes how comfortable it's been to have less responsibility for the children, allowing for that rewarding career focus and personal satisfaction. He or she is no longer so sure about joint custody and now feels the child support is too generous.

Typical "Fair" Divorce Settlement

Even without the numerical details, to be provided shortly, it's evident that the spouses will live distinctly different dreams, one in vivid Technicolor and the other in drab black and white. Of course, this isn't the only "typical type" of divorce, and in many marriages that simply end with 50-50 splits, both spouses end up OK. However, in most divorce-case rulings or settlements involving marriages with young children where one spouse has been the primary bread-winner or continues in a good job while the other has partially or fully dropped out of the workforce, equal (shares) rapidly diverges from equity: the noncar-eer spouse ultimately ends up living much less comfortably than the other one after having shared a comfortable lifestyle for a number of years.

This happens because it's difficult to recover lost earning-power growth, and the cost of running a single-parent postdivorce household isn't much less than that of the two-parent marital household. Yet once spousal support, if any, runs out, only a fraction of that departed spouse's income is now available, and it is in the form of child support. Let's "run" with this idea a little bit by thinking of your financial life after divorce as an economic marathon. When the divorce settlement awards the lower-earning spouse a few years of alimony, he or she might keep pace or edge ahead for a while, but at alimony's end, the higher earner quickly pulls ahead and away with naturally higher earning speed. Although he or she trains hard to improve earning speed, the domestic spouse is encumbered by career-inactivity pains—the growing pains of the kids to whom he or she has been primarily devoted.

It's impossible to totally compensate for this earning-speed difference with-out giving the lower earner virtually all of the higher earner's assets, so that those assets can earn investment income to supplement the lower income. But for the ex-spouses to even stay in sight of one another, the faster-earning spouse must "handicap" the lifetime economic marathon by giving up a head-start larger share, and by providing longer or larger spousal support than might otherwise seem equitable. The handicap should enable the slower-earning spouse to per-manently boost (running) earning speed by hiring a massage therapist (ample, top-notch child care) to become more (time) flexible, and a personal trainer (education) to become more (financially) durable and powerful.

Why Fair Isn't Fair

Before running too wild with this analogy, let's look at the economic track record of long-term marriage "fair divorces"—"fair" thee well often resulting in one spouse's faring far less well. The inequities fall in these major categories:

- *Career growth and benefits limitations of domesticity:* When one spouse, whether employed or stay-at-home, assumed the primary domestic role, the other had the career freedom to more rapidly advance, which is usually what he or she continues to do after divorce. Meanwhile, the domestic spouse, although trying for more rapid advancement, remains tethered to children, with the result that he or she is automatically put on the plateau mommy (or daddy) career track when his or her employers learn or suspect that he or she is not available 24/7. Consequently, the domestic spouse often tries self-employment or more flexible jobs that pay less and offer fewer or no benefits—increasing his or her health-care costs while limiting access to pension or other employer-based retirement-savings plans.

- *Living longer is (female-finance) deadly.* Not only are women more often limited by their domestic roles, they're also stung by the double whammy of longer average life spans, further widening their retirement-savings gap. See the Resource Appendix for details on female old-age poverty excerpted from a Social Security Administration Web site entitled Women and Retirement Security.
- *Later learning, less future earning:* Returning for more education does boost pay, but domestic spouses who do it after a 40+ (age) divorce get less benefit due to outright or institutional age discrimination.
- *Silver-spoon versus plastic-spoon spouses:* Not infrequently, one party enters a marriage with substantial separate property, endowing the marriage in a way that allows both spouses to live a higher lifestyle than marital earnings alone allow. If that silver-spoon spouse is careful not to commingle the bulk of the separate property with marital assets, then it's usually not subject to division upon divorce—often relegating the other spouse back to a plastic-spoon life.

An Alternative Approach to Equitable Settlement

So when equality (of marital property share) doesn't make for an equitable settlement, what does? The problem with traditional methods is that they're based on two points in time, the wedding and divorce days. But just as Einstein discovered in physics, understanding events that take place over time is all relative, and you must consider the entire continuum.

In divorce, that means defining the financial life of each spouse not by just the two precise moments when the marriage began and ended but by the continuum of what happened financially immediately leading up to and during the marriage, and what is expected to happen afterward. So far, we've seen how the before and during play a huge part in determining a settlement, but courts are increasingly recognizing the equally important after. Testimony concerning the future financial effects of alternative divorce settlements is rapidly gaining acceptance in courts around the country. In 1998, a Tennessee appeals court refused to overturn a lower court's ruling in *Dellinger v. Dellinger* that awarded 65 percent of the property to the homemaker spouse in a 28-year-old marriage. The ruling had been influenced by the persuasive testimony of a certified financial planner who presented financial projections to the court. The grounds for the appeal, that only current circumstances be considered, were rejected.

Where Do You Need to Be in N Years?

So let's go back to the future in thinking about settlement equity and view negotiations the way an employer might question you during a job interview. Where do you want (in this case, need) to be in 5 years? In 10 years? In 25 years? In divorce, though, it's where you need to be for the settlement to be considered equitable that matters; getting to the "want to be" is up to your extra initiative after the divorce.

A "reasonable settlement," though, alone won't necessarily get you to where you need to be. Courts are loathe to rule that one spouse totally owes another an all-expenses-paid vacation. But a good settlement will put you on the trajectory to live at something like the lifestyle you enjoyed during a long-term marriage; and after a short-term marriage, it will at least put you on your feet for long enough that you can maintain your balance and start moving forward.

What Kind of Settlement Will Get You Where You Need to Be?

So here's where Einstein's physics comes in, or at least Isaac Newton's. With calculus, Newton showed how determining where a cannonball needs to land enables you to determine what explosive force to apply and how to aim the cannon. With the financial planner's equivalent of calculus, cash flow analysis, you can determine how a given combination of a property and support settlement can combine with a budget and investments to reach your targets.

Think of the settlement as where the cannon is aimed. A lousy settlement will have you in debt immediately or heading there soon, while an equitable one will have you pointed in the right direction. You can then think of the budget as the munitions mixture needed to propel the cannon. You must come up with the proper mixture of education and investment management to increase earning power, and work to realize that earning power—all while carefully controlling expenses to meet only needs, until wants are affordable—to propel your cash flows toward your goals.

Charting a Settlement's Net Worth

Figures 9-1 through 9-3 illustrate the three basic possible outcomes over time of any given financial strategy in terms of its effect on your net worth, the difference at any given time between the sums of your assets and your liabilities. Each shows net worth, cumulative income, and cumulative savings projected over 30 years from divorce:

Figure 9-1 shows you starting with a modest net worth and maintaining it by balancing spending and income. Figure 9-2 shows the effects of reducing spending below income so that your net worth continually increases. In contrast, Figure 9-3 shows an all-too-common outcome, the domestic spouse's net worth heads south as spending exceeds income, and assets must be eaten into in order to support even a subsistence level of living. Eventually, it goes

FIGURE 9-1   Flat Net Worth

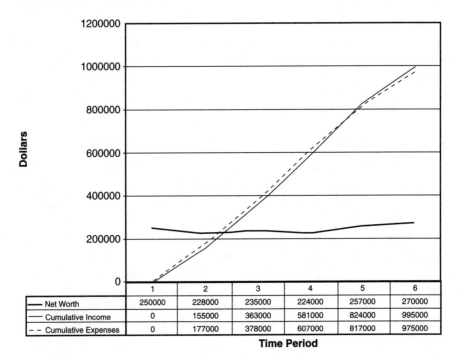

	1	2	3	4	5	6
Net Worth	250000	228000	235000	224000	257000	270000
Cumulative Income	0	155000	363000	581000	824000	995000
Cumulative Expenses	0	177000	378000	607000	817000	975000

Time Period

FIGURE 9-2 Increasing Net Worth

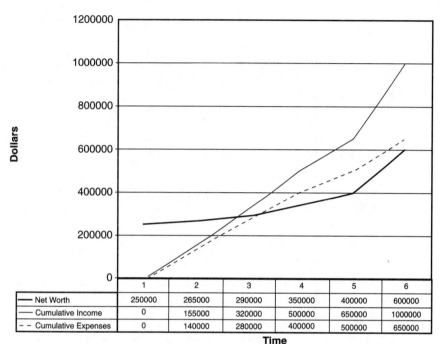

	1	2	3	4	5	6
—— Net Worth	250000	265000	290000	350000	400000	600000
—— Cumulative Income	0	155000	320000	500000	650000	1000000
– – Cumulative Expenses	0	140000	280000	400000	500000	650000

Time

negative when all assets are consumed and debt must be taken on just to meet necessities.

Charting a Better Net Worth Course

Given this new orientation, let's revisit this chapter's earlier case and illustrate the difference between the equal split, traditional equal view of equity, and the forward-looking split that comes from an enlightened view of equity. Using two software packages available to consumers, *Split-Up* and *Support 2004*, Figure 9-4 gives a more detailed look, for each scenario, at where the spouses stand at the time of divorce and where they'll be over the 30-year time horizon that follows.

Figure 9-4 shows the equal distribution soon becoming wildly inequitable right at the time the spousal support payments have stopped; the domestic spouse's net worth plummets toward six-figure debt, while the other spouse's net worth spikes upward.

FIGURE 9-3   Decreasing Net Worth

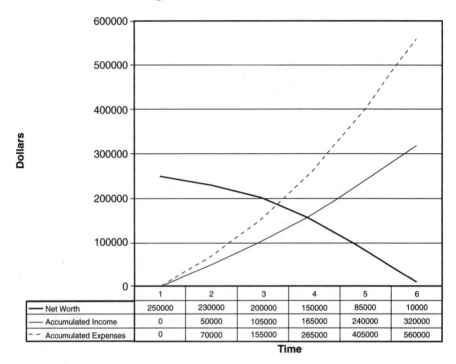

	1	2	3	4	5	6
—— Net Worth	250000	230000	200000	150000	85000	10000
—— Accumulated Income	0	50000	105000	165000	240000	320000
– – Accumulated Expenses	0	70000	155000	265000	405000	560000

Time

Figure 9-5 shows how some less-than-draconian adjustments to the settle-ment—50 percent higher spousal support payments and a two-thirds to one-third split—tilt it toward the domestic spouse. By sacrificing dubious equality to move toward desired equity, the domestic spouse stays a bit north of debt, while the higher-earning spouse remains comfortable—although having to wait a bit longer to become a millionaire, and no longer qualifying for the filthy-rich club.

Why It's a Win-Win for Both Sides

So, what's the problem; why haven't courts always handled divorce this way? For starters, professional financial planning for individuals didn't emerge until the 1970s—divorce planning in the 1990s. While businesses have long used cash flow analysis to determine the worthiness of proposed strategies and some individuals borrowed those concepts for themselves, until today's personal com-puters, most people lacked the capability to do the needed calculations.

FIGURE 9-4   An Equal Distribution Look at Differing Financial Fortunes

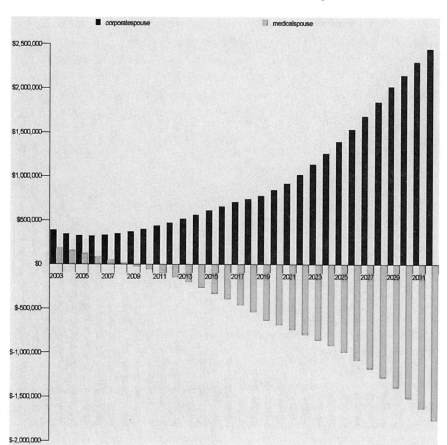

Net worth by year of custodial/medical (light shade) spouse and high-earner/corporate (dark shade) spouse.

Even with the calculations, though, one spouse often "gives up" what he or she considers to be his or hers using the traditional view of equity. Furthermore, until the advent of no-fault divorce, which emerged not long before financial planning and personal computers did, divorce was played as a zero-sum moralistic or immoral game in which the parties generally went for everything they could get because they were either entitled to it or had the power to get it. Now, however, as a consequence of the changing family dynamic and research on divorce's effects, conscionable individuals are increasingly recognizing a responsibility to do the right thing—even if it's just because they're aware of how not doing so can come back to haunt them.

FIGURE 9-5 An Equitable Distribution Look at Similar Financial Fortunes

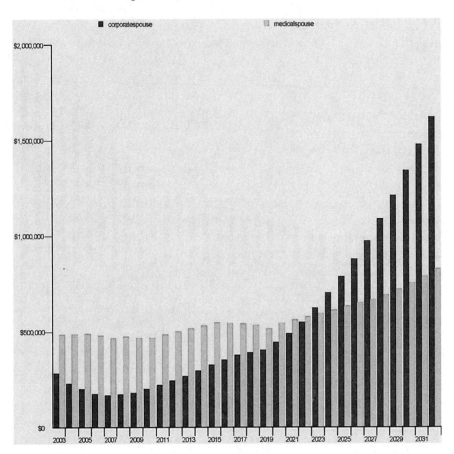

Net worth by year of custodial/medical (light shade) spouse and high-earner/corporate (dark shade) spouse.

Moving ahead in life is hard enough, particularly to successfully form a new family. But it's almost impossible if you leave contraband baggage behind, in the form of resentful children and spouse, without eventually facing up to the deleterious effects on new relationships and the lifelong problems it causes kids. In this age of tell-all television, highly publicized studies of our societal ills, universal access to information, too many attorneys ready to litigate, and pooper-scooper laws, it's in most people's best interests not to leave a mess behind.

Win-Win Scenarios

We're assuming you're among those that see it that way and see the wisdom of a win-win divorce resolution that could feel a little bit like losing. But even if you buy into this view of equity, it's often no simple matter to determine an equitable settlement. Why? Because every case is different; rulings and settlements based on long-range equity is just coming into its own, so there are no hard and fast rules. But even with these uncertainties, you can always act with a sense of fairness, while striving for equity. Chapter 10 models how you might do that with two detailed hypothetical cases showing how legal principles, the quest for equity, and old-fashioned horse trading can come together in settlements constructed with the application of fairness toward the goal of equity.

Meanwhile, we'll end this chapter with Figure 9-6, which is a table showing general scenarios that include a general settlement structure for each that often leads to fairness, if not equity. Keep in mind that this doesn't comprehensively cover all possible scenarios, and the scenarios are not detailed enough for you to know whether they apply to your case or whether that's how the case would be settled or decided in court.

Family Profile	Property Split	Spousal Support	Child Support(CS) and Other Issues	Comments
Short-Term, No Children	50-50 Marital	None	None	In a short marriage involving no children, neither spouse's life is far-removed from what it was, so split the marital-property difference.
Medium-Term, No Children Well-Off Big Salary Gap	50-50 or possible larger share for lower-paid spouse in non-community states.	None	None	When neither spouse's career development has been constrained, then in marriages long enough for a high-earner's contribution to have greatly increased marital property, (s)he might give a higher share to the lower earner who would not otherwise be able to maintain a similar lifestyle or provide for retirement.
Long-Term, Childless, Well-Off Big Salary Gap	50-50 marital	Lower earner might merit it even if marital role caused no career constraints.	None	The long-term marriage established a marital lifestyle that the lower earner might not be able to match. The higher earner may prefer paying deductible spousal support in lieu of additional property.
Med/Long Childless, Well-Off, Lower Earner Domestic	Possible larger share for lower-earning spouse in non-community states.	Possible Spousal Support for lower-earning spouse — especially in community states.	None	When one spouse in LT marriage sacrifices career development in a dead-end job to provide extensive domestic support (entertaining spouse's business associates, community socialite, etc.) for the other spouse, compensation is often in order.

Scenario	Property	Spousal Support	Child Support	Fairness/Equity
Short/Medium-Term with Young Kids, Middle Income, OK Financially, DS left job-job	More for Domestic Spouse (DS), but may need to sell house to have more cash.	2 to 6 yrs of lower-than-normal spousal-support payments in conjunction with more than 50-50 property share.	Statutory CS + college-fund supplement. Adjusted some down later for higher DS earnings.	A medium-income non-domestic spouse has trouble affording "normal" spousal support in addition to child support and college savings, especially because spousal-support payments don't provide as much tax benefit as they do for higher-income payers. So the payer compensates by giving more property.
Medium-Term DS left Career 2 Teen(ish) Kids, Good Income, Solid Finances	Even split, except when the DS gets a house with an equity value that's more than half of the total value of the couple's property; more for DS if home equity exceeds half of property if DS gets house.	4 to 6 years spousal support possibly increased depending on when domestic spouse can reduce child rearing responsibilities to retrain and re-enter the job market. Payments reduced if DS gets more than 50-50 property due to getting a high-equity house.	Statutory plus college-fund supplement. Adjusted way down later for higher DS earnings.	If home equity much less than half of property than they might want to give less than half of property to the domestic spouse and increase spousal support for more payer's deduction in high tax bracket.
Medium-Term 30's Couple, Unequal Earners, 2 Teen(ish) Kids, Good 1st Income, Solid Finances	Even	4 to 6 years spousal support to lower-earning spouse, even if fully joint custody.	Statutory plus college-fund supplement. Adjusted some down later for higher DS earnings.	Except in short-term marriages, a lower-earning spouse is entitled to continue the marital lifestyle to the extent possible after divorce. Spousal support is often awarded or negotiated for a period equal to $\frac{1}{2}$ the years of the marriage for medium term marriages.

FIGURE 9-6 General Scenarios for Possible Settlement Fairness/Equity

Family Profile	Property Split	Spousal Support	Child Support (CS) and Other Issues	Comments
Med/LongTerm 40's Couple, DS left Career, 4 Teen(ish) Kids, Good Income, Solid Finances	DS gets half or more, depending on spousal support.	6 to 10 years of higher-than-normal rehab spousal support to compensate and catch up after DS lost vital career-advancement.	Statutory plus college-fund supplement. Continual adjustments down as kids age out and DS earns more.	Tax situation favors the higher spousal support but couple might decide to give DS higher share of property if child support for 4 kids limits affordability of spousal support.
Long-Term, 50's couple, grown children, DS now works, Ok finances, big salary gap	Lower earner gets half or more, depending on spousal support.	Long-term spousal support as former DS will never come close to equal earnings. Might front load higher for fewer years.	None	Classic situation in which one spouse was a homemaker for most of the marriage. (S)he's entitled to maintain marital lifestyle, so needs either long-term spousal support or shorter term with decidedly favorable property settlement.
Medium-Term, 50's couple, grown children, DS now works, Ok finances, salary gap	Lower earner gets half or more, depending on spousal support.	Medium-term equalizing spousal support.	None	Here the lower-earning spouse is entitled to maintain the marital lifestyle for a limited period of time because the marriage wasn't long-term—this despite the fact that (s)he might not have enough time before retirement to catch up earnings.

FIGURE 9-6 Continued

Chapter 10

Financial Self-Defense in Action: Specific Settlement Scenarios and Solutions

Like Gene Hackman as the basketball coach in *Hoosiers* who takes his small-town team to an Indiana high school state championship, we believe that you must commit to the team system for the best chance of divorce success. In the coach's case, success required a committed belief in his leadership, no-holding-back participation in " basketball boot camp," and no room for prima donna stars or their meddling parents. Here, it means commitment to our constructive approach to divorce and willingness to work hard to thoroughly educate and prepare yourself as much as possible; working with your divorce professionals—and your spouse's, if possible, in a team effort; and not being influenced by friends, family, or gladiator divorce lawyers egging you on to "win."

Just as Gene Hackman lacked enough players for a full intra-squad practice scrimmage to simulate game conditions, we can't completely simulate your experience going through divorce. But we intend this chapter's two example cases as the next best thing, in which you should find several elements similar to your own situation and you can see how they reach equitable resolutions that don't require a "Hoosiers miracle."

The Stein Case

Rachel and Michael Stein, ages 51 and 54, respectively, are divorcing after 25 years of marriage. Their three teenagers—David (18, twelfth grade), Rebecca

(16, tenth grade), and Joel (14, eighth grade)—will all live with Rachel, who'll get the house. The Steins will mutually assume responsibility to pay for their Michigan in-state college educations. Until Joel enters college, Rachel—who was primarily a homemaker after David was born but worked as a physician's assistant until then—will upgrade her skills by getting a master's degree while working part-time and being available as much as possible for her kids, who are shocked and upset. She'll make $15,000 to $20,000 annually the next few part-time years, $40,000 annually when she begins work full time, and about $50,000 once promoted a few years later after (re)proving herself.

Unfortunately, financial pressures have played a significant role in the divorce. Michael has just taken essentially forced early retirement from a large company where he has been a high-level computer professional. He has received a five-year sweetener on his pension, so he'll start receiving payments at age 65 (2013) as though he'd worked 35 years and retired in 2013. But he loses a great benefit package, including health insurance, and to stay above water, he's taken a position as a traveling computer-systems consultant/contractor with a national technical outsourcing firm, for which he'll start at $75,000 after having last made almost $100,000 annually.

Rachel and Michael do trust each other and intend to put the kids' needs first, so Michael intends to travel from wherever he's living as much as possible to see them. But they remain somewhat far apart on the property division and spousal support issues. Rachel's salary will improve significantly in 7 or 8 years but still lag considerably behind even Michael's reduced salary—which is expected to keep up with inflation. But she hasn't earned any pension benefits and has no 401(k) savings—and she feels that her efforts at home allowed Michael to always put his job first and ratchet up his salary.

Meanwhile, while Michael understands Rachel's desire to maintain the house for the kids—and maybe very young grandchildren for a few years—he feels it's a luxury they can't afford. He thinks everyone will be far less deprived by selling the house before the divorce. The Steins have always been good budgeters, so he's prepared to live cheaply the next 8 years or so while paying both child support and spousal support, the spousal support ending when Rachel reaches full earning power in about 5 years and the child support in 8 years.

Stein Base Case Scenario

We'll analyze this case with three alternative scenarios that follow, comparing their net-worth projections (and also providing settlement details for the first scenario to give you an appreciation of the way *Split-Up* analyzes a case). In addition to the key elements already mentioned, each of these scenarios incorporates the following additional data:

- *Tax filing:* Michael will file as single, taking "advantage" of his higher tax bracket by claiming the three children's exemptions (until age 21). As custodial spouse, Rachel will file as head of household, usually offering a lower overall composite tax rate than filing as single.
- *Property and lifestyle:* Michael and Rachel have always been fiscally responsible, but living on one income has resulted in their only significant assets, other than the future pension, being Michael's 401(k) and the equity in the house.
- *Investment returns:* Other than a 5 percent annual appreciation rate on the home, we assume annual pre-tax returns of 6 percent on reinvested cash (net income after taxes and expenses), 6 percent capital and 1 percent dividend return on stocks, and 7 percent on tax-deferred IRA and 401(k) investments.
- *Debt:* They have a zero-interest loan for their oldest child's car and, after just completing automobile leases, have each just bought inexpensive ($15,000) new cars, taking advantage of no-interest-loan promotions. Other than the 6 percent rate on the mortgage, we use 7 percent on both the unsubsidized college loans and the cumulative debt that results from an excess of expenses over net income in any given year.
- *Major expenses:* Michael has agreed to pay 75% of their daughter's wedding costs, with Rachel paying the other 25%. In addition to his share of current and future college loans that will be split in the property division, Michael will also pay an additional $30,000 toward college expenses over the next 8 years.

Stein Scenario 1: Keep House

This settlement scenario is basically "by the book,"—in which Michael and Rachel essentially split their assets, and Michael pays both child support and spousal support in line with Michigan's guidelines. We calculate the support amounts with a nifty personal computer software product, MarginSoft's *Support 2004* (www.marginsoft.net), developed by 25-year Michigan family law attorney and mediator Craig Ross. Many Michigan family court jurisdictions have relied on it for decisions like this one,

Support 2004 computes 11 to 12 years of about $12,000 in spousal support annually. However, Michael and Rachel decide to "front-end" the support by making it 5 years of $24,000 annually, to best cover Rachel during the particularly lean years until the youngest child is in college and she's earning a solid professional wage. In addition, Michael and Rachel use the *Support 2004* calculation as a guideline to come to a compromise agreement of higher-than-normal child support of $15,000 annually initially, decreasing to about $10,000 annually, then $5000 annually, and finally nothing as each child graduates from college. We've simplified this, when in reality, in the absence of a long-term agreement, child support should be recalculated annually because the parents' incomes and children's circumstances are most likely changing.

(Caution: This is just meant to be a realistic but hypothetical example; do not assume that a Michigan court would have rendered this decision under these facts. Furthermore, Michigan only requires child support until age 18 or high-school graduation, but several states now require child support until college graduation, so we're going to assume the couple agrees to child support until the youngest child graduates college.)

Figures 10-1 and 10-2 show, respectively, the property division and a 30-year projection of each spouse's net worth, calculated by the *Split-Up* software package. The results are based on the assumptions we've covered here, plus details on expenses and other items that the program requires that we don't show here.

Note that Figure 10-1 shows a zero value for the pension being divided. That's because, instead of determining its lump-sum value, Rachel and Michael have agreed to divide the marital portion of future payments in the same ratio as they decide for other property. Because Michael started earning the pension before marriage, the marital portion is only 83 percent, the ratio of years married (25) to total pension-earning years (30) actually worked (not including the 5 additional sweetener years). The agreed split applies only to that divisible (shared) pension portion, so Michael gets 57 percent of total pension payments, and Rachel 43 percent.

Unfortunately, Rachel's increased earning, alimony subsidy, and home appreciation don't offset the high property tax and maintenance costs of their almost-50-year-old home. Despite her higher earning power, Rachel's net worth begins plummeting the year after spousal-support payments end, as she must eat into savings to pay living costs. By the time she's 74 her net worth will go negative and she'll be almost $400,000 in the hole by age 81.

Meanwhile, Michael's net worth declines slightly during the 8 years until he no longer must pay either spousal support or child support. His net worth exceeds $1 million by age 75 and hits $1.5 million by age 84.

FIGURE 10-1   Property Division for Michael-Rachel Scenario 1

Property Division Report

Property division report for Michael Stein and Rachel Stein.

This report shows each item of property, its current value, allocation between marital and separate, and who is keeping it. It also shows totals for each property type.

	Michael Amount	Pct	Rachel Amount	Pct	Total Amount
Cash					
Total Cash	$53,248	64%	$29,952	36%	$83,200
Investments					
Stock	$100,000	100%	$0	0%	$100,000
Total Investments	$100,000	100%	$0	0%	$100,000
Cars, Furniture					
Rachel's Furniture	$0	0%	$25,000	100%	$25,000
Rachel's car	$0	0%	$15,000	100%	$15,000
Michael's car	$15,000	100%	$0	0%	$15,000
Michael's Furniture	$5,000	100%	$0	0%	$5,000
Total Cars, Furniture	$20,000	33%	$40,000	67%	$60,000
Residence Equity					
	$0	0%	$243,324	100%	$243,324
Michael's Rental	$0	0%	$0	100%	$0
Rachel's Rental	$0	0%	$0	100%	$0
Total Residence Equity	$0	0%	$243,324	100%	$243,324
Businesses	$0	0%	$0	0%	$0
IRAs and 401(k)s					
401(k)	$168,000	84%	$32,000	16%	$200,000
Total IRAs and 401(k)s	$168,000	84%	$32,000	16%	$200,000
Defined Benefit Pensions					
Total Pensions	$0	0%	$0	0%	$0
Life Insurance Plans					
Life Insurance	$0	0%	$0	0%	$0
Bank and Credit Card Debts					
Home Equity	$0	0%	$0	100%	$0
Michael Car Loan	$15,000	100%	$0	0%	$15,000
Rachel Car Loan	$0	0%	$15,000	100%	$15,000
Kids Car Loan	$9,600	100%	$0	0%	$9,600
Michael College	$10,000	100%	$0	0%	$10,000
Rebecca College	$0	0%	$11,000	100%	$11,000
Joel College	$0	0%	$12,000	100%	$12,000
Bank and Credit Card Debt	($34,600)	48%	($38,000)	52%	($72,600)

Prepared by Alan Feigenbaum. Copyright (c) 1997-2003. SU Software v 6.01   www.FamilyLawSoftware.com / 1-877-477-5488

FIGURE 10-1   Continued

Family Debts

Family Debts	$0	0%	$0	0%	$0
Bank and Family Debts	($34,600)	48%	($38,000)	52%	($72,600)

Notes (Debts) btw Spouses

Mortgage on residence	$0	0%	$0	0%	$0
Notes on businesses	$0	0%	$0	0%	$0
Total Notes btw Spouses	$0	0%	$0	0%	$0
Total Property	**$306,648**	**50%**	**$307,276**	**50%**	**$613,924**

Total Property Graph (not including debts):

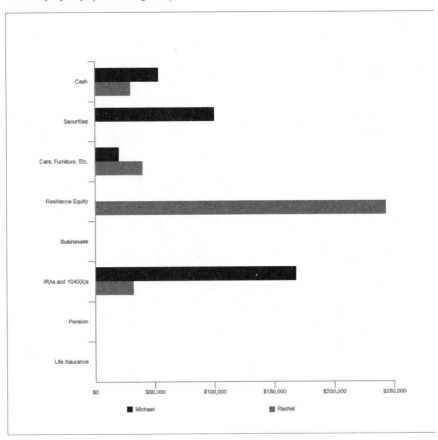

FIGURE 10-2   Net Worth Projections for Michael-Rachel Scenario 1

Projected Net Worth: Table

	Michael	Rachel		Michael	Rachel
2004	$ 304,088	$ 281,746	2019	$ 744,865	$ 260,732
2005	$ 296,379	$ 277,733	2020	$ 791,080	$ 265,253
2006	$ 287,235	$ 272,598	2021	$ 838,915	$ 243,909
2007	$ 278,221	$ 282,784	2022	$ 888,424	$ 219,044
2008	$ 270,773	$ 294,054	2023	$ 939,663	$ 190,339
2009	$ 286,366	$ 283,906	2024	$ 992,697	$ 157,447
2010	$ 279,261	$ 266,025	2025	$ 1,047,680	$ 119,997
2011	$ 299,759	$ 249,225	2026	$ 1,104,602	$ 77,585
2012	$ 320,295	$ 236,112	2027	$ 1,163,653	$ 29,777
2013	$ 347,218	$ 217,567	2028	$ 1,224,926	($ 23,888)
2014	$ 405,793	$ 225,967	2029	$ 1,288,680	($ 83,919)
2015	$ 487,825	$ 233,998	2030	$ 1,354,912	($ 150,852)
2016	$ 533,503	$ 241,598	2031	$ 1,423,933	($ 225,270)
2017	$ 603,000	$ 248,670	2032	$ 1,495,899	($ 307,796)
2018	$ 700,209	$ 255,149	2033	$ 1,571,663	($ 399,109)

Projected Net Worth: Graph

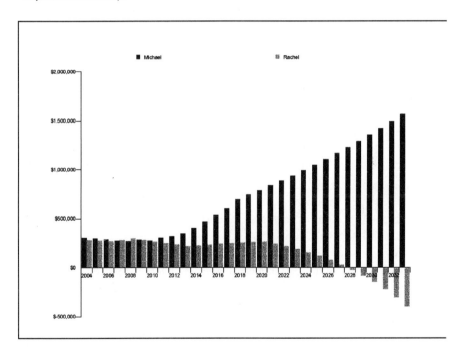

Prepared by Alan Feigenbaum. Copyright (c) 1997-2003.   SU Software v 6.01   www.FamilyLawSoftware.com / 1-877-477-5488

Stein Scenario 2: Keep House 8 Years

To help Rachel recover from this hole, let's see, in the chart in Figure 10-3, if Michael was onto something when he thought she should sell the house—which she'll do in this scenario in 8 years, after the kids have finished college.

Indeed, Rachel's financial position does improve, her net worth peaking at about one-third of a million at age 70. It then steadily declines and she's almost in debt by age 81. This improvement occurs despite having to start paying rent after 8 years and after becoming mortgage free in just 5 years. That's because she benefits so much from eliminating maintenance and other home-owning expenses such as property taxes. Therefore, we'd expect her to do even better if she completely cut those expenses by selling the house immediately. However, she is unwilling to consider selling the house before all the kids have graduated, and feels Michael should make a further financial concession to go along with her willingness to give up the house in 8 years.

Stein Scenario 3: Give Rachel More Property

In trying to find a way to improve Rachel's position, increasing spousal support is out of the question, as Michael is already paying more than half his gross income toward support during the next five years. And he's unwilling to extend the number of years. The only thing left is property, in the form of all of a stock portfolio and 84 percent of a 401(k) that he would get in Scenarios 1 and 2. So Scenario 3 gives her 45 percent of the stock portfolio and more of the 401(k), resulting in a 60/40 split favoring Rachel. In addition, they adjust the pension the same way, giving Rachel 60 percent of the marital portion, which comes out to 50 percent of each actual pension payment.

As Figure 10-4 reveals, Rachel would be foolish to deep-six the 60/40 offer. Her net worth slowly but steadily increases to almost $600,000 by age 76, declining only slightly thereafter. Meanwhile, Michael's net worth declines initially, even more so than before, but starts rising when he reaches age 65, reaching $600,000 by retirement at age 70 and exceeding $1 million by age 82. While it's true that Michael does better, it's partly due to his willingness to work until age 69, while Rachel's financials are based on retiring at age 68. By working until age 70, Rachel will not only improve this net-worth projection by adding a few additional years of savings, she'll also increase her Social Security monthly benefit.

FIGURE 10-3 Net Worth Projections for Michael-Rachel Scenario 2

Projected Net Worth: Table

	Michael	Rachel			Michael	Rachel
2004	$ 304,088	$ 281,746		2019	$ 744,865	$ 311,907
2005	$ 296,379	$ 277,733		2020	$ 791,080	$ 330,533
2006	$ 287,235	$ 272,598		2021	$ 838,915	$ 324,699
2007	$ 278,221	$ 282,784		2022	$ 888,424	$ 317,122
2008	$ 270,773	$ 294,054		2023	$ 939,663	$ 307,651
2009	$ 286,366	$ 283,906		2024	$ 992,697	$ 296,126
2010	$ 279,261	$ 266,025		2025	$ 1,047,680	$ 282,376
2011	$ 299,759	$ 249,225		2026	$ 1,104,602	$ 266,217
2012	$ 320,295	$ 228,822		2027	$ 1,163,653	$ 247,452
2013	$ 347,218	$ 207,842		2028	$ 1,224,926	$ 225,878
2014	$ 405,793	$ 224,013		2029	$ 1,288,680	$ 201,269
2015	$ 467,825	$ 240,659		2030	$ 1,354,912	$ 173,390
2016	$ 533,503	$ 257,795		2031	$ 1,423,933	$ 141,987
2017	$ 603,000	$ 275,405		2032	$ 1,495,899	$ 106,795
2018	$ 700,209	$ 293,511		2033	$ 1,571,663	$ 67,853

Projected Net Worth: Graph

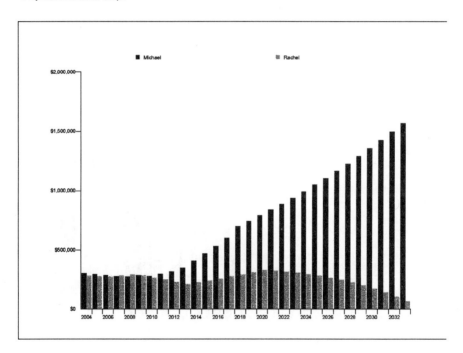

Prepared by Alan Feigenbaum. Copyright (c) 1997-2003. SU Software v 6.01   www.FamilyLawSoftware.com / 1-877-477-5488

FIGURE 10-4   Net Worth Projections for Michael-Rachel Scenario 3

Projected Net Worth: Table

	Michael	Rachel		Michael	Rachel
2004	$ 237,564	$ 344,907	2019	$ 567,497	$ 497,464
2005	$ 225,668	$ 344,615	2020	$ 600,055	$ 530,417
2006	$ 215,529	$ 344,219	2021	$ 633,455	$ 540,439
2007	$ 204,534	$ 359,477	2022	$ 667,713	$ 549,661
2008	$ 191,869	$ 376,174	2023	$ 702,829	$ 557,992
2009	$ 202,289	$ 371,833	2024	$ 738,827	$ 565,328
2010	$ 189,718	$ 360,165	2025	$ 775,793	$ 571,562
2011	$ 204,389	$ 350,013	2026	$ 813,673	$ 576,575
2012	$ 218,732	$ 336,229	2027	$ 852,577	$ 580,241
2013	$ 239,053	$ 321,669	2028	$ 892,538	$ 582,431
2014	$ 287,100	$ 348,227	2029	$ 933,727	$ 582,996
2015	$ 338,450	$ 375,863	2030	$ 976,078	$ 581,785
2016	$ 393,092	$ 404,624	2031	$ 1,019,807	$ 578,634
2017	$ 450,927	$ 434,536	2032	$ 1,064,986	$ 573,373
2018	$ 535,832	$ 465,513	2033	$ 1,112,362	$ 566,308

Projected Net Worth: Graph

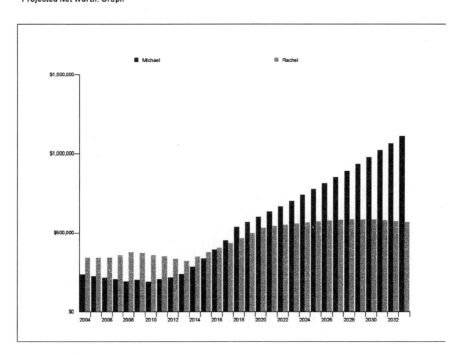

Prepared by Alan Feigenbaum. Copyright (c) 1997-2003. SU Software v 6.01   www.FamilyLawSoftware.com / 1-877-477-5488

Stein Case Comments

It's nice to know that in comparing different settlement options, you can sometimes improve one spouse's lot without further weakening the other one's—as we found in Scenario 2. In fact, had Rachel been willing to sell the house immediately, she would have done even better (a scenario we didn't show). If she changes her mind Rachel and Michael might do further number crunching to see if they can balance out and make things better for the kids. They should test having Rachel stay in the house for only five years, until all the kids have entered college, which might allow them to lower spousal support a bit while keeping Rachel as well off as she ended up in Scenario 3. After all, Michael is as responsible an ex-spouse as anyone could want, willing to become a professional nomad in order to pay needed child support and spousal support.

Finally, with so few assets, to start getting only 40 percent of the property in Scenario 3, you might be wondering how Michael can swing those substantial combination child and spousal support payments for the next 5 to 10 years. The calculations we show assume that he had to rely on credit card debt when his outflow exceeded his income. However, he did have another alternative that might work better, tapping his 401(k) without an early withdrawal penalty. IRS regulations allow for the special case in which 401(k) funds can be disbursed without penalty under the provisions of a QDRO if used to pay support obligations. So if you have a large 401(k) and few liquid assets, consider that alternative. But don't forget that you'll be giving up tax deferral on that part of your earnings, paying income tax on the distributions, and cracking your humpty-dumpty retirement nest egg in a way that you can't put all back together again.

The Byrnes Case

Unlike Michael and Rachel Stein, Ted and Samantha Byrnes have lived more like their typical spendthrift early-boomer American peers—perhaps because of their one-fell-swoop family, fraternal twins Thomas and Traci, born the year after marriage and graduating from college this year. After the children were born, Ted and Samantha agreed that Samantha would quickly return to her fast-track career as a new-media marketing whiz, while nontraditional Ted, a teacher, combined a leave of absence with part-time status during the twins first few years and then continued as the primary parent once he returned to full-time teaching.

It's just as well Ted was flexible because Samantha's star took them on a multistate corporate-climb tour during which Ted never did more than a 5-year stretch in any public school system, and also taught in many private schools. That rootless existence and Samantha's continued salary spikes when taking new jobs perhaps made it easier to spend almost their means. That left them with hardly any savings, significant credit card debt, and no pension—although Ted might still earn a small one in the 15 years until most systems' maximum retirement age should he get another public school position after the divorce.

No such pension awaits Samantha, who decided to finally stop chasing the rainbow and is parlaying her expertise into her own business. Despite the financial risk, Ted shared Samantha's optimism and looked forward to finally putting down roots and enjoying more time together in their now-empty nest. Unfortunately, it quickly became evident that Samantha's success required substantial domestic and even international travel, so they mutually decided to end the marriage.

On his own, Ted feels he can be comfortable living a more modest lifestyle on a teacher's salary and start building up retirement savings, but he is worried about whether he can accumulate anywhere close to enough. He knows he's facing high medical costs in retirement, beyond what Medicare covers, because of his high blood pressure and adult-onset diabetes. He also foresees Samantha building the business from its initial success and retiring well off, and he feels that his marital contributions and career sacrifices—including giving up pension service years and normal teaching salary-ladder growth—played a significant role in establishing a base for that business and success.

Therefore, even though Samantha now earns only a $60,000 annual salary from the business, he feels entitled to spousal support that takes into account her $100,000-plus salary she earned before she started the business—and to which she could easily return. Furthermore, he knows that she projects business revenues growing well beyond 10 percent annually, which will allow her to increase her salary at least 10 percent a year. While Samantha agrees that Ted is entitled to spousal support, perhaps even more than would normally be awarded given her current salary, she's concerned about high support payments, particularly in the next few years, draining available capital for her business.

However, Ted knows that long-term spousal support is unlikely, so he's returning to another state's school system where he'll bridge 5 previous years of service with 15 more, retiring at 65 on a partial 20-year-service pension of about $24,000 annually. (This is significantly less than typical full 30-year teacher pensions of about 60 percent of final-year salary.) Because the Byrneses were married during 5 of Ted's 20 pension-earning years, they agree that Samantha is entitled to 5/20ths of an equal share of Ted's pension, $3000 annually.

Byrnes Base Case Scenario

In addition to the key elements already mentioned, the three following scenarios use this data:

- *Property:* Samantha owns a $45,000 car because she feels it is essential to project the appropriate business image.
- *Retirement accounts:* Other than the pension Ted will earn by returning to one of his previous school systems, the only other retirement account is Samantha's IRA. It consists mainly of rollovers—for continued tax deferral—from the 401(k) accounts she had at her various employers. Although we don't cover it here, once Samantha can afford it, she should start a *simplified employee pension* (SEP) *plan, saving incentive match plan for employees* (SIMPLE), or Keogh plan that will enable her to shield some current income from current taxes and build up additional retirement savings.
- *Business value and Ted's buyout:* A valuation done by a CPA/CVA (certified valuation analyst) established a value of $200,000. Samantha contends that this should belong entirely to her because the business didn't begin until the separation. Ted feels that his overall marital contributions helped Samantha get to the point where she could succeed in the business. In addition, during the planning and setup phase, he provided substantial editing and production services for promotional literature and a Web site, and drafted several proposals (he's an English teacher) that have turned into business for Samantha. Thus, he feels entitled to a $75,000 share of its current value. We'll reflect this difference of opinion in the different scenarios. Also, we assume that the business value grows at a rate of 2.5 percent annually and will be sold at the amount that growth comes to when Samantha reaches age 65, the proceeds going all to Samantha after capital-gains taxes.
- *Business income:* Although Samantha has hopes that the business might make as much as $70,000 this year, we use only $60,000 with growth of 10 percent annually in the base case.
- *Filing status:* Ted and Samantha will file as single—neither with dependents—after divorce.
- *House and debt:* Ted and Samantha have almost $500,000 in personal, kids' college, mortgage, and business-related debt embedded in their current net worth of about $240,000. They'll both rent modest apartments after agreeing to sell the home now—splitting the little equity in it. They're also refinancing the remaining debt and assigning all but one

debt in Ted's name to Samantha, which of course means she gets most of the positive assets as well to counterbalance the debt.

- *Work plans:* The results assume Ted, now age 49, and Samantha, now 45, will both work until age 65—at which point Samantha will sell the business. However, we'll discuss how working longer might change things.

Byrnes Scenario 1: Even Split of Nonbusiness Assets, Limited Spousal Support

Once again, we start by splitting the net assets (combined assets and debts) equally, except for the business, which in this scenario we assume belongs totally to Samantha. Thus, her starting net worth will be $200,000 higher than Ted's. In turn, although Samantha is entitled to a small share of Ted's pension, we give it all to him in this scenario. In addition, Samantha pays Ted a modest spousal support award based on a "compromise salary" for Samantha of $80,000 annually. Although Ted and Samantha aren't from Michigan, we've used *Support 2004* to estimate spousal support of about $8000 annually for 7 years.

Once again, we provide the most detail for the first settlement scenario, shown in Figures 10-5 and 10-6.

Ted's concerns were well founded; his net worth peaks at a paltry $155,000 a few years after retirement and then declines sharply until he's in debt by age 79. Meanwhile, after Ted reaches his maximum net worth figure the year after Samantha stops paying him spousal support, her net worth shoots back up as the college debt and car loan are paid off and her company more than triples its annual revenues. She'll be worth more than $1 million after selling the company at age 65. From there, her net worth remains steady through age 75.

Byrnes Scenario 2: Business Buys out Ted

This differs in two respects. We recognize that Ted has contributed $75,000 to the current $200,000 value through his marital intangible contributions, editing and promotion services, and share of marital loans that helped fund the business startup that he's assuming in the property split. Samantha buys Ted's $75,000 contribution by paying him 16 years of level payments at an interest rate of 5 percent, working out to about $6900 annually. (Note that the software reflects this in two ways in the reports: first, in the initial net worth difference from Scenario 1 by assigning Samantha a debt of $75,000 and Ted being owed $75,000; and second, in income and expenses, respectively, with payments from Samantha and to Ted when they actually occur.) In addition, we assume that Samantha gets her rightful pension share, $3000 of the $24,000 annual payments.

As Figure 10-7 shows, the buyout gets Ted above water, with a net worth that rises to a peak of just over $340,000 at age 70, declining slowly from there to about $275,000 at age 79. However, it immediately drops from there to just over $100,000 by age 78 and will go negative if Ted lives into his 80s. Meanwhile, Samantha barely dips into debt during the years she's paying spousal support, but her net worth rises rapidly afterwards to a peak of $1.3 million at age 68, declining slowly from there to remain over $1 million at age 75.

Byrnes Scenario 3: Trade Partial IRA for Buyout

Ted might be able to outlast his slowly declining net worth if he doesn't live into his 90s, but he'd like to feel more secure. The gap between him and Samantha seems unwarranted given the length of their marriage, his being primarily responsible for holding the family together during it, and his contributions to Samantha's business. So we look to make a few minor adjustments that will improve Ted's position without damaging Samantha's too much.

Unlike Michael and Rachel's case, there's not enough property to accomplish this by changing the property split, so we look to increase Ted's cash flow at Samantha's cash-flow expense. We do this primarily by giving Ted a full half of the current value of Samantha's business. So she must now pay off a $100,000 buyout instead of $75,000—accomplished by increasing the 16 years of annual payments by about $2000 annually to a little over $9000 each. In addition to helping Ted's front-end cash flow, we also help him on the back end by giving him all of his pension, transferring Samantha's $3000 annually to him starting at age 65.

Figure 10-8 shows that these changes result in Ted reaching almost a half-million in net worth by age 77 before slowly declining, while Samantha's peaks at almost $1.2 million at age 65, declining gradually to a little over $900,000 at age 75. Although she ends up worth about twice as much Ted at comparable ages, that seems relatively equitable. They'll have been married about the same number of years as the number of years from the divorce until retirement, and Samantha will continue putting heart and soul into the business to reap its rewards.

FIGURE 10-5   Property Division for Samantha-Ted Scenario 1

Property Division Report

Property division report for Ted Byrnes and Samantha Byrnes.

This report shows each item of property, its current value, allocation between marital and separate, and who is keeping it. It also shows totals for each property type.

	Ted Amount	Pct	Samantha Amount	Pct	Total Amount
Cash					
Total Cash	$12,000	40%	$18,000	60%	$30,000
Investments					
Long Term Winning Stock	$0	0%	$100,000	100%	$100,000
Long Term Losing Stock	$25,000	50%	$25,000	50%	$50,000
Short Term Winning Stock	$15,000	25%	$45,000	75%	$60,000
Short Term Losing Investm	$0	0%	$30,000	100%	$30,000
Total Investments	$40,000	17%	$200,000	83%	$240,000
Cars, Furniture					
Samantha Fancy Car	$0	0%	$45,000	100%	$45,000
Ted Cheap Car	$5,000	100%	$0	0%	$5,000
Samantha Furniture	$0	0%	$47,000	100%	$47,000
Ted Furniture	$13,000	100%	$0	0%	$13,000
Total Cars, Furniture	$18,000	16%	$92,000	84%	$110,000
Residence Equity					
	$0	0%	$50,000	100%	$50,000
Ted Rental	$0	0%	$0	100%	$0
Samantha Rental	$0	0%	$0	100%	$0
Total Residence Equity	$0	0%	$50,000	100%	$50,000
Businesses					
Samantha Stationary B	$0	0%	$200,000	100%	$200,000
Total Businesses	$0	0%	$200,000	100%	$200,000
IRAs and 401(k)s					
Consolidated Rollover IRA	$0	0%	$150,000	100%	$150,000
Total IRAs and 401(k)s	$0	0%	$150,000	100%	$150,000
Defined Benefit Pensions					
Total Pensions	$0	0%	$0	0%	$0
Life Insurance Plans					
Life Insurance	$0	0%	$0	0%	$0
Bank and Credit Card Debts					
Leg Breaker Lenders	$0	0%	$200,000	100%	$200,000
College Loans	$0	0%	$100,000	100%	$100,000
College Loans2	$0	0%	$0	100%	$0
Fancy Car Loan	$0	0%	$40,000	100%	$40,000
Samantha Crunched Credit	$0	0%	$150,000	100%	$150,000
Ted Crunched Credit	$50,000	100%	$0	0%	$50,000
Bank and Credit Card Debt	($50,000)	9%	($490,000)	91%	($540,000)

Family Debts

Family Debts	$0	0%	$0	0%	$0
Bank and Family Debts	($50,000)	9%	($490,000)	91%	($540,000)

Notes (Debts) btw Spouses

Mortgage on residence	$0	0%	$0	0%	$0
Notes on businesses	$0	0%	$0	0%	$0
Total Notes btw Spouses	$0	0%	$0	0%	$0
Total Property	**$20,000**	**8%**	**$220,000**	**92%**	**$240,000**

Total Property Graph (not including debts):

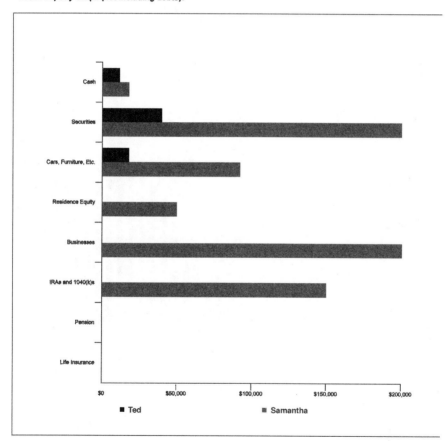

FIGURE 10-6   Net Worth Projections for Samantha-Ted Scenario 1

Projected Net Worth: Table

	Ted	Samantha		Ted	Samantha
2004	$ 24,401	$ 149,467	2019	$ 151,719	$ 600,439
2005	$ 28,936	$ 140,457	2020	$ 153,979	$ 727,535
2006	$ 34,215	$ 135,872	2021	$ 154,795	$ 877,289
2007	$ 39,629	$ 133,921	2022	$ 154,036	$ 1,052,624
2008	$ 48,404	$ 136,733	2023	$ 151,557	$ 1,276,776
2009	$ 58,090	$ 134,648	2024	$ 147,204	$ 1,535,174
2010	$ 68,731	$ 137,426	2025	$ 140,814	$ 1,536,003
2011	$ 73,847	$ 148,870	2026	$ 132,176	$ 1,559,960
2012	$ 79,556	$ 167,090	2027	$ 120,714	$ 1,583,686
2013	$ 85,862	$ 192,802	2028	$ 106,258	$ 1,586,139
2014	$ 93,379	$ 227,779	2029	$ 88,357	$ 1,584,504
2015	$ 101,565	$ 273,579	2030	$ 66,658	$ 1,578,330
2016	$ 110,400	$ 331,919	2031	$ 40,059	$ 1,567,129
2017	$ 119,279	$ 404,705	2032	$ 7,844	$ 1,550,373
2018	$ 128,182	$ 493,560	2033	($ 27,608)	$ 1,528,156

Projected Net Worth: Graph

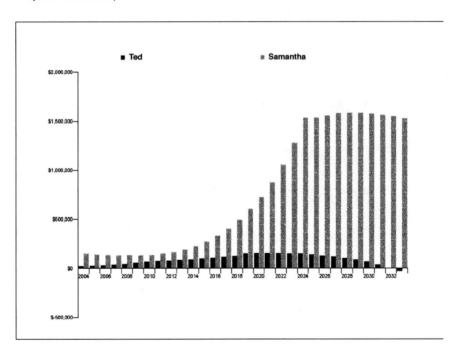

Prepared by Alan Feigenbaum. Copyright (c) 1997-2003. SU Software v 6.01   www.FamilyLawSoftware.com / 1-877-477-5488

FIGURE 10-7   Net Worth Projections for Samantha-Ted Scenario 2

Projected Net Worth: Table

	Ted	Samantha			Ted	Samantha
2004	$ 173,913	($ 2,100)		2019	$ 310,530	$ 402,346
2005	$ 178,035	($ 12,215)		2020	$ 318,718	$ 519,545
2006	$ 182,999	($ 18,646)		2021	$ 325,819	$ 659,496
2007	$ 188,195	($ 22,074)		2022	$ 331,721	$ 825,321
2008	$ 196,853	($ 20,807)		2023	$ 336,303	$ 1,039,435
2009	$ 206,563	($ 24,700)		2024	$ 339,434	$ 1,287,193
2010	$ 217,368	($ 24,019)		2025	$ 340,978	$ 1,276,744
2011	$ 222,726	($ 14,988)		2026	$ 340,786	$ 1,288,746
2012	$ 228,843	$ 472		2027	$ 338,700	$ 1,299,799
2013	$ 235,755	$ 23,539		2028	$ 334,549	$ 1,288,819
2014	$ 244,090	$ 54,993		2029	$ 328,152	$ 1,272,945
2015	$ 253,327	$ 96,817		2030	$ 319,315	$ 1,251,678
2016	$ 263,478	$ 150,686		2031	$ 307,832	$ 1,224,478
2017	$ 273,945	$ 218,460		2032	$ 293,480	$ 1,190,763
2018	$ 284,746	$ 301,713		2033	$ 276,373	$ 1,150,569

Projected Net Worth: Graph

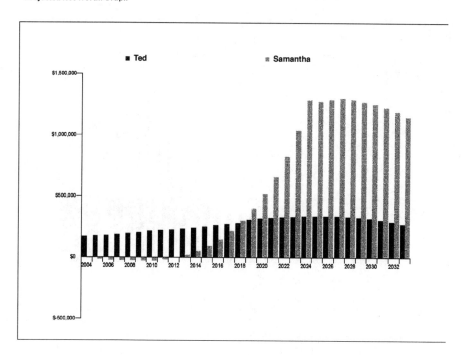

Prepared by Alan Feigenbaum. Copyright (c) 1997-2003. SU Software v 6.01   www.FamilyLawSoftware.com / 1-877-477-5488

FIGURE 10-8 Net Worth Projections for Samantha-Ted Scenario 3

Projected Net Worth: Table

	Ted	Samantha		Ted	Samantha
2004	$ 223,749	($ 52,622)	2019	$ 363,490	$ 336,550
2005	$ 227,748	($ 63,105)	2020	$ 378,456	$ 445,543
2006	$ 232,603	($ 70,004)	2021	$ 392,741	$ 576,714
2007	$ 237,723	($ 73,855)	2022	$ 406,258	$ 733,144
2008	$ 246,353	($ 73,089)	2023	$ 418,912	$ 938,127
2009	$ 256,071	($ 77,569)	2024	$ 430,600	$ 1,176,206
2010	$ 266,927	($ 77,570)	2025	$ 441,213	$ 1,155,497
2011	$ 272,357	($ 69,325)	2026	$ 450,635	$ 1,156,624
2012	$ 278,612	($ 54,766)	2027	$ 458,740	$ 1,156,150
2013	$ 285,730	($ 32,724)	2028	$ 465,392	$ 1,132,951
2014	$ 294,336	($ 2,434)	2029	$ 470,446	$ 1,104,125
2015	$ 303,924	$ 38,077	2030	$ 473,747	$ 1,069,128
2016	$ 314,514	$ 90,468	2031	$ 475,130	$ 1,027,375
2017	$ 325,518	$ 156,583	2032	$ 474,415	$ 978,234
2018	$ 336,957	$ 237,982	2033	$ 471,765	$ 921,688

Projected Net Worth: Graph

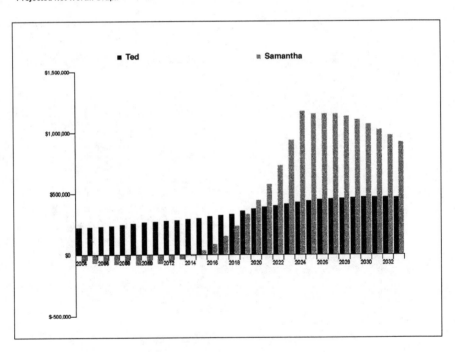

Prepared by Alan Feigenbaum. Copyright (c) 1997-2003. SU Software v 6.01   www.FamilyLawSoftware.com / 1-877-477-5488

Byrnes Case Comments

Given their respective financial lifestyles, both Ted and Samantha should have about the same level of minor concern that they each might outlive their money based on the seemingly most-equitable Scenario 3. Therefore, upon divorce, they each might want to independently consult with their own advisors regarding the possibility of working to age 70 if possible. In Samantha's case that would make an enormous difference, because given the rate at which her business is projected to grow, she could easily add more than a million in net worth in those 5 extra years. In Ted's case, the extra years would increase both his pension and Social Security annual payments a bit, while also adding substantially to his savings.

Additional Cases

We could have provided additional cases, but instead we are offering something even better. You can examine additional cases we've also prepared using the *Split-Up* software (in conjunction with *Support 2004*) on the Split-Up Web site (www.split-up.com/financial_book/more_case.htm), where you'll be able to read the cases and actually download demo *Split-Up* software with all the case details so you can look at all the various reports. That's not all; we've also put these cases into that demo version, so that you can try out the powerful what-if capabilities of *Split-Up* to quickly evaluate various additional scenarios.

If you like what you see, you can also download a full-calculation-capability lim-ited-time trial version of *Split-Up* that will enable you to enter your own data and get the results on your screen, but it won't allow you to print out reports. You can then choose to activate it as a full-function version (without losing your data) if you buy it online at a special discount for this book's purchasers; see very last page.

Obviously, we like *Split-Up*, but whether or not you use it, it is critical that either you or a professional do the type of analysis we used it for in these cases. Some financial advisors have more powerful customized software to do even "finer" analysis, so if you're trying to determine a settlement on your own— with either *Split-Up*, a new competitive product, or your own spreadsheet—consider running your outcome by a financial advisor before committing to it. If nothing else, we urge you to base any settlement on either doing the math or having it done for you; any other approach to settlement is just sp(l)ittin' in the wind.

Resource Appendix

We hope you've found this book to be a key source of information to help you understand and work through the financial and other issues in your divorce. But we'd be doing you a disservice if we didn't point you to many other outstanding sources of information that you might find helpful.

Hence this Resource Appendix, which lists well over one hundred different sources, including comprehensive divorce Web sites, divorce sections of Web sites, comprehensive online articles about divorce-related topics, specific books, software and online calculators and other tools, other divorce-related products and services, and many directories of divorce professionals. Many of these were referred to in various book chapters, but you'll find numerous new ones here.

Remember that you—acting with emotional maturity and common sense—are by far your most important resource in surviving this difficult life passage in a way that will allow you and your children to eventually thrive.

General Information Sources

General Divorce Web Sites

Here are the best comprehensive Web sites devoted to divorce issues:

- *Divorce Source and sister sites:* These sites (www.divorcesource.com, www.betterdivorce.com, www.divorcesupport.com, and www.divorce-topics.com) collectively offer the most comprehensive source of articles, directories, and other divorce information that you'll find anywhere: financial matters, laws and cases, family issues, professional and support resources, chat rooms and bulletin boards, products and services, a research center to find additional information, and links to other helpful sources.

- *Pension Appraisers, Inc.* (www.pensionappraisers.com) is also related to Divorce Source, but it is primarily devoted to comprehensive information about how to handle pensions during and after divorce. It also contains an e-book on divorce that you can download for free: *Pension Issues in Divorce* (www.pensionappraisers.com/freedownload.shtml)
- *Lee Borden's Web site* (www.divorceinfo.com), Lee, a veteran Birmingham, Alabama divorce attorney frequently quoted in this book, offers a wealth of compassion and helpful information to help take the sting out of divorce—with special emphasis on leaving the failures of marriage behind and being the best possible parents afterward.
- *DivorceNet:* This site (www.divorcenet.com) was originally created by a Newton, Massachusetts, law firm, and it now involves a consortium of attorneys and other divorce professionals around the country. It offers a similarly comprehensive compendium of divorce material to that offered by the Divorce Source sites. The site's best features are its separate bulletin boards on a whole range of divorce-related subjects, and links to online articles from *The Family Law Advisor,* published by the site's owners, The LawTek Media Group, LLC.
- *Divorce Headquarters* (www.divorcehq.com) is yet another site sponsored by a national consortium of divorce professionals, also offering a broad range of articles on divorce topics from its online and e-mail newsletter, and other sources. Its unique features include a growing archive of divorce humor a page devoted to recent news stories on divorce issues, and many state-specific FAQS on divorce issues and procedures.
- *Divorce Magazine* (www.divorcemag.com/index.shtml) is the online home of the print publication with a number of excellent articles, including some specific to Canadian divorce. Its unique features include a few advice columns, and statistics on divorce in the United States and internationally. It also has an extensive directory of all types of divorce professionals and a few good forums on divorce issues.
- *Millennium Divorce, LLP* (www.millenniumdivorce.com), sponsored by a New York law firm, offers a less-extensive but still wide range of helpful divorce information. Its best features include an online divorce primer (www.millenniumdivorce.com/webbooks/divorceprimermn.asp), and a set of useful calculators related to financial issues during divorce such as credit management, home financing, and budgeting.
- *American Academy of Matrimonial Lawyers* (www.aaml.org/). In addition to a highly readable online divorce manual (www.aaml.org/Manual.htm), you'll also find more detailed additional

information if you're willing to wade through more technical explanations of almost every conceivable legal divorce issue.

- *Divorce Helpline* (www.divorcehelp.com): This site, sponsored by a California law firm with a collaborative law specialty, offers good overall information on divorce but it is particularly oriented to California collaborative divorce and community property laws. It includes an excellent online divorce short-course, a downloadable e-book for purchase, and a number of helpful articles.
- North Carolina Divorce Law (www.rosen.com): While this divorce-specialist law-firm site is specific to North Carolina law and cases, but is also a thought-provoking resource for "divorce consumers" from any state—especially its descriptions of actual recent cases that cover a broad spectrum of areas of emphasis ranging from alimony to domestic violence.
- Other sites include one meant for men only (www.dadsdivorce.com/) and another for women only (womansdivorce.com), and several more with some useful information:
  Divorce Recovery 101 (www.divorcerecovery101.com),
  Americans for Divorce Reform www.divorcereform.org/,
  Divorce Transitions (www.divorcetransitions.com/),
  Divorce Central (www.divorcecentral.com), and
  Divorce Interactive (www.divorceinteractive.com)

Divorce Sections of Web Sites

Here are several Web sites with excellent sections totally devoted to divorce:

- Managing Your Divorce: A Guide for Battered Women
  www.nationalcouncilfvd.org/pubs/images/managing_divorce.pdf
- American Bar Association (ABA) Family Law Section
  www.abanet.org/family/home.html
  ABA (Online) Guide to Family Law
  www.abanet.org/publiced/practical/books/family/
- Equality in Marriage
  www.equalityinmarriage.org/d/News/headlines.html
- Street Law Family Law Page, www.streetlaw.com/casesun5.html#ch34
- Cornell Legal Information Institute
  www.law.cornell.edu/topics/divorce.html
- Prairie Law Family Law Channel
  www.prairielaw.com/channels/channel.asp?channelId=18

- FindLaw Family Law Section,
  www.findlaw.com/01topics/15family/index.html
- AllLaw Family Law Section, www.alllaw.com/articles/family/divorce/
- Women's Institute for Financial Education (Suddenly Single),
  www.wife.org/suddenlysingle.htm
- Martindale-Hubbell,
  www.lawyers.com/legal_topics/browse_by_topic/index.php (Then click
  on "Divorce" then under "Family.")
- Women's Institute for a Secure Retirement (Divorce Page),
  www.wiser.heinz.org/divorce_detail.html
- Kids and Divorce, www.bol.ucla.edu/~jeffwood/
- Heart Choice, www.heartchoice.com/divorce/index.php
- Divorce Handbook, www.divorceandfinance.com/info/handbook.shtml
- NOW Legal Defense Fund Short Course,
  www.nowldef.org/html/pub/kits/divplan/divplancontents.shtml
- Equality In Marriage, www.equalityinmarriage.org
  "During Divorce," www.equalityinmarriage.org/wd.html
  "After Divorce," www.equalityinmarriage.org/ad.html
  "In New Relationships,"www.equalityinmarriage.org/nr.html

Books and Other Print Publications

Here are several books that mostly focus on how to best psychologically and
emotionally get through a divorce and work with your spouse to make the best
of a difficult situation in the interest of your children. In addition, though, there
are a few books concerning the overall strategy, custody considerations, and
financial issues in reaching a divorce agreement.

Ahrons, Constance. 1995. *The Good Divorce: Keeping Your Family
Together When Your Marriage Comes Apart.* Harper Collins.

Baris, Mitchell A., and Carla B. Garrity. 1997. *Caught in the Middle:
Protecting the Children of High-Conflict Divorce*: Jossey-Bass.

Blakeslee, Sandra, Gary M. Neuman, Patricia Romanowski, and Judith
S. Wallerstein. 1999. *Helping Your Kids Cope With Divorce the Sandcas-
tles Way*: Random House.

Blakeslee, Sandra, and Judith S. Wallerstein. 1996. *2nd Chances: Men,
Women, and Children a Decade After Divorce*: Mariner Books.

Brennan, Carleen, and Michael Brennan. 1999. *Custody for Fathers: A Practical Guide through the Combat Zone of a Brutal Custody Battle*: Brennan Dalsgard Publishers.

Briles, Judith, Edwin Schilling, and Carol Ann Wilson. 1998. *The Dollars and Sense of Divorce*: Dearborn Financial Publishing.

Dachman, Kenneth A., and Jeffrey M. Leving. 1998. *Fathers Rights: Hard–Hitting and Fair Advice for Every Father Involved in a Custody Dispute*: Perseus.

Gardner, Richard A. 1998. *The Parental Alienation Syndrome: A Guide for Mental Health and Legal Professionals*: Creative Therapeutics.

Hamilton, Michael J., and Martin M. Shenkman. 2000. *Divorce Rules for Men: A Man-to-Man Guide for Managing Your Split and Saving Thousands*: John Wiley & Sons.

Johnson, Laura. 1997. *Divorce Strategy: Tactics for a Civil Divorce*: Wolf Hollow Publishing.

Klatte, William C. 1999. *Live-Away Dads: Staying a Part of Your Children's Lives When They Aren't a Part of Your Home*: Penguin.

Krantzler, Mel, and Patricia B. Krantzler. 1999. *The New Creative Divorce: How to Create a Happier, More Rewarding Life During—and After—Your Divorce*: Adams Media.

Levy, David L. 1993. *The Best Parent Is Both Parents*: Hampton Roads.

Margulies, Sam. 2001. *Getting Divorced without Ruining Your Life*: Simon & Schuster.

McClure, Daniel F., and Jerry Saffer. 1999. *Wednesday Evenings and Every Other Weekend: From Divorced Dad to Competent Co-Parent. A Guide for the Noncustodial Father*: Penguin.

Mercer, Diana, and Marsha Kline Pruett. 2001. *Your Divorce Advisor: A Lawyer and a Psychologist Guide You through the Legal and Emotional Landscape of Divorce*: Simon & Schuster.

Oberlin, Loriann Hoff. 2000. *Surviving Separation and Divorce: A Woman's Guide to Making it through the First Year*: Adams Media.

Ricci, Isolina. 1997. *Mom's House, Dad's House: Making Two Homes for Your Child*: Random House.

Smith, Gayle Rosenwald, and Sally Abrahms. 1998. *What Every Woman Should Know about Divorce and Custody*: Berkeley Publishing.

Warshak, Richard A. 2002. *Divorce Poison: Protecting the Parent-Child Bond from a Vindictive Ex*: Regan Books.

Wittman, Jeffrey P. 2001. *Custody Chaos, Personal Peace: Sharing Custody with an Ex Who's Driving You Crazy*: Penguin.

Woodhouse, Violet. 2002. *Divorce and Money: How to Make the Best Financial Decisions during Divorce*: Nolo.

Supplementary Material Specifically Referred to in Chapters

The following document (www.divorcehq.com/billrights.html) is from Divorce Headquarters, a comprehensive Web site listed earlier in this Appendix. Neither the document nor Web site is marked as copyrighted.

Children's Bill of Rights (Referenced in Chapter 4)

We the children of the divorcing parents, in order to form a more perfect union, establish justice, insure domestic tranquility, provide for the common defense, promote the general welfare, and secure the blessings of liberty to ourselves and our posterity, do ordain and establish these Bill of Rights for all children.

1. The right not to be asked to "choose sides" or be put in a situation where I would have to take sides between my parents.
2. The right to be treated as a person and not as a pawn, possession, or a negotiating chip.
3. The right to freely and privately communicate with both parents.
4. The right not to be asked questions by one parent about the other.
5. The right not to be a messenger.
6. The right to express my feelings.
7. The right to adequate visitation with the noncustodial parent which will best serve my needs and wishes.
8. The right to love and have a relationship with both parents without being made to feel guilty.
9. The right not to hear either parent say anything bad about the other.
10. The right to the same educational opportunities and economic support that I would have had if my parents did not divorce.
11. The right to have what is in my best interest protected at all times.
12. The right to maintain my status as a child and not to take on adult responsibilities for the sake of the parent's well being.
13. The right to request my parents seek appropriate emotional and social support when needed.

14. The right to expect consistent parenting at a time when little in my life seems constant or secure.
15. The right to expect healthy relationship modeling, despite the recent events.
16. The right to expect the utmost support when taking the time and steps needed to secure a healthy adjustment to the current situation.

Women and Retirement Security (Referenced in Chapter 9)

These facts are excerpted from the Social Security Administration Web site (www.ssa.gov):

- *Women have lower income in retirement than men, thus higher poverty.* In 1997, the median income for elderly unmarried women (widowed, divorced, separated, and never married) was $11,161, compared with $14,769 for elderly unmarried men and $29,278 for elderly married couples. Thus, the poverty rate for elderly women was higher than that of men. In 1997, the poverty rate of elderly women was 13.1 percent, compared to 7.0 percent among men. Among unmarried elderly women, the poverty rate was significantly higher—about 19 percent. Divorced women are a growing share of the elderly population, and their poverty rate is higher than the overall elderly poverty rate.
- *Women tend to live longer and have lower lifetime earnings than men.* A woman age 65 expects to live to 85, while a 65-year-old man expects to live to 81. Women reach retirement with smaller pensions and other assets than men do. Only 30 percent age 65 or older were receiving a pension in 1994 (either worker or survivor benefits), compared to 48 percent of men. Among new private-sector pension annuity recipients in 1993–1994, women's median annual benefit was $4800, or only half of the men's median benefit of $9600. And among women approaching retirement, pension wealth is much smaller. For example, single women had average pension wealth that was 34 percent of the single men's average. Overall, fewer women workers have pensions through work: 40 percent of women compared to 44 percent of men. However, women in full-time jobs are equally likely to have pension coverage as men. In 1997, 50 percent of women in full-time jobs had pensions compared to 49 percent of men. It is important to note, though, that women are much more likely to work part-time or be out of the labor force than men.

Web Links to Useful Documents and Additional Supplementary Material

- Diagram of Family Law Process (in Santa Clara, California), www.scselfservice.org/fam/process.htm
- Estimated Total Cost of Divorce Calculator, www.msnbc.com/onair/msnbc/bwilliams/divorcecalc.asp
- National Center on Women and Family Law Documents, www.nowldef.org/html/pub/index.shtml#ncw
- Client Information Forms for Divorce Attorney, www.divorceinfo.com/downloads/worksheets.doc
- Client Marital History Form (for Divorce Attorney), www.sherridonovan.com/marital.htm
- Family Law Depositions, www.nicholslaw.com/CM/Publications/doc1.pdf
- Sample Marital Settlement Agreements, www.pjhoskins.com/divorce/Divorce%20Settlement%20Agreement.html and http://laweasy.com/disagreement.htm
- Budgeting: How to Develop a Workable Plan, www.gofso.com/Premium/LE/04_le_fp/fg/fg-Expense.html
- Life Insurance: How Much and What Kind to Buy, www.gofso.com/Premium/LE/08_le_bi/fg/fg-Life_Ins.html
- Financial Documents and Valuable Papers Needed for Divorce, www.extension.iastate.edu/Publications/PM1719.pdf, http://ohioline.osu.edu/pdf/l237.pdf
- Wisconsin Proposed Marital Settlement Agreement (filled in). http://firms.findlaw.com/Romero/memo14.htm
- Sample Attorney Case-Closing Checklist and QDRO Prep Checklist, www.nicholslaw.com/FSL5CS/Publications/DivorceIssues2.pdf
- Connecticut Financial Affidavits, www.larcc.org/pamphlets/children_family/financial_affidavits.pdf
- Sample Collaborative Law Participation Agreements, www.collaborativelaw.com/Documents/Participation%20Agrmt-summary.pdf, and www.collaborativelaw.com/Documents/clcfaq.doc
- Simple Separation Agreement, www.rosen.com/ppf/ID/114/issues.asp
- Who's Liable for What Debts? (chart),www.raggiolaw.com/chart.htm
- Example Financial Disclosure Form, www.kemplegal.com/id34.htm
- Alzheimer's Financial Organizer,www.aricept.com/financialorganizer.pdf We hope you don't have Alzheimer's, but we have included this Web site

because it is an excellent resource for *anyone* to organize important financial information.

- When Your Marital Status Changes (What to Do), www.usaaedfoundation.org/pdf/541.pdf
- Checklist for Divorce Self-Representation, www.peoples-law.org/family/divorce/self%20rep%20list.html
- One Attorney's "Fee Agreement" Form, http://www.divorcegroup.org/Fee_Agreement.pdf
- Description of Divorce "Discovery" Process, www.dfwlawyer.com/family_law/discovery.html
- Child Support Project: Termination of Child Support and Support Beyond Majority (Table Showing State Policies) www.ncsl.org/programs/cyf/educate.htm

Online Federal, State, and Local Divorce Information

- State Child Support Guidelines on the Web, www.supportguidelines.com/links.html
- State Bar Associations and Family Law Sections, www.supportguidelines.com/famlawsections.html
- Where to Write for Vital Records, (regarding your spouse, for example) www.cdc.gov/nchs/howto/w2w/w2welcom.htm
- Overview of Federal/State Marriage/Divorce Laws, www.law.cornell.edu/topics/divorce.html
- Divorce Laws by State, www.divorcelawinfo.com/ state information
- Divorce Law Information Center, www.divorcelawinfo.com/ (can purchase forms for each state)
- Detailed State Divorce Statutes (bottom of page) http://www.law.cornell.edu/topics/Table_Divorce.htm
- Divorce Resources in Santa Clara County, California, www.scselfservice.org/fam/divorce.htm
- Family Law Manual for Santa Clara County, California, www.sccsuperiorcourt.org/family/rule3toc.htm.
- Divorce in Maryland, www.peoples-law.com/family/divorce/divorce%20home.htm. Check whether your locality has similar resources. This is a model resource.

Directories and Web Sites of Divorce Professionals Organizations

- Institute for Divorce Financial Analysts, https://www.institutedfa.com/
- Military Divorce Online, www.militarydivorceonline.com
- Pension Appraisers, Inc., www.pensionappraisers.com
- College for Divorce Specialists, www.cdscollege.com
- The Divorce Resource Network, www.divorceresourcenetwork.com/
- Split-Up Divorce Professionals (Referral Directory Page: 317),www.divorcesoftware.com/prodir/pro_search.htm
- The Association of Divorce Financial Planners, www.divorceandfinance.com/info/mprofessionals.shtml
- *Divorce Magazine* Professional Referrals, www.divorcemagazine.com/XX/prodserv/index.shtml
- One Planner's Referral List and Advice on Using Experts, www.kathleenmiller.com/TheWorkGroup.htm www.kathleenmiller.com/pdf/usingqualifiedexperts.pdf
- International Association of Divorce Professionals, www.iadp.net/.
- Divorce Choice (Referral Directory), www.divorcechoice.com/savmarriages/prosThatHelp.html
- Conflict Resolution Resources, www.mrn.org/Mediation/crlinks.html
- Divorce Headquarters Referral Directory, www.divorcehq.com/servicedir.html
- The Internet Legal Resources Guide, www.ilrg.com/
- International Academy of Collaborative Professionals, www.collabgroup.com
- Coalition for Collaborative Divorce, www.nocourtdivorce.com
- The Collaborative Law Center, www.collaborativelaw.com/
- Association for Conflict Resolution: Divorce Mediator Referrals www.acmet.org/referrals/ap=family.htm
- Financial Planners with Specialties in Divorce, www.smartdivorce.com/divorce1.htm
- American Bar Association Commission on Domestic Violence, www.abanet.org/domviol/home.html

Divorce Support Groups and Services

- MSN Marriage/Divorce Support Groups, groups.msn.com/browse.msnw?catid=173
- Stay-at-Home Dads' Web Site, slowlane.com

- An Author's List of Divorce Support Groups,
  www.smartdivorce.com/support.htm
- Second Wives Club, www.secondwivesclub.com/
- Local Area Support Groups (example),
  www.considering-divorce.com/namenumber.html (Look for similar
  resources in your local area)

Commercial Divorce Products and Services

Divorce Software, Online Calculators and Worksheets

- Split-Up (Comprehensive Divorce Financial Software),
  www.split-up.com
- FinPlan (Divorce Financial Software),
  www.divorceplanner.com
- Divorce Power Analyzer, www.floridom.com/medwin2.html, and
  www.floridom.com/medwmi.html
- Support 2004 (Alimony and Child Support Software),
  www.marginsoft.net
- Social Security Administration Downloadable Benefit Calculator,
  www.ssa.gov/OACT/ANYPIA/download.html
- Online Child Support Calculators, www.divorcehq.com/calculators.html
- Child Support Calculators on the Web,
  www.supportguidelines.com/calcs.html
- Property Division Spreadsheet, www.divorceassist.com/tools.html#ps
- Income/Expense Chart, www.divorceassist.com/tools.html#ec
- Cash Flow Calculator,
  www.millenniumdivorce.com/Calculators/Calculatorcash.asp
- Income and Expense Worksheet,
  www.extension.iastate.edu/Publications/PM1720.pdf
- Nolo Press Worksheets to organize Divorce, www.nolotech.com/WR/

How-to Books, Handbooks, and Divorce Kits

- Divorce Yourself: The National No-Fault Divorce Kit,
  www.smartdivorce.com/selfhelp.htm
- *Divorce Survival Guide,*
  www.edutainingkids.com/reviews/bkjugglingactkit.html

- *Plans for Parting Divorce Kit,*
  http://www.divorceinfo.com/plansforparting.htm
- *The Property Division Handbook,*
  www.divorcefind.com/a/divorcelawinfo/property.shtml
- *The Child Support Handbook,*
  www.divorcefind.com/a/divorcelawinfo/childsupport.shtml
- *The Father's Child Custody Handbook,*
  www.divorcefind.com/a/divorcelawinfo/childsupport.shtml
- *Successful Divorce Workbook* (California),
  www.pjhoskins.com/books/prod01.htm
- *Enforcing Orders* (California), www.pjhoskins.com/books/post_divorce.htm
- *The Mother's Child Custody Handbook,*
  www.divorcefind.com/a/divorcelawinfo/mothercustody.shtml
- *The Divorce Primer* (e-book),
  www.millenniumdivorce.com/webbooks/divorceprimermn.asp
- *Your Pocket Divorce Guide,*
  www.divorcetransitions.com/books/ypdg.htm
- *The Divorce Process: Empowerment Through Knowledge,*
  www.divorceprocess.com/divprohomepage.htm

Organizers and Related Materials

- Divorce Record Keeper,
  www.divorcefind.com/products/recordkeeper.shtml
- Divorce Diary, www.1800calendar.com/index.cgi?jp=floridalawyer
- Divorce Log, www.yradvantage.com/divorce-.htm
- Divorce Personal Information Planner,
  www.smartdivorce.com/personal.htm
- Document Locator System,
  www.gofso.com/Premium/LE/21_le_ot/fg/fg-Doc_Locator.html
- Divorce Recovery Journal, www.smartdivorce.com/recovery.htm
- Parenting Time Calendar, www.parentingtimecalendar.com/
- Pre-Divorce Checklist—Finding Hidden Assets and Income,
  www.divorcenet.com/predivorce-check.html

Online Divorce Forms and Other Related Services

- Asset Searches/Public Records,
  www.yourdivorceadvisor.com/resources.html#asset

- www.ourdivorceagreement.com/
- www.divorcedirect.com
- www.completecase.com
- www.divorcesite.com
- www.legalzoom.com/doityourselfdivorce.html
- INFOAMERICA No-Fault Divorce Kit, www.divorcekit.com

Index

277

About the Authors

Alan Marc Feigenbaum is a CERTIFIED FINANCIAL PLANNER® certificant who after more than 25 years of corporate work and secondary/college mathematics teaching, writes primarily about personal finance. His previous books were *A Parent's Guide to Money: Raising Financially Savvy Children* (co-authored with his middle of three daughters) and *Alpha Teach Yourself Retirement Planning in 24 Hours* (Macmillan, September 2001). He has written regular columns and frequent features for *Bloomberg Wealth Manager*, CBS MarketWatch, WORTH Interactive, *Raleigh News & Observer*, and *Chapel Hill News*—and has been published in the *New York Times*, *Boston Globe*, LA Times Syndicate, and *Journal of Financial Planning*.

Alan has covered virtually every aspect of personal money management with a passionate consumer advocacy flavored with a sense of humor. He has also written op-ed and humor pieces in the *Boston Globe* and other publications, as well as recently indulging a lifelong competitive passion with a column in *The ACBL Bulletin* (American Contract Bridge League).

Heather Smith Linton, a CPA and CERTIFIED FINANCIAL PLANNER®, founded Linton & Associates in 1989. She received her B.A. summa cum laude from the University of Delaware and her MBA from the University of North Carolina at Chapel Hill—and is also a Certified Valuation Analyst (CVA), and Certified Divorce Financial Analyst (CDFA).

Ms. Linton is past president of the North Carolina Association of CPAs. She now serves on the national CPA governing body, the AICPA Council. Additionally, she is or has been active in the following professional and community organizations: Wachovia Bank (local) board, Durham Chamber of Commerce board, Chapel Hill Country Club (past-president), Leadership Triangle (past-president), Durham-Orange Estate Planning Council, Council of Entrepreneurial Development, Durham Technical Community College Foundation, and the North Carolina Global Center.

Ms. Linton's first book, *Streetwise Business Valuation: Proven Methods to Easily Determine the True Value of Your Business* (February 2004) follows extensive contributions (cited in the forward) to *Alpha Teach Yourself Retirement Planning in 24 Hours* (Macmillan, September, 2001). She has written several professional articles, appeared on several local and statewide radio and television programs, and has been quoted on tax and business topics by many high-profile and local publications such as: WORTH Interactive, CBS MarketWatch, *Wall Street Journal*, *Bloomberg Wealth Manager*, *Raleigh News & Observer*, *Durham Herald-Sun*, *Business North Carolina*, *The Business Leader*, *Triangle Business Journal*, and *Chapel Hill. News*.

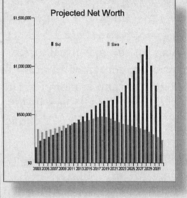